KEEPING
YOUR
BALANCE

KEEPING YOUR BALANCE

Approaching theological & religious studies

Edited by Philip Duce & Daniel Strange

APOLLOS

INTER-VARSITY PRESS
38 De Montfort Street, Leicester LE1 7GP, England
Email: ivp@uccf.org.uk
Website: www.ivpbooks.com

First published 2001

British Library Cataloguing in Publication Data
A catalogue record for this book is available from the British Library.

ISBN 0–85111–482–2

Set in Garamond
Typeset in Great Britain
Printed and bound in Great Britain by Creative Print and Design (Wales), Ebbw Vale

Inter-Varsity Press is the publishing division of the Universities and Colleges Christian Fellowship (formerly the Inter-Varsity Fellowship), a student movement linking Christian Unions in universities and colleges throughout Great Britain, and a member movement of the International Fellowship of Evangelical Students. For more information about local and national activities write to UCCF, 38 De Montfort Street, Leicester LE1 7GP, email us at email@uccf.org.uk, or visit the UCCF website at www.uccf.org.uk.

Contents

Foreword

People do not usually expect a vocational training to make them question their vocation or leave them uncertain how to pursue it. At the end of a course in chemical engineering, one expects to have a better knowledge of how to do the task. A course in philosophy or literature, however, may be somewhat different and students may find that their previous understandings in these areas require radical reformulation. Study of the Bible, theology and religious studies seems to belong in both worlds. On the one side, such studies are still an essential part of preparation for a career in Christian ministry in any of its many forms. On the other side, these studies involve a critical understanding of Christian belief that may seem to call into question those very beliefs on whose basis Christian ministry and Christian living generally depend. In the opening chapter, David Field notes some of the ways in which a theological education may make students incapable, to a greater or lesser extent, of fulfilling their intended vocation.

The writers of this book are all theological teachers and learners who are united by a desire to show that theological education, properly addressed, need not have such undesirable results. A recurring theme, reflected in the title of the collection, is the need for integration, so that theological study is not carried on in a vacuum from one's personal spiritual life and vice versa. Such a proposition, to be sure, can look like a recipe for disaster. It may be difficult to read the Gospel of John devotionally while wrestling with questions of the historicity of its picture of Jesus, or to take a balanced view of the validity of the traditional arguments for the existence of God if you think that rejection of them is not an option in view of your faith that God does exist. Nevertheless, I have no doubt that the approach that is developed here is the right one.

Many students' problems arise from facing up to the scepticism about the truths of Christianity voiced by unbelievers or by persons who do not share their particular understanding of Christianity. Even before I became a student I was helped immensely by a little booklet by F. F. Bruce, *Are The New Testament Documents Reliable?*, which I bought as a birthday present for my father, but really so that I could read it myself! It tackled many of the problems relating to the reliability of the New Testament, especially in the Gospels, and it was so obvious that the author knew what he was writing about and could take on the sceptics from a position of profound knowledge that it gave me confidence to enter into an area where at times one could easily be driven to despair and despondency. I learned the vital lesson that to deal with historical scepticism one needs to go back to history and not turn a blind eye to the problems. The resultant understanding may not be entirely the same as that with which one began (any more than mature medical students will hold the same naïve understandings of disease as they started with), and there will be areas where frequently we shall have to say 'We do not know'; but as 'faith seeks understanding' there will be development of enough understanding to justify continuing to believe. The scope of the present book obviously prevents detailed attention to the kind of issues addressed by Bruce, but here there are helpful pointers in the right direction, not least in the discussion of 'Faith and certainty'. One point that emerges throughout the book, and that I can confirm from my own experience, is the importance of maintaining your own Christian life of worship and service, both personal and corporate. To see Christianity at work in the life of Christians and in their impact upon society puts theological studies into perspective and helps to keep us from thinking that the last word lies with scholars. The divine revelation is given to 'little children' rather than to 'the wise and learned' (Matt. 11:25), though to say this is not to commend naïvety nor to despise wisdom and knowledge.

Readers will not find the answers to all their problems in theological and religious studies in this book, but they will find that, with its writers as their companions, their journey through difficult territory will be eased considerably. The contributors have been this way before them, and know where the dangers are and where help is to be found.

It is a privilege to introduce the essays in this book, and I pray that they will help many students to be confident in upholding their faith and commending it to others.

Howard Marshall
Honorary Research Professor of New Testament in
the University of Aberdeen

Editors' preface

Thinking about, and reflecting on, the reality of God – in short, *theology* – is inescapable for all Christians. Those who take up formal theological or religious studies do not have greater access to God's wisdom, or belong to a 'special breed'. However, as they study the Bible, the church, religion and the many topics which relate to their own faith, they do face particular challenges in the contexts of their academic communities and curricula. Such challenges, of course, can be very stimulating, but the tension between personal faith and academic study can also be uncomfortable, disorientating or distressing.

This collection of essays offers excellent guidance and wise counsel. The authors are senior scholars, recent graduates and an ordained minister. Between them they provide a range of complementary perspectives on the issues with which students have to grapple. From our own experiences, both of us can testify to the quality and good sense of this practical advice and orientation. One of us studied at a residential evangelical college, and subsequently undertook some theology tutoring. The other studied at a British university, and now works full-time in providing support for theology and RS students. Both settings bring their own challenges, to Christians in general and to evangelicals in particular.

Most of these essays were originally published as monographs by the Religious and Theological Students' Fellowship (part of the Universities and Colleges Christian Fellowship and the International Fellowship of Evangelical Students). Through collaboration between the RTSF and Inter-Varsity Press, we are now pleased to present the essays, suitably revised and edited, in this new format. We are very grateful to Elizabeth Fraser for her assistance in the RTSF office, to the authors for permission to include their essays, and to Howard Marshall for writing the foreword.

Some of these essays have already served students for many years. We gladly commend this whole collection to new generations, in the hope that it will help and encourage them to 'keep their balance' through (and beyond) their time of study, and grow into mature followers and servants of the Lord Jesus Christ.

Philip Duce
Daniel Strange
Leicester, May 2001

1. Approaching theological study
David Field

David Field is now retired. He was Patronage Secretary for the Church Pastoral Aid Society (1994–2000) and Vice-Principal and Lecturer in Christian Ethics at Oak Hill Theological College, London (1968–1993).

'*Instant insanity*', the caption read, a new game which '… is the cheapest way to go crazy'. Whether or not it was a humorous touch on the editor's part to set this particular advertisement at the foot of *The Times*' ordinations list will probably never be known, but to many readers the positioning must have seemed extraordinarily appropriate. 'What could be calculated to drive someone more quickly to the verge of insanity,' they might ask, 'than two or three years at a theological college in preparation for the ministry?'

Cautionary tales abound of those whose understanding of the Christian faith has been clouded rather than clarified by a university or college course in academic theology, and it would be foolish to pretend that all the stories are exaggerated. Indeed, one does not have to look far to find first-hand examples of apparently excellent candidates for the ministry who seem to have lost much of their Christian enthusiasm between entering and leaving a theological college. Some went in with a simple faith and have come out with complicated doubts. Others have emerged as sophisticated professionals, their minds bursting with new knowledge which simply bores and bewilders those whom they are fondly hoping to 'educate'. Others who had hoped to find a faith have emerged little further forward. While others again still continue to say and do all the right things, but without the obvious sincerity and concern which used to characterize their less polished preaching and teaching days.

This essay seeks to tackle, in particular, the difficulties of those who are anxious to undertake theological study as convinced Christians, wanting to equip themselves better to serve God and others. Surrounded by so many sobering object-lessons, some have wondered whether they should study academic theology at all. It has been an understandable reaction, both in view of the contemporary theological atmosphere which, with its inherited naturalistic bias and scaling down of the supernatural, is particularly repugnant to those with doctrinal convictions, and also because God has so obviously blessed the work of men and women who have enjoyed little or no formal theological training. If an 'amateur' can reach others effectively with the gospel, it is tempting to conclude that theology can be separated off safely from ordinary Christian living and service as an optional extra for the very strong or ultra-foolhardy.

However, this is a gross over-simplification. Theology is basically the attempt to think and talk about God, and by this definition every Christian is a theologian of sorts whether or not he or she studies the subject academically. If we do not have a good theology, we will inevitably have a bad one. We cannot simply opt out.

To put the same thing in a different way, theology is the theoretical basis for religion, and while the two cannot be equated (any more than the study of botany is the same thing as a growing plant), it would be just as wrong to set one against the other as mutually exclusive alternatives. A theologian without a deep religious experience of his own cannot hope to warm the hearts of those he teaches, but the Christian minister who lacks a sound grasp of theological theory runs the equally great risk of saying untrue things about God. Most people would think twice before committing their bodies to a 'doctor' who had not bothered to learn his or her facts at medical school, however warm-hearted and enthusiastic he or she might be.

It is interesting to compare the example of biblical leaders in this respect. From the patriarchs through to the prophets, and on into New Testament times, we find a great deal of evidence to support Paul's observation that 'God chose the foolish things of the world to shame the wise' (1 Cor. 1:27). Although some of those called to leadership were educated adequately by contemporary standards, others were far less well-equipped intellectually. Nevertheless, the degree of theological knowledge displayed is uniformly high. In the first twelve chapters of Jeremiah, for example, fifty echoes of Deuteronomy have been detected, while the prayer in Jonah 2 quotes from ten psalms and Stephen's short speech in Acts 7 is studded with over seventy references to or direct quotations from the Old Testament. The leaders of God's people in Bible times were steeped in knowledge of the Scriptures. Jesus himself clearly went to considerable lengths to show his disciples how his teaching related to the Old Testament, as he took time to interpret to them 'what was said in all the Scriptures concerning himself' (Luke 24:27). They may not have attended a residential training college or sat a BD examination, but they were subjected to rigorous personal tuition in the great biblical subjects with which the theological student still has to grapple.

Now all this may sound hopelessly naïve to a twenty-first-century student struggling with the authorship of Isaiah or Barth's *Christian Dogmatics*. Even modern 'biblical' theology has so many ramifications that straight Bible knowledge often seems far less important, particularly for examination purposes, than the ability to understand and reproduce the theories of scholars. If the kind of knowledge encouraged by Jesus can be described as truly theological, there does seem to be a gap between this and much that is included under the label of theology today.

It is one of the functions of this essay to acknowledge such difficulties and to attempt to face them realistically, but it is only right to recognize from the outset that mastery of the facts and doctrines of the Scriptures themselves is in the long run the sole major *academic* criterion by which any theological theory can be assessed. It is obviously important to learn as much as possible from what others are saying about the Bible, but a fresh glance at the syllabus on which the course is based will usually be enough to set the theories and the source-material in their correct perspective. Students who spend a great deal of time acquainting themselves thoroughly with what the Bible says are only being faithful to their brief as biblical theologians. And the reverse must also apply.

It is unfortunate that some of those who are most anxious to approach their work in this way are particularly prone to confuse a determination to respect the contents of the Bible with a refusal to engage in the strict intellectual discipline which all theological study demands. They want straight answers to straight questions. Impatient to get on with the vital work of teaching the faithful and evangelizing the unbeliever, they tend not to be over-sympathetic towards such 'peripheral' concerns as language study, church history and questions of dating and authorship. In other words, they want to be indoctrinated rather than educated, and in this they are usually, particularly at university level, disappointed.

In common with all academic disciplines, academic theology is concerned with education, not indoctrination. Its primary aim is to teach students *how* to think, not *what* to think, and if they attempt to short-circuit the system, the loss will be theirs (the very practical one of exam marks if they are content to assert conclusions instead of arguing their way to them from evidence). It is important to notice how Jesus himself replied to some questions by raising others. Even the implications of his parables were not always immediately obvious, and we hear of special supplementary teaching seminars when the Lord further unravelled the meaning of his public teaching. During these times with Jesus the disciples' minds were stretched rather than straight-jacketed.

Jesus taught that men and women should love God with their minds, and the capacity to analyse statements, detect hidden presuppositions and distinguish the primary from the secondary are all important intellectual benefits which theological study, when rightly approached, will yield. Modern students who are prepared to have their minds stretched while faithfully remaining humble before their Lord have nothing to fear from an academic study of the Bible. It will not inevitably either confuse their minds or cool their love. (It is sometimes forgotten that Wesley felt his heart 'strangely warmed' after listening to an intellectual preface to a theological commentary on the most doctrinal of the New Testament epistles!) And on the positive side, their preaching and teaching will increase in value as their knowledge of Scripture deepens, because true theology is as inextricably bound up with proclamation as the gospel is involved in the total message of the Bible. It was not with any desire to belittle the value of academic study that the theologian James Denney wrote: 'I have not the smallest interest in a theology that cannot be preached.'

Open mind or empty mind?

It used to be thought that in order to write an accurate account, honest historians must first decontaminate their material by ridding it of all personal colouring and private judgment. The result might be very dull, but at least it would be clinically sterile. It is the only way the reader could be sure that he or she was getting at the facts and not an individual's interpretation of them.

In rather the same way, it has sometimes tacitly been assumed that if theological students want to be really honest and 'scientific', they must first go through the mental exercise of stripping off all the prejudices and bias they have inherited from their past. If they happen to be convinced Christians from a particular tradition, at the very least they must be willing to approach their academic study with the recognition that other people's positions are as likely to be correct as their own. Although personally convinced of the historicity of the resurrection, for example, in order to maintain their intellectual integrity as scholars, they must be able to think themselves into a position from which they can see that a diametrically opposite view may equally well be right.

For many years now the pendulum has tended to swing in the other direction, so that Professor Alan Richardson could write: 'It is recognised in a new way that in history and in theology the stand-point of the observer and his personal judgements cannot, and should not, be excluded in the name of "science".' No historian or theologian can approach his or her work in a mental vacuum; nor can either justly be charged with dishonesty if he or she fails to measure up to the impersonality of a detached observer. Indeed, whatever a person's background and convictions, any claims to absolute detachment in itself must be partially dishonest if only because it presupposes an impossible standard.

All this, of course, raises difficulties for those who come to college with definite convictions. But here a vital distinction has to be made. *An open mind is not the same as an empty mind.* Failure to distinguish clearly between these two alternatives can be utterly disastrous. Time and time again one hears of students who are being reproached for '*closing* their minds to the assured results of modern scholarship', when in reality they are simply refusing to *empty* their minds of basic convictions in order to make a fresh start.

There are times, of course, when such a charge is fully justified. It is quite possible for theological students with decided convictions to approach their course as a kind of spiritual survival test, to cringe from contact with anything that calls into question part of their faith and to reject all new ideas on principle. If a book without the right imprimatur has to be read for exam purposes, every attempt must be made to seal away its contents in a special 'examinations only' compartment of the mind which can later be emptied and thoroughly fumigated. Even the apparently sound insights of an otherwise unsympathetic tutor must suffer the same fate in case subliminal heresy is absorbed unawares. When the last day of the final term arrives, college dust can be shaken off sensitive feet with a sigh of relief. The test has been passed safely and they emerge untainted, eager to get on with the work to which God has called them and sincerely grateful that the college or university has left no distinguishable mark on their mind or soul.

Of course the picture is overdrawn. And yet it cannot be denied that some students have tended to think in this way in the past, and quite understandably so in situations where they have found the theological scales heavily loaded against them. Nevertheless, in any academic discipline a closed mind and a refusal to face criticism are basically unhealthy attitudes. This is particularly so in the case of the convinced Christian whose presuppositions include belief in Jesus as truth. The truth does not fear examination.

Any theological student who deliberately presents a closed mind to distasteful teaching is simply a bad student. But again, the vital difference between openness and emptiness must be appreciated clearly. A willingness to open one's fundamental convictions to scrutiny is one thing. To be required to jettison the same after little or no examination in the name of academic integrity is something entirely different. Or, to change the metaphor, there is a world of difference between examining the roots of one's faith and deliberately tearing them up.

Everyone, consciously or unconsciously, brings his or her own presuppositions to bear on the study of theology, and students whose faith is grounded in the Bible are no exception. They believe in a God who redeems and reveals. They believe that this God has used words in history to make his mind known and, to avoid loss or perversion, has caused them to be written in a book. They believe that the doctrine of an inspired Bible is part of the wholeness of redemption. These beliefs will be challenged, and such students must expect to put in a lot of hard work to examine their position. In doing so they may well discover that some of the things they have been brought up to accept are not in fact part of the Bible's testimony at all, but as they lay their convictions open to rigorous scrutiny they will not *for this reason* try to empty their minds of the 'prejudices' of faith. To come to the Bible in an attitude of faith that it is the inspired, authoritative and wholly reliable Word of God is to be neither basically dishonest nor inevitably blind to other viewpoints.

An attitude of humility towards God as Revealer (and therefore of submissiveness to his revelation) will lead to two important practical controls on theological study. In the first place, students will be aware constantly of the feebleness of their own understanding. They are looking at the facts of revelation 'through a glass, darkly', and, particularly at the beginning of a course, new questions will be asked to which there are no ready answers. Even when students sense that a logical answer *is* there, they may not be able to articulate their thoughts in a way that will satisfy the higher-powered critics at their own level. As a beginner this should hardly be a surprise! Often 'I don't know' is a more satisfactory reply than either a desperate attempt at a slick solution or an over-readiness to label difficulties as discrepancies.

Strangely enough, it is also surprisingly easy to over-estimate the extent of one's knowledge early on in the course. Solutions to problems that have baffled the best theological brains for centuries may seem irritatingly obvious to the first-year theolog. (I well remember beginning my first essay for a tutorial with the sentence, 'I profoundly disagree with Professor Dodd ...', only to be told that Professor Dodd happened to be in the next room and would like to have it out with me personally!) Again, intellectual humility is the best counsel. The amount of learning absorbed in one term may seem colossal when compared with former ignorance, but becomes very tiny when set in the context of all that there is to be known.

The Athanasian Creed is wise as well as impossibly tortuous when it asks for belief in 'the Father incomprehensible, the Son incomprehensible and the Holy Ghost incomprehensible'. Behind the comprehensible in theology there will always stand the incomprehensible, and Christians who preserve a humble relationship with God in their work will not be lured easily into a false position where they either expect to know all the answers, or are under the impression that they actually do.

This leads directly to a second control which Christian students will want to apply to theological investigation. As well as acknowledging the impossibility of ever fully comprehending all that is revealed, they will also take care to respect the limits imposed upon theology by the scope of revelation itself; for behind the revealed there will always be the unrevealed.

An illustration which may help here is that of a motorist driving through the countryside at night. The Highway Code demands that he drive within the limits of his lights. As he does so he can see the road ahead of him clearly enough for safe and reasonably fast motoring. But he does not expect to see very much of the surrounding landscape.

Like headlights, God's revelation is strictly functional. Its aim is the very practical one of imparting enough information to enable anyone to live in a godly way. There are other things we should *like*, but do not actually *need*, to know, and on these the Bible is often silent. Beyond the light is darkness, and the wise student is the one who is careful, theologically speaking, to drive within the limits of his or her lights. It is interesting in this connection to examine the history of the Creeds and to see how they originated in order to combat the heretical teaching of brilliant scholars who were trying to bridge the intellectual gulf between Christianity and their contemporary culture, by filling in the gaps of revelation. At one time the Roman authorities offered the state's express stage-coaches to church leaders free of charge for travel to ecclesiastical synods, and we are told how the imperial postal service was reduced to chaos as bishops scurried from council to council to thrash out their doctrine. Church history may seem dull at times, but it has its uses in exposing modern counterparts of these extra-revelational 'theologicies'. As Professor Paul Woolley of Westminster Theological Seminary wrote: 'Church history saves so much time by avoiding a lot of unnecessary, and sometimes tragic, experimentation.'

The Christian's approach to theology, then, will be controlled by the nature and scope of revelation. It is a lesson which the pastoral epistles are most anxious to get across. Timothy and Titus are told to *guard* what has been 'entrusted' to them (1 Tim. 6:20); to *follow* 'the pattern of the sound teaching' (2 Tim. 1:13); to appoint as presbyter/bishops those who '*hold firmly* to the trustworthy message as it has been taught' (Titus 1:9, my emphasis). Those who teach 'false doctrines' and 'promote controversies' are in fact going astray into a 'wilderness of words' (1 Tim. 1:6, NEB). Positively, the Christian preacher and teacher is to 'encourage others by sound doctrine' and to 'refute those who oppose it'.

Many today, of course, chafe at this kind of dogmatic restriction. In the words of Schubert Ogden, 'The New Testament sense of the claim "only in Jesus Christ" is not that God is only to be found in Jesus and nowhere else but that the only God who is to be found anywhere – *though he is to be found everywhere* – is the God who is made known in the word that Jesus speaks and is' (my emphasis). Others do not consider themselves at all obliged to accept on trust everything within the boundaries of biblical dogma. 'Is it possible to have faith without dogma?' asked Pierre Berton in his analysis of the Anglican Church in Canada. 'I should think the answer would be in the affirmative. More, I should think that in the late twentieth century it would be almost impossible to have faith *with* dogma.' The New Testament, however, would beg to disagree. Faith, in its biblical usage, is never to be divorced from 'the faith' – the body of doctrine, prophetic and apostolic, which declares what God has done and why he has done it.

So the wheel turns full circle. The kind of faith Christian students exercise in their study of theology is that of people making their way up a narrow mountain path (hard and difficult to distinguish in places, but always defined), not that of a death-wish leap from the path into a ravine of doubt, for it is no virtue to be agnostic where God would have us certain. They will willingly submit their deepest convictions to theological scrutiny, but as they do so they will be careful not to stray beyond the data of revelation. Their minds will be open – but not empty.

The professional

No worth-while occupation is without its special hazards, and the study of theology is not an exception to the general rule. On the 'forewarned is forearmed' principle, therefore, the next few pages will be devoted to some of the specific pitfalls Christian theological students must expect to meet as they begin their academic courses. There are no pat solutions to many of these problems, but the main danger nearly always lies in failing to spot each as it arises, and if the warning signals can be sighted early enough, the hazard itself is often easier to meet and overcome. In military terms, it is usually a case of crossing a mine-field rather than storming a barbed-wire entanglement.

By far the most insidious trap into which any theological student can fall is that of *professionalism*. It is not that there is anything inherently wrong in being a professional. Indeed the whole purpose behind theological training is to turn amateurs into professionals, in the same way that a course in engineering is designed to make a professional out of a do-it-yourself expert, and the function of a medical school is to turn a first-aid enthusiast into a doctor. However, at the student level there is a very important personal adjustment to be made (more so for the medic and the theolog than for the engineer) if the professional attitude encouraged by the course is going to be a healthy one. The medical student, for example, may go home after her first term of anatomy for a rest, only to find herself meeting an interesting cross-section of crania and rib-cages instead of people, as she walks down the street. She has to adjust, to assimilate her new professional knowledge so that it helps rather than hinders her attitude to the society in which she moves, and the contribution she eventually hopes to make to it.

For Christian theological students, the problem becomes more acute if they fail to understand what is happening to them and why. As Christians, they will probably be fairly well-acquainted with the contents of the Bible before going to college. In more optimistic moods, they may even have looked forward to nine terms of theology as a glorious opportunity to spend days and days doing just the kind of Bible study they have always longed to do if only time had permitted. This is a refreshingly positive attitude, but the process of disenchantment can be swift if students do not also appreciate that the way in which they are required to study the Bible as theological students (i.e. professionally), is subtly but vitally different. Previously they will have opened their Bibles only when they have been on their knees (figuratively or literally), seeking to apply God's Word to their lives in a personal way. Now, as students, the devotional handbook becomes an academic textbook which has to be analysed and dissected on the desk. There is nothing irreconcilable in the two approaches, but a great deal of needless trouble will be avoided if the difference of attitude is recognized right from the outset.

Students may react in one of three ways if they fail to integrate their academic and devotional approaches to Scripture. They may rebel against studying the Bible academically at all (the 'closed mind' attitude outlined in the last section); they may go to the other extreme and become so involved in technical niceties that the Scriptures no longer have any vital devotional meaning, even though they are still preoccupied with them academically; or they may adopt a middle course, recognizing the value of both approaches but striving to keep them as far apart in their own minds as possible. The second and third 'solutions' need fuller treatment, but at this stage the purpose is only to spot the problem. Theological students, whether they like it or not, have become professionals.

There are, of course, many other textbooks that theological students will be expected to read in addition to the Bible. For example, Bright, Kümmel and Guthrie will jostle for attention, and so crammed is the average theological course that most students will find themselves reading far more books about the Bible than the Bible itself. The dangers are obvious. To mention but one, most biblical references in the main textbooks are not quoted in full in the text, and although it is a really worthwhile exercise to see just how the verses cited support the author's case (and sometimes how they do not!) it is only the most conscientious who will ever get round to looking them up, let alone examine them in context. It cannot be over-stressed that Christians who mean business theologically must make it their primary aim to read deeply and widely in the Scriptures themselves. For examination purposes they will rightly be expected to know what the scholars say, but if they can add to this their own considered judgment based on an independent study of the text, they will be marked up, not down. So much theological work is little more than a playing-off of scholar against scholar, and most examiners as well as students get heartily fed up with the game.

It is not only in their approach to the Bible that Christian students need to exercise great care. Their relationships with other people, in the latters' eyes at least, will be on a slightly different level. It would be quite wrong to over-emphasize this change, but they will almost certainly become marked men and women in their home church (their Christian Unions, too, if at university). At some point in a Bible study, for instance, the leader will say in deferential tones, 'We had better turn to our tame theolog for some help on this', and it is so easy to take the bait and pontificate at great length, dragging in the involved technicalities of the lecture room when only the straightforward meaning is required. Given the very best of intentions, a correct adjustment between the academic seminar and the practical or devotional meeting is far more difficult to achieve than it may seem at first sight. Many Christian Unions complain that their theological contingent is far more of a hindrance than a help, making irrelevant points which bog down the flow of a discussion and raising questions that no-one else is asking. This is a great pity, because one or two theological students can make a really helpful contribution to a Bible study if only they are sensitive enough to know when and how to make it.

A similar lack of sensitivity bedevils a great deal of preaching and teaching. It probably accounts more than anything else for the warm reception a non-professional speaker receives ('Of course, I'm no theologian but ...'), and indeed for the way his blunt, well-directed words reach targets which the professional has tried but failed to hit. The young minister fresh from college tends to shy away from the 'great texts' because he feels that they are as much old hat to his congregation as they are to him. Often he is quite wrong, and he succeeds only in confusing his people with what appear to them as abstruse irrelevancies. Spurgeon was talking about sound, biblical preaching when he wrote, 'No chloroform can equal the sleep-giving properties of some ministers' discourses.' And again, 'If some men were sentenced to hear their own sermons they would soon cry out like Cain "My punishment is greater than I can bear".'

The *patronizing* professional is absolutely nauseating, of course, in any walk of life. One might assume that the Christian would be safe from this particular peril at least, but unfortunately it is not always so in practice. Not a few ministers have found themselves put kindly but theologically in their place by students during vacations. In term-time, too, the Christian Union programme may seem intolerably shallow and naïve. From what he had to say, last week's speaker might never have heard of Bonhoeffer, and the committee's obstinacy in refusing to lay on more talks with some solid doctrinal content simply has to be seen to be believed. And so on.

If the criticisms are not brought out into the open they may buzz around below the surface over coffee, which is probably more damaging to the fellowship in the long run anyway. Frequently the points made are extremely valid. Some Christian Union programmes *do* need to make room for more solid doctrinal teaching. Perhaps last week's talk *would* have been more valuable if the speaker had referred to Bonhoeffer – particularly if it had been predigested Bonhoeffer presented in such a form that it was immediately relevant to the uninitiated. But often the approach is so blunt and insensitive that the impression created is of the theolog on his pedestal attempting (usually in vain) to haul the reluctant Christian Union up to his own new-found heights of Christian maturity.

Maturity itself is a fine word. Paul encourages the Christians at Corinth not to be babes in understanding 'but in your thinking be adults' (1 Cor. 14:20). According to Hebrews, the believer ought to be able to 'leave the elementary teachings about Christ and go on to maturity' (Heb. 6:1). Immaturity, by contrast, is exemplified by those who are 'tossed back and forth by the waves, blown here and there by every wind of teaching' (Eph. 4:14). It is part of every Christian's vocation, then, to attain to doctrinal maturity, and it is those with theological training who are best equipped to encourage their fellowships towards this kind of high doctrinal standard. But true Christian maturity is further defined in the New Testament as 'the whole measure of the fulness of Christ' (Eph. 4:13); that is, not only being adult in *doctrine* (and in passing it is worth noticing that 'leaving the elementary doctrines of Christ' is not the same thing at all as *cutting loose* from set doctrinal standards), but also grown-up in *Christ-likeness*. 'A student', said Jesus, 'is not above his teacher, but everyone who is fully trained' (or 'mature' – the word is the same) 'will be like his teacher. Why do you look at the speck of sawdust in your brother's eye and pay no attention to the plank in your own eye?' (Luke 6:40–41). Jesus taught advanced doctrine, but he was never repugnantly doctrinaire in his attitude towards those he was trying to enlighten.

'In the eyes of many, his sincerity is now tainted with professional*ism*.' So wrote the Rev. A. M. Stibbs many years ago to describe the changed attitude a newly ordained man might expect from his parishioners, and although his collar may still be the right way round the theological student has already placed himself in a similar position. Christian 'amateurs' read the Bible because they want to, and do their Bible study in non-working hours. Theological students have their Bibles open on their desks; they must read it whether they want to or not, because if they do not they will fail their exams. They are professionals, and others are quick to recognize the fact, even if the students are reluctant to do so themselves.

Nevertheless, the professional tag is not one to regret, if the dangers of professional*ism* are recognized and avoided. Theological students who have rightly integrated their devotional and academic approaches to Scripture, who take care to soak in the actual words of the Bible as well as the thousands of words written about it, and who maintain a humbly sensitive attitude towards others, will find that the extra knowledge they are acquiring will be put to the best possible use. They will become part of the muscle of their fellowships, instead of being irritating thorns in their spiritual flesh.

Dypsychos

'As I go on, I get to know and more about less and less.' This is the specialist's testimony, and we live in a specialists' world where anyone who wants to make a serious contribution on anything must shut himself up to his own specialized field of investigation with barely a disciplined glance beyond its boundaries. The biblical research worker, for example, in searching for a good thesis subject, will often have to focus down his main interest to a mere handful of verses in order to achieve anything original at all. Most theological students will not aspire to such heights, but even the average theological college course calls for a marked degree of specialization. The Bible, in particular, tends to be fragmented. The Old Testament will be divided off from the New, and then further whittled down into history, prophecy and wisdom literature. Isaiah will be trisected, perhaps, and the sources of the Pentateuch analysed. There will be the special New Testament set book(s) to be studied in Greek. We may even set a computer to work on Paul.

The advantages of specialized study are enormous and it would be wrong to question them simply because one cannot immediately see the relevance of, for example, the date of the Exodus to the evangelization of the world. Nevertheless, there is an implied criticism behind such a comment which is absolutely valid. The Christian theologian is concerned with the *communication* of the whole biblical message to the world, as well as with the academic study of its constituent parts. One may excuse the scientific boffin who is so immersed in his research on an aeronautical instrument that he forgets all he has ever known about getting a plane into the air (after all, someone else can fit his device into a machine and get it to fly). But the theological boffin who separates off his or her academic work from his or her devotional life and its practical usage in the world is defenceless by New Testament standards.

There are in particular three pressure-points which theological students should watch with special care.

The academic and the devotional

'One thing I learned at theological college', said the new curate in his first sermon, 'was how easy it is to forget God.' The congregation, with good British ecclesiastical calm, did not bat an eye-lid, but there must have been some who were inwardly quite disturbed. Surely a theological course is designed to teach more about God. How could one possibly forget about God at a *theological* college?

Any student beyond his or her first few months would have known exactly what the preacher meant. The truth is that it is fatally easy to learn a great deal about God in a theological course without ever growing in personal knowledge of him. Sometimes one hears it said, rather disparagingly, that a Hindu could live through a degree course of theology at an English university without the least fear of getting converted. In so far as this is true it is hardly a reflection on the university, which exists to impart and further knowledge, not to convert souls or build up a Christian student's devotional life. Its function is frankly an academically specialized one, and it is up to the Christians to recognize this fact and to make sure that they supplement their specialist academic training with disciplined devotional living.

This is more easily said than done. It is not hard, for example, to rationalize away the need for a daily time of prayer and devotional Bible study, by arguing that as a theological student one is preoccupied with reading and thinking about God's things all day anyway. Even the mental adjustment needed to look at a passage devotionally rather than academically may take considerable effort, particularly if the same verses have been the subject of a recent lecture or essay. One student admitted that since attending a course of lectures on the Pentateuch the first books of the Bible had 'gone dead on him'; he found he had to look elsewhere for devotional help. And he was not the only one with this kind of problem.

There is no simple answer to this one. Often a really good devotional commentary will help, as may the simple expedient of using different copies of the Bible for devotional and academic use (possibly in different translations). Ultimately, however, the only worthwhile solution is for individuals themselves to integrate the two approaches to their own satisfaction, so that their devotional life is fed constantly with academic knowledge, and academic problems softened by being set in a context of humble prayer. Some find the process of integration relatively easy and barely have to think about it; others have to work fairly hard to achieve any positive results.

Theological colleges, of course, are concerned to produce ministers and other workers as well as academic theologians, people of prayer as well as men of knowledge. For this reason, theological college students will almost certainly find that they are expected to attend chapel services in addition to lectures and tutorials. Compulsory chapel attendance may become an irksome duty, but it can also play a most valuable part in helping to encourage devotional discipline – provided it is not accepted as a substitute for a regular private time alone with God. Theological students need more, not less, time for personal devotions. When problems are prayed over unhurriedly and a warm personal relationship with God is maintained and deepened, only then will the dry harshness of a purely academic approach to theology be avoided.

The academic and the practical

If over-specialization can deaden the devotional life, it can also drive a wedge between the academic and the practical. One symptom of this is an inability to 'get across' in preaching and teaching. Someone who has been able to interest others in God and Christ in a simple, straightforward way before becoming a student may emerge from theological college (or university) rather more erudite but also much duller. Some of his friends will shake their heads in disappointment at his stuffiness and blame theology, while he himself murmurs thoughtfully about the difficulties of communication.

In all probability the root of the problem lies in neither. It is far more likely to be the direct result of an imbalance in the student's own life between academic intake and practical output. Theological obscurity is certainly neither a sign of grace nor a mark of academic prowess, so that if you are difficult to understand it probably means either that you are grossly insensitive to your audience, or that you have an inadequate grasp of your subject. As far as the Christian is concerned, academic study will bear its proper fruit only when it elucidates, not complicates, God's truth. Jesus' own example is significant in this respect. He was certainly keen to train his disciples in the exegesis of the Old Testament Scriptures and to teach them as much academic theology knowledge as they could possibly assimilate in a hectic three-year course, but his tuition was never conducted in an artificially 'world-tight' atmosphere. Reading through the gospels we find that teaching and practice sometimes coincide and sometimes alternate. 'He appointed twelve', Mark 3:14 tells us, *'that they might be with him'* (in order to learn) *'and that he might send them out'* (in order to practise). Their theoretical learning was never divorced from practical training in real-life situations.

It is not considered to be part of a university's function to build such bridges between the academic and the practical (though the individual tutor may sometimes take it upon himself to do so), and the faculty student will generally have to do the relating and applying for himself. If he is of an academic turn of mind this side of things may be allowed to slip, but only with disastrous consequences to his usefulness as a Christian leader in later years. Often Christian Union local activities will provide the theolog with helpful outlets for practical service. Should this source fail, another valuable way to keep 'earthed' is to help out with a local young people's organization where boring irrelevancies will get the merciless treatment they deserve. In fact, anything will help that will bring home forcibly the need to translate technical terminology into language which bites on non-theological minds and that will encourage Christ's stewards to be not only faithful but wise in the way they distribute the food from their well-stocked larder.

Life in a theological college is in some ways rather easier. Lectures in homiletics and applied pastoral theology supplement the purely academic approach to the Scriptures, and opportunities to preach and teach in a wide variety of situations are usually built into the course. Nevertheless, a representative group of students at a conference sponsored by the British Council of Churches could complain in the strongest terms about the gulf they felt to exist between 'the theological insights of the gospel' and their practical application. 'We are convinced,' they reported, 'that training in these matters in our theological colleges at present leaves much to be desired.'

Colleges differ in their approach, of course, and it would be foolish to generalize, but it would be equally wrong for the individual student to imagine that, just because the subject of Homiletics appears on his time-table and opportunities are provided for him to speak at a local remand-home once a week, he is thereby relating his academic knowledge to real-life problems. More often than not he will find himself preparing his remand-home talk without the slightest reference to anything he has picked up in lectures, and his academic and practical lives may go their separate ways quite happily until the course ends and he has to confess that his academic training has been utterly irrelevant to the practical challenges of the world. At one American seminary the students are required to relate the theme of their weekend sermons to something they have learned from lectures or seminars during the preceding week – a terrifying exercise but perhaps not altogether valueless!

Academic study and personal belief

A particularly difficult situation arises when there is a clash between the teaching emphasis of the college (or university) staff and the student's personal convictions. There are many evangelicals, for instance, who feel the force of this problem very acutely. Unless they have the chance to opt for an all-evangelical college, they will find themselves almost certainly in a minority group in the student body; and if they are not at a university, and therefore unable to enjoy the benefits of Christian Union fellowship, it may be quite hard to find regular opportunities to talk and pray over specific difficulties with like-minded people. There are always those, of course, who really thrive on the cut-and-thrust of fierce theological debate (for them such a situation is a stimulus rather than a burden), and many lasting friendships are made across theological barriers; a 'mixed' college has its advantages. But there are always others who feel so unbearably lonely and oppressed that they long for the time when they can escape from the academic pressures and the well-intended jibes of college life, and get away into the outside world which, by comparison, is a friendly place.

These latter will be especially prone to find refuge in a Jekyll-and-Hyde approach to their academic course. For the sake of peace they will dutifully master a set of facts and memorize some eminent scholarly opinions, reproduce these whenever they are required to do so without comment or criticism, and at the same time attempt in private to keep their minds intact from what they are inwardly convinced is rank heresy. Arguments with tutors will be avoided and the necessary examinations passed.

Although it is easy to criticize such a mental dichotomy as negative and obscurantist, there are obvious practical advantages to it. Sometimes the pressures to change one's theological position build up very quickly indeed. There have been instances of students deserting well-founded convictions under the force of superior arguing power before the alternatives have been examined at least as thoroughly, which is unsatisfactory from everyone's point of view. Perhaps the best advice that can be offered to evangelicals who know they are likely to find themselves in this kind of minority situation is that they should spend as much time as possible, preferably before starting the course, mastering the main tenets of their own position, particularly the doctrine of Scripture which is nearly always the main debating-point. If they are quite clear, for example, what is *really* meant by such terms as 'inspiration' and 'inerrancy', they will not be so clumsy in presenting the conservative case as they might be otherwise. They will also run less risk of indignantly defending non-essentials while the really important issues are allowed to go by default.

It is so tempting, when facing a theological position with which one has little or no personal sympathy, to set up and demolish an Aunt Sally or straw man that bears as much resemblance to the real thing as a caricature does to an accurate portrait. The only remedy is to make quite sure that the case under fire (whether yours or the other person's) is presented at its strongest. Honest students will be unable to rest content with an airy dismissal of other points of view they have reluctantly learned for exam purposes. It will also mean, of course, that the willingness to think and be informed must be reciprocated. It is surprising, for example, to discover how few conservative books some will have read before feeling able to pronounce judgment on a whole range of conservative theology.

'That man should not think', writes the very practical James, 'he will receive anything from the Lord; he is a *double-minded* man, unstable in all he does' (Jas. 1:7–8).' The word is *dipsychos*, literally 'of two minds', and in this context it refers to those who vacillate in their personal faith, unsure whether God is to be trusted or not. James uses the same word once again towards the end of his letter in rather a different sense, to warn those whose practical living fails to match their Christian profession. It is as though an impenetrable barrier stands between their attitude to faith and their outlook on life; they are split personalities morally and spiritually. 'Wash your hands, you sinners, and purify your hearts, you *double-minded*' (Jas. 4:8).

This is teaching which theological students need to take to heart and apply to their own situation with the greatest of care. There will be many pressures upon them to compartmentalize their lives, either by splitting away their academic interests from devotional living and practical witness, or by erecting a barrier between their academic intake and their personal convictions. The New Testament strongly encourages the person with intellectual gifts to develop them to the full, but it nowhere condones a split-minded attitude towards the totality of Christian living. Disciples who would serve their Master best must make it their primary aim to lead a fully integrated life of devotion, learning and service.

Personalia

One disadvantage of a discussion like this is that it may give the impression that theological students are in some sense a class apart from 'ordinary Christians', rather fragile oddities who can fulfil a highly useful function in Christian society if they are protected with the utmost care from the special perils to which they are continually exposed. Nothing, of course, could be further from the truth. There are certainly particular dangers which confront theological students because of the nature of their work, but the same is true of any other discipline. Art and natural science students face problems in their own fields which the theologian escapes. Even the 'pressure-points' mentioned in the last section will ring true with some people and leave others wondering why they were included at all. Personalities differ, even theological ones, and many apparently technical difficulties turn out, on closer examination, to be problems of personal adjustment on one side or the other.

This is not to belittle the problems themselves. They are just as real, whatever their origin. But it will help towards solving some of them if their true nature is appreciated. The appeal of a particular theological system, for example, may have its roots in the personal charm of its chief advocate rather than in any particular merits of its case, and it can be quite hard to disentangle the one influence from the other. At the other end of the scale, a feeling of victimization may be due far more to the unpleasantly awkward attitude of the victim than to any real feelings of hostility on the part of his supposed tormentors. He may be unable to take criticism, in which case he will get far more of it than he otherwise would. He may be bad at producing routine work on time, and feel (quite wrongly) that his theological views are under fire when he is chased by his tutors.

The necessity of maintaining right personal relationships is especially vital in the artificially close atmosphere of a theological college, where men and women from all walks of life are thrown together and there are inevitably a few occasions when personalities conflict. Hard-boiled extroverts will feel that their timid, shy neighbours need to be taken out of themselves, and the shy scholarly types, who usually form the main target for ragging, while outwardly they take it all in good fun, inwardly may be seething with indignation that such practical jokers should ever intend to enter a serious occupation like the ministry. It is at times like these that 'academic' categories like intercession, penitence and sanctification will either come alive or die miserably. A vice-senior student at one of the happiest, best-integrated colleges in Britain could still write: 'It could be argued with some force that

Christians are usually content with far too low a standard in this respect. We talk about a personal relationship with God, meaning that we surrender all we have and are to him, and yet we happily accept an entirely different standard where relationships with fellow-Christians are concerned.' The personal rights which are surrendered willingly to God are often indignantly defended when it comes to sharing out the college chores (particularly if you happen to be married, with divided loyalties in the evenings). Significantly, Jesus taught the pupils of his itinerant theological college, with the utmost emphasis and clarity, that they should learn to love *one another* first and foremost. 'All men will know that you are my disciples, if you love one another' (John 13:35).

Loving sensitivity will produce tact, patience and insight into the needs and susceptibilities of others. It will encourage the practical discipline of turning down a volume control, returning borrowed property, forestalling irritability by an early night (one wonders how many 'spiritual crises', particularly near exam times, might be averted by a little more physical exercise and a couple of good nights' sleep), and being scrupulously – but not neurotically – sensitive to the effect on others of actions and words which in themselves may be perfectly harmless.

It is one of the banes of the ministry to substitute expertise for love, and no doubt Jesus was anticipating this particular peril when he laid such stress on his 'new commandment'. The Rev. Eric Alexander of Glasgow underlined the point very effectively when he told of a goodwill New Year's message from a local firm with a fatal misprint; it read: 'We try to *fake* an interest in all our customers.' With a little professional skill it is not hard to become a passable fake, and even to imagine that a genuine concern for others exists when it is really little more than skin-deep. There are usually the few at a theological college, sometimes rather unattractive individuals, who nurse private doubts and worries which they are afraid to bring out into the open. At a university these people can simply be avoided (which is hardly the way of Christ), but not so at a residential college. Sometimes a particularly sensitive student or member of staff will go out of his or her way to understand and help. But unfortunately it does not always work out like that.

Examples could be multiplied, but it is perhaps unnecessary to spell out the consequences of a right or wrong attitude towards others in any further detail. It will be enough for the Christian that Jesus himself returned again and again to the importance of *love among* disciples for the success of his work of love in the world. Above all, faithful disciples will recognize that their relationships with other people can stay right only if their relationship with God is close and fresh. Avoiding spiritual flippancies, which are a first sign of spiritual staleness, they will be careful to walk each day in the presence of the Saviour who alone can sharpen their sensitivity to the needs of others. 'As the Father has loved me, so have I loved you; *abide in my love*' (John 15:9, my emphasis).

An Indian theological student once paraphrased 1 Corinthians 13 in words which provide a fitting commentary on the theme of this section. It is worth quoting in full as a conclusion:

> If I have language ever so perfect and speak like a pundit, and have not the knack of love that grips the heart, I am nothing.
>
> If I have decorations and diplomas and am proficient in up-to-date methods, and have not the touch of an understanding love, I am nothing.
>
> If I am able to worst my opponents in argument so as to make fools of them, and have not the wooing note, I am nothing.
>
> If I have all faith and great ideals and magnificent plans and wonderful visions, and have not the love that sweats and bleeds and weeps and prays and pleads, I am nothing.
>
> If I surrender all prospects and, leaving home and friends and comforts, give myself to the self-evident sacrifice of a missionary career, and turn sour and selfish amid the daily annoyances and personal slights of a missionary life, and though I give my body to be consumed in the heat and sweat and mildew of India, if I have not the love that yields its rights, its coveted leisure, its pet plans, I am nothing, nothing. Virtue has ceased to go out of me.

If I can heal all manner of sickness and disease, but wound hearts and hurt feelings for want of love that is kind, I am nothing.

If I can write books and publish articles that set the world agog, and fail to transcribe the word of the cross in the language of love, I am nothing.

'I urge you to live a life worthy of the calling you have received', wrote Paul to the Ephesians. 'Be completely humble and gentle; be patient, bearing with one another in love' (Eph. 4:1–2).

This edition © David Field, 2001

2. A survivor's guide:
Things I wish I'd been told *before* studying theology
Laura Jervis

Laura Jervis graduated with a First Class Honours degree in Theology from St John's College, Oxford, in 1998. She was vice-president of the Oxford Inter-Collegiate Christian Union. Currently she combines working for The Bible Talks at Christ Church, Mayfair with MA studies at Oak Hill Theological College, London.

I don't know what made you want to study theology. Maybe it was your Christian conviction that theology is the subject to study. Or maybe, like me, you chose it by a process of elimination. It's a bit like playing *Twenty Questions* with yourself. It cannot be a subject involving numbers. There must not be any compulsory nine-o'clock lectures. I've got to be able to do it at a college where I will be able to live-in for the entire three years, and where there's good food and a tiddly-winks team (or whatever!). In that case, perhaps your personal beliefs were incidental. But whatever your reasoning was, and whether you like it or not, you are now facing three years of theological study as a believing Christian.

I wonder what reaction you had from Christian family and friends, or people in your church, when you told them you were planning to study theology. A number of people warned me that I was being unwise. It was dangerous. I was likely to 'fall away' and 'lose my faith'. Frankly, that was an attitude that frustrated me. Surely if we believe that we know the truth, then we have nothing to fear or hide. A bit of honest questioning could only strengthen my faith, or so I thought. I felt that people were patronizing me and that their attitudes were misguided and unhelpful. Surely they should have been encouraging me? It put my back up that they were implying that I would not be able to cope.

So I arrived at university quite confident, but totally unprepared

for the real difficulties and challenges that were ahead. If only those
kindly concerned Christians had told me *why* studying theology
could be dangerous. It is not that the Christian faith doesn't stand
up to rigorous critical enquiry. Not at all! But the academic study
of theology *can* pose problems for the spiritual health of the
Christian.

That, then, is why I have sub-titled this brief essay 'Things I
wish I'd been told *before* studying theology'.

The pros ...

It is all too easy to dwell on the problems of theological study, so I
want to begin by being very positive. It is an amazing privilege to
study theology. Just stopping to think about all that true
theological study ought to be makes me want to do my degree all
over again. Well, nearly! All Christians are theologians in a very real
sense because they study the Bible, thinking through their faith as
they seek to know God better. The difference is, you get to do it as
your degree. This really came home to me in the run-up to finals.
My friends and I were doing seven or eight hours work a day. (It
may sound virtuous, but it is amazing what fear can do.) While
everyone else was poring over Contract Law cases or scrutinizing
German textbooks, I was digging into the Word of God!

It is possible to study some pretty exciting options later on as
you home-in on areas that particularly interest you and, believe it
or not, Greek is great! You may think I am getting a bit desperate
in my attempt to find something to be positive about, but once
you have done a bit of hard work, it is brilliant to be able to read
the gospels in the original language.

I am risking sounding like a total geek, so I will move on. My
basic point is this: studying theology is a great privilege. Try not to
take it for granted.

And cons ...

It is difficult to stay spiritually healthy, however, and I want to
explain briefly why I think that is before giving some practical tips
on how to 'survive'! Hopefully, with God's help, we will do much

more than 'survive' and our time of studying theology will be one when we reach increasing Christian maturity.

It is who you know that counts

There is an important distinction to be made between two different types of religious knowledge: knowledge *about* God and knowledge *of* God. The former is all in the third person, whereas the latter is personal, relational knowledge in the second person. My French is not very good, but I suppose it's like the two verbs *savoir* and *connaître*.

As we study theology, we talk a great deal about God. In your first year you will be tackling all sorts of questions: 'What does it mean to say that God is creator?'; 'What does Mark's Gospel emphasize about Jesus and the kingdom of God?'; 'How do the different gospel accounts of Jesus' ministry relate to one another?' and 'What were the factors in the development of Chalcedonian orthodoxy?'

You will be taking in a huge amount of information about God and wrestling with it daily (well, often!).

But the problem is that the Bible's aim is for us to know God, not just for us to know about him. The reason the Bible teaches us all these things about God is so that we can come to know him personally as Lord and Saviour. That is the point we see Jesus making to the Pharisees in John 5:39–40: 'You diligently study the Scriptures because you think that by them you possess eternal life. These are the Scriptures that testify about me, yet you refuse to come to me to have life.'

The human circulatory system works by quantities of blood being pumped around the body by the heart. If a surgeon has a human body laid out on the operating table in front of him and the heart has stopped beating, then the problem is not solved by pouring more blood into the arteries and veins. Blood in the veins, even in vast quantities, is no good unless the heart is beating. That is the way the whole system is designed to work. Similarly, what you are learning is useless – it is not serving its purpose – unless it is causing you to know, love and serve God more fully.

When you are studying God for your academic degree, it is

difficult for the rate at which your heart is beating to keep pace with the large amount of blood which is being pumped in. In fact, I think it is probably impossible. No doubt the analogy of the circulatory system is a very imperfect one – I am no scientist – but I hope you understand what I'm writing. You must take steps to keep your spiritual life healthy, or sooner or later you will find that your relationship with God has died. Make every effort to be sure that you are getting to know God better as you study theology. Your spiritual maturity is not measured by whether or not you can discuss theological issues for hours and is far more important than what you know. It is easy for us to mix up those two types of knowledge of God and fall into the trap of mistaking a passion for theological correctness with a passion for God. No, spiritual maturity is better measured by your prayer-life, your love for God's Word and the extent of your daily obedience to it in the way that you live.

Do try to stand back and examine yourself from time to time. When I went home after my finals, I found that I did not really like the person I was becoming. I'd be chatting to Christian family and my heresy-hunting antennae would be twitching overtime! They would be talking about praying to Jesus, and I would be thinking that it might be better if they prayed to the Father through the Son by the Spirit. I had begun to look down on other Christians just because they had not received the privileged theological education and the good Bible teaching that my degree and my church respectively had given me.

So don't mistake knowing about God for a personal relationship with him.

What are you doing with your knowledge of God? It is important that knowledge about God becomes personal knowledge of God, so that we are spiritually healthy, but I would also argue that knowledge of God that is not put to its proper use of helping us to love and serve both God and others, actually damages us.

To use another unpleasant medical illustration: I help with an outreach to some elderly ladies in my local area and recently we had a social meeting at which someone came to talk about healthy eating. I was massively convicted about almost every area of my diet, but particularly my fibre intake. Apparently most Europeans eat nowhere near enough fibre. Everything can appear to be functioning healthily but actually undigested food is accumulating in our stomachs and intestines, so that by the time you are 30 or 40 you could be carrying up to 5lbs of undigested rotting food around with you! If you do not digest your food properly as you go along, by eating enough fibre regularly, then it will have nasty repercussions later. (There is a point to all this – I'm not being sponsored by a cereal manufacturer). In the same way, if we are receiving a lot of knowledge and not putting it to use or doing anything with it, it will go rotten on us and damage us spiritually.

How is your heart?

This brings our motives for theological study into sharp focus. To quote from J. I. Packer's excellent book, *Knowing God*, where he speaks about beginning the study of Christian doctrine:

> We need to ask ourselves: what is my ultimate aim and object in occupying myself with these things? What do I intend to do with my knowledge about God, once I have got it? For the fact that we have to face is this: that if we pursue knowledge for its own sake, it is bound to go bad on us. It will make us proud and conceited. The very greatness of the subject-matter will intoxicate us, and we shall come to think of ourselves as a cut above other Christians because of our interest in it and our grasp of it; and we shall look down on those whose theological ideas seem to us crude and inadequate, and dismiss them as very poor specimens ... To be preoccupied with getting theological knowledge as an end in itself, to approach Bible study with no higher a motive than a desire to know all the answers is the direct route to a state of self-satisfied deception. We need to guard our hearts against such an attitude, and pray to be kept from it.[1]

From Psalm 119 it is evident that the writer is studying the

Word of God with a very clear and noble motive. He says:

> How can a young man keep his way pure?
> By living according to your word.
> I will seek you with all my heart;
> do not let me stray from your commands.
> I have hidden your word in my heart
> that I might not sin against you.
> (Ps. 119:9–11)

He was interested in biblical teaching and in theological enquiry not as ends in themselves, but as a means to the greater aims of spiritual life and godliness. His ultimate concern was to know the awesome God whom he sought to understand.

Is this your attitude in studying? Do you want to get to know the living God better, or is your focus on knowing the doctrines of his attributes more adequately?

This really is an urgent question. At the end of the Sermon on the Mount, Jesus tells of those who will come before him on judgment day and expect to enter his kingdom because they did all sorts of things in his name – teaching and performing miracles. Jesus says to those people, 'I never knew you'. 'Away from me you evil doers!' It seems to me that many theologians will be in a similar position.

'But I wrote a dissertation on the Trinity.' – 'I never knew you.'

'But I did a PhD on the atonement.' – 'I never knew you.'

'But I lectured all over the world defending truth and ortho-doxy.' – 'I never knew you.'

It is vital that we do not neglect our relationship with Jesus and mistakenly think that theological knowledge alone amounts to the same thing. We need to get our motives right for studying theology.

Be bold!

We need not be embarrassed about our motives. People might say that *they* are studying theology with an open mind, with absolute scholarly objectivity and free from all presuppositions, but we know that is utter nonsense! Everyone without exception has his or her own set of presuppositions. The difference is that you, as a Christian, will have thought through yours and be more fully aware of them. When there is no conclusive evidence on a particular question of dating, authorship or reliability, and even if most fashionable scholars side against the Bible, there is no reason to be ashamed of sticking with Scripture. That is not blind faith. I never had to make myself believe something that flew in the face of all the evidence. Rather, I am calling for loyalty to God's truth when it may not yet be crystal clear to you how a particular problem should be resolved. You might be made to feel stupid in front of your slightly sarcastic tutor, but that is where not being ashamed of the gospel – the simple saving news about Christ crucified – really kicks in. So do not be surprised by the sneers or those raised eyebrows over the half-moon spectacles. Do not worry about your tutorial partner's patronizing smirk. Jesus tells us we should expect persecution when we stand for him. If we are not getting this sort of flak, perhaps it is because we are not contending for the gospel as we should be.

I often used to go back to 1 Corinthians 1:18–25 after a particularly stressful tutorial.

To summarize, then: studying theology is a wonderful privilege, but there are real dangers to our spiritual health in gorging ourselves on lots of knowledge about God for the duration of our course, without taking the time and effort required to digest it as we go along, applying it and obeying it in our relationship with God.

Six top tips on how to stay spiritually healthy

Don't take yourself too seriously

This may sound like a total contradiction of everything you hear from your tutors, but in fact it is eminently good sense, both spiritually and academically. There are bound to be moments when you are thrown by your studies. It might be that you cannot work out how the gospel accounts of the resurrection of Jesus could possibly fit together, or maybe one of the books on your reading list has a pretty convincing critique of the morality of Jesus' sacrificial death. It is tempting to take yourself terribly seriously, to have a major spiritual crisis and to suppose that the entire Christian faith is collapsing around you. It isn't! You have probably read four or five books on the subject (if you're really keen) and they were all by people your tutor has put on the reading list. Maybe you will have thought seriously about the question for a week, or even a term. You have been studying theology for six months altogether and you are about twenty years old!

I can honestly say that I would happily burn most of the essays I wrote in my first year. At the time I was utterly convinced by what I was arguing, but even a few years on, having read a lot more and studied other aspects of theology, having gained some experience of how lecturers and tutors work, I am embarrassed by many of my shallow analyses and spoon-fed conclusions. If you need convincing on that point, dig out your GCSE English books some time!

I sometimes think that theology files should be like *The Hitch Hiker's Guide to The Galaxy*, with 'Don't Panic' emblazoned across the front in huge fluorescent letters. My advice is: Chill out! You will be surprised how many things that baffle you now will soon fall into place. I can say honestly that I didn't have an overall grasp of how to approach liberal theology until the start of my third year. Until then there were a lot of unresolved questions and no clear 'framework' for tackling them. To some extent I kept my academic studies and my Christian life at arm's length from each other. I do not think that is necessarily evil and dishonest. It can be very sensible to recognize that you cannot expect to understand a subject entirely on the basis of four books, one tutorial and an essay, which you wrote at three in the morning the night before (or after) it was due in. Work out the difficulties in your own time. Don't suddenly drop your relationship with God because of a glitch in your understanding.

Don't let your personal time with God be squeezed out

Regular prayer and Bible reading are vital. When you read the Bible, don't treat it as a theology textbook, but as it really is, as God's personal word to you – almost God's love-letter to you! It is easy to get into dry academic study of the Bible, so make sure you guard against it. Perhaps get some reading notes that will push you towards practical applications. Make sure you spend time in prayer. It is a great sadness when theology students lose the joy of their salvation. You may write essays about grace, but forget the wonder of the fact that God gave his precious Son to die for you while you were a rebellious sinner deserving only his judgment.

Wonderfully, God promises to keep all those who are his, whether or not they are studying theology! But we are urged to trust him, and one of the main ways to keep our hearts pumping is by reading and applying his Word prayerfully to our lives.

Seek out good teaching and Christian support

Try to settle quickly into a church where the Bible is taught clearly and faithfully. Don't go somewhere where you will be subjected to yet another academic lecture. Look for a church where you will be encouraged by meeting up with others who love the Lord Jesus and who will support you. Get involved with the Christian Union and try to spend some time with people who are concerned to know Jesus better by living according to his word. Something I found invaluable was to meet regularly with an older Christian to study a passage of the Bible and pray briefly and chat together. Don't be proud and independent. You *need* other Christians. Perhaps look out for one or two particular friends with whom you can be honest about your struggles and be committed to praying for one another.

Find out about resources

There are lots of useful books written by credible evangelical scholars, but they will not always appear on your reading list. Some alternative reading list suggestions are available from the RTSF (write to RTSF, 38 De Montfort Street, Leicester, LE1 7GP or visit www.uccf.org.uk/rtsf). Ask older Christian theology students which books they found helpful. You are not the first person to face these challenges, and those who have 'survived' may well be keen to help. Hopefully you will find the opportunity for mutual support and encouragement through the local RTSF group and you may even be able to put on evangelistic events together.

Always read the primary text for essays and pray for wisdom

It is so easy to write an essay on Job without actually reading the book itself. You are pushed for time and so you go straight to the nearest Bible dictionary and, for example, the Sheffield OT Study Guide, and never read the text. To study theology effectively you will need to know what the Bible actually says! Make sure you grapple with Scripture first before you take on a load of second-hand ideas about it. It is amazing how many times some critic will say, 'and this is clearly what Paul says in 2 Corinthians 4', for example, and when you look up the reference that is blatantly *not* the point Paul is making at all. So always check up what the Bible actually says. Believe it or not, your tutors will love to see a detailed first-hand engagement with the text, and so will the examiners! Hardly any candidates comment on the actual text. They just trot out the same two critics and weigh up their theories. That must be bad theological method and it will not do wonders for your spiritual health either.

When you are reading the Bible or writing an essay, pray to God for wisdom. God has not written the Bible to confuse and he does not leave us on our own to understand it (cf. Jas. 1:5; 2 Tim. 2:7). You still need the Spirit of God to help you understand the Word of God, and you need humility to take it on board and obey it, not just to analyse it for your essay.

Be humble

In my third week at college I decided that one final year student at a Christian Union meeting really needed all the benefit of my extensive theological research. I came out with something that I had swallowed hook, line and sinker from my tutor about most Christians misunderstanding the OT sacrificial system. Fortunately, the person was not taken in, but told me very clearly that I did not know what I was talking about and showed me some parts of the Bible on the subject! It makes me blush to write it, but it is so easy to be proud and to think that you are on some higher level than other 'simple' Christians who just read their Bibles. I urge you to keep fairly quiet while you are settling in to the study of theology, just as men are advised not to sing while their voices are breaking. For example, those in your college Bible study probably won't benefit much from your 'superior' knowledge, which in any case you may well rethink after another term's study. Young Christians certainly do not need to be dragged into your confusion over some of the technical questions which liberal theology has thrown up. A good rule of thumb is that if you cannot express your ideas in ordinary language that the person in the pew could understand, then they are probably not worth airing. If you need to talk about 'realized eschatology' and 'redaction critical technique' then either you haven't grasped the ideas very firmly yourself or they are probably pretty irrelevant.

Be careful. I know from experience that it is very easy to become proud. As Paul said to the Corinthians: 'Knowledge puffs up, but love builds up' (1 Cor. 8:1). Keep asking yourself two questions: First, are you living by what you know and, second, are you seeking to explain the gospel to non-Christians? *That* will keep you humble. Who cares if you got the highest grade for your last essay and are heading for the top first in the university. If you are not living it out, and if you cannot explain the Christian faith to the other guys in your rugby team or to those girls on your corridor, then, as far as God is concerned, you are not a good theologian. You are a failed theologian. Keep asking yourself these searching questions and you'll realize that you are no better than any other Christians and desperately in need of God's forgiveness and help.

Note

[1] J. I. Packer, *Knowing God* (Hodder & Stoughton, 1975), p. 20.

3. Evangelical foundations for 'doing' theology
Nigel M. de S. Cameron

Professor Nigel M. de S. Cameron is former Provost and Distinguished Professor of Theology and Culture at Trinity International University, Deerfield, Illinois. He was also Warden of Rutherford House, Edinburgh.

Introduction

'The great question is that of method, everything else follows in due course.'[1]

How do we 'do' theology?

Is it a matter of finding your favourite theologian, and following him? Or choosing the kind of theology which most appeals to you, and justifying it? Or what? The picture of most theological faculties is not an encouraging one. Professors and lecturers seem to arrive at a dozen different conclusions about God, and why? Because they start from a dozen different premises, and allow different methods to determine the course and the conclusions of their study.

Little wonder that theology today has difficulty in keeping its traditional image as a 'scientific' discipline, in which the great facts of the faith govern people's imaginations. God is dead, Jesus is a revolutionary, the gospel is all about social reform – today's theologies take many forms. Is it still possible, in the middle of all this, for an evangelical Christian to claim that there is only *one* true theology, and that it is the faith 'once delivered to the saints' of New Testament days?

This essay is written with the conviction that it is still possible.

What is more – and this gives a particular cogency to the evangelical position today – any other brand of Christianity is fatally flawed by its arbitrary and selective character. The 'theologies' that have blossomed in recent decades have taken their point of departure in attempts to improve upon biblical Christianity. However, biblical Christianity cannot be open to improvement, not because we find nothing in it with which we may disagree (it is a sign of the authority of the Bible over us that we believe it while not liking all that it says), but because once we begin to tamper with a revealed, God-given, religion it immediately ceases to have that fundamental character. It becomes something man-made. The selection of truths which is accepted is our selection, not God's. What began as an attempt to bring faith up to date or to round it out ends up destroying the faith itself.

I was asked to write on 'theological method'. How dry and very uninteresting! And yet, of course, how *crucial*. For the method that we use in our theology – our thinking about God – determines whether we discover him. Get the method wrong and you get God wrong. Get it right, and your mind can come to grips with him. After all, for what greater work were our minds made? It has been the great desire of thinkers down the ages to find God. That indeed was the purpose of God, as Paul told the gathered philosophers of ancient Athens (in Acts 17). God made people 'so that [they] would seek him and perhaps reach out for him and find him' (17:27). Yet it was his purpose also, even as men and women sought him, to find *them*. He is not awaiting discovery, he has revealed himself; and in the Holy Scriptures we are provided with his own means whereby we may come to learn of him. 'Theological method' is the proper use of God's self-revelation to understand him and know him as he has intended.

The alternative is mere madness, the attempt to pit the little wits of human beings against an unknown God who must be worshipped in ignorance (the God of the philosophers), or to tamper with the God-given faith in a vain and self-destroying effort at up-dating it. Evangelicals, pinning their hopes on the Bible and trusting it as God's own Word, can 'do' theology in a way no-one else can; because if historic Christianity be true, they are doing it the way God intended.

What is theological method?

The phrase 'theological method' is used for different purposes, and given different meanings. Here it is assumed to have one specific meaning. 'Theology' is derived from the Greek *theos* (God), and *legein* (to discourse, or speak); so the *Oxford English Dictionary* defines it as follows: 'the study or science which treats of God, his nature and attributes, and his relations with man and the universe; "the science of things divine" (Hooker)'. 'Method' derives from the Greek *methodos*, which means 'pursuit of knowledge' or 'mode of investigation', and once again the *OED* definition well suits our purpose: 'a special form of procedure adopted in any branch of mental activity, whether for the purpose of teaching and exposition, or for that of investigation and inquiry'. So we shall take 'theological method' to be the special procedure whereby the study of God is properly carried on.

It is important to recognize at the outset that, although we may think of 'doing theology' as simply an academic course of study in which it is largely *theologians and their ideas* that are in view, theology is properly *the study of God*. Not that the two are necessarily in conflict. God may be studied by means of the works of others who have studied him. But, while it may be convenient to speak of 'theology' as an academic discipline along with medicine and English literature, it is vitally important to realize that, if we may speak in such terms, the *object* of theological study does not lie in theological study itself. Languages, history, archaeology and a dozen other subjects may all be laid under tribute by the theologian, but if his investigations end with them and do not penetrate beyond them, his study has failed completely. Theology proper is not the study of humanity's thought about God; it is that only in so far as it enables the theologian to study God for himself. And that is why the term 'theologian' is used here not simply for people of great learning or academic distinction, but of everyone who engages in theology.

So when we say that theological method is 'the special procedure whereby the study of God is properly carried on' we are defining it in a strict sense. That is entirely appropriate to Christian theology. To a pagan, 'theological method' could be the way of investigating many different gods; to an agnostic or a student of comparative religion, it might be the study of a variety of religions and their claims. Someone who did not believe that God had revealed himself could scarcely have confidence that he or she could learn anything of him. So it is evident that our religious position plays an important part in our definition of theology and its scope.

To a Christian, therefore, 'theology' may mean, quite strictly, the study of God. But how is that possible? How may God be studied? He is not accessible to us, not part of the world of phenomena around us. He can be studied only if he has made himself known, only if he has revealed himself. The foundation of Christian theology is that he has done so. He has revealed himself, in order that men and women might come to know him. So it is possible to study him, 'his nature and attributes, and his relations with man and the universe' (*OED*) and Christian theological method is the appropriate means. What then is that method to be?

The approach of this essay is positive and constructive. Many theological systems, or 'theologies', differ from each other for the plain reason that they are constructed by different methods. Method profoundly affects, and can determine, conclusions. Theologians may never state what they conceive their method to be, and why they have adopted it. They may proceed as if their use of the available materials were the only use possible. Yet, in the face of the widely divergent conclusions which characterize theological writing today, that can hardly be the case. It is not as if the starting-points of these theologies were different. Virtually every theology that claims the name 'Christian' formulates its theological propositions on the basis of the Bible, or at least it seeks to *justify* them by appeal to the Bible. The Bible, interpreted in this way or that, is the 'given' of Christian theology, and there is well-nigh universal agreement about that at least. Other elements – tradition, criticism on the basis of philosophical or other factors, and so on – may all have their place, but if theologians who share the same fundamental starting-point end up so widely scattered, the answer must lie in the methods by which they 'do' their theology.

That gives some indication of the importance of this subject. Our aim in these few pages will be to suggest the outline of a method for evangelical theology.

Where do we start?

If theology is the study of God, and if God has revealed himself, then that revelation is the proper immediate object of the theologian's attention. And where is the revelation of God? Traditionally a distinction has been drawn between his *general* revelation, in the natural order and the human consciousness, and his *special* revelation in Scripture. According to Scripture itself, the general revelation has a real, though limited, role to play in making God known (Ps. 19; Rom. 1). Whatever that may be, the principal locus of revelation is not in nature, but in Scripture. That is the datum of Christian theologians, and the interpretation of Scripture is the foundation of all their theology. Even the general revelation in nature and conscience is properly understood and acknowledged as valid only because we learn of it in Scripture. It may be all unbelievers can see of the revelation of God, resulting in their being 'without excuse' before him; but believers can learn nothing of God in nature that they have not first learned in Scripture. It is by means of Scripture and the light it sheds on everything they see that nature may speak to them of God, for the special revelation illumines the general.

A word must be said, at this stage, all too briefly, about the place of Jesus Christ. In much recent theology the emphasis placed on Christ as *the* revelation of God has seemed to displace the Bible from its station as the focus of the Christian theological task. Christians who look principally to the Bible are accused of 'bibliolatry', worshipping the book rather than the God it reveals. The control, we are told, on our theological enquiry should not be the Bible, it should be Christ. Now, if it were true that orthodox Christian theology exalted the Bible above Christ, this would be a terrible error. The Bible, whatever may be special about it, is a book; and the book must serve God, not rival him. But it is doubtful that ever a Christian did worship the Bible. The accusation of 'bibliolatry' is polemical, a smear directed against the high view of the Bible which orthodox Christians maintain. There is no contradiction between reverence of the Bible as the recorded revelation of God, and the worship of Christ as his personal revelation. There are a number of reasons why, far from competing with each other, the two must go hand-in-hand. For one thing, the Bible and Jesus Christ play different and distinct parts in the plan of salvation. Jesus Christ is the Saviour, who, in his incarnation, brings humanity and God together and achieves redemption through his death. The Bible is the trustworthy record of God's dealings with the world and his people, culminating in his dealing with them in Jesus Christ. These are separate functions, and should not be confused. Again, the only knowledge that we have of Jesus Christ is through the medium of the Bible. Theologians who pretend otherwise deceive themselves. Apart from a few scattered references in other ancient records, some reliable and some not, our knowledge of Jesus Christ stems from the pages of the Bible. We may know him in experience too, but if the content of that experience is not always controlled by what is revealed in the New Testament then it is purely subjective and simply untrustworthy. We cannot know Christ apart from the Bible. Further, from what the Bible says of Christ we discover that he too revered the holy Scriptures, and indeed described them in language that few would use today. He passed on to his disciples the highest regard for his and their (Old Testament) Bible, and he promised that they would be inspired to recall the final chapters of the history of redemption.[2] So a proper reverence for Christ upholds, and does not detract from, the highest regard for the Bible; indeed, we may say that it requires it. And, what is more, the Bible unitedly witnesses to and exalts Christ himself – looking forward in the Old Testament, backward in the New. He is its focus and theme.

We may ask, however, what is the meaning of saying that Christ, rather than the Bible, should be the control of our theological thinking? How can a person, knowledge of whom we gain from the Bible itself, teach us about God *except by means of the Bible*? It is an incoherent notion that we should make Christ *rather than* the Bible the revelation of God by means of which we 'do' our theology, and it is no surprise that at a time when many speak in this way we have unprecedented theological pluralism. Personal preference and simple ingenuity become the subjective guides of self-contained 'theologies' that have little contact with each other or with the Christ of the Scriptures.

This leads us inevitably to the question of what form the

revelation in the Bible actually takes. The Bible, as its name reminds us, is a book (correctly, it means 'the books'). It is a great collection of prose and poetry. It is composed of sentences, phrases and words. We could also say that it is composed of statements or propositions. That is why Christians have spoken of it as 'propositional revelation', a phrase that in fact says something simple, no more than is implied in our assent to the belief that the Bible is God's revelation of himself and to the evident fact that it is composed of words and sentences. However, this whole area is a controversial one, in which, increasingly, some who would call themselves 'evangelical' and who share a common theological heritage would disagree with the use of such traditional phrases. In fact, there is a growing number who, while accepting other distinguishing marks of evangelicalism – belief in the virgin birth, the substitutionary atonement, the physical resurrection, the second coming, and so forth – would wish to depart from the view of the Bible maintained by former generations of orthodox Christians. We face a spectrum of opinion, including defence of the old doctrine in new language, retention of the old language with the abandonment of important elements of the old doctrine, and, thirdly, innovation in terminology and belief.

It is easy for arguments about terminology to obscure the truth as much as they are intended to illuminate it, but in order to lay some basis for what follows, and in the interests of clarity, we must devote some time to several central concepts in the Christian view of Scripture.

Inspiration

There is no property more generally attributed to Scripture than that of inspiration, and it is a feature of almost every strand of 'Christian' theology. But what does it mean to say that the Bible is 'inspired'? It need not mean very much. Many have acknowledged 'inspiration' in Scripture as they would in, say, Shakespeare and other elevated writings. They may feel that inspiration in the Bible goes beyond, perhaps far beyond, inspiration exhibited elsewhere; but the difference is one of degree, not of kind. Others, while recognizing inspiration of an altogether different order in the

Bible, would see its proper locus as outside the Bible itself in the lives of its authors. The Scriptures are not, it is said, *inspired writings*: they are *the writings of inspired men*. This may seem an insignificant difference, but it is not, for it seeks to drive a wedge between God and the Bible. If inspiration is but an elevated quality in the lives of the biblical writers what effect need it have on their writings? Historically, when Christians have spoken of the inspiration of Scripture, it is *the Bible* to which they have attributed inspiration, whatever may have been the talents and experiences of its human authors.

Our chief reason for believing this, is that it is what the Bible says about itself, and we may comment here on a familiar objection often raised at this point. It is said that this is a circular argument, and that therefore it is not valid; but in fact it is not as simple as that. Every Christian is prepared to start from the Bible, to see the Bible as the 'given' of theology, the source-book, to put it at its lowest. So it is reasonable, before we make further use of this source of revelation, to enquire of it what it says about itself. It would be irrational to employ it as a guide to other theological questions while ignoring its testimony to itself. The fundamental problem of theology since the rise of the 'critical' view of the Bible has been its attempt to use the Bible as the basis for theological statements while flatly rejecting the Bible's view of itself. This is a deep-rooted problem of method to which we shall return.

The biblical idea of inspiration is expounded classically by B. B. Warfield, the greatest evangelical theologian of his day, in his essay on the subject. He defines inspiration as 'a supernatural influence exerted on the sacred writers by the Spirit of God, by virtue of which their writings are given divine trustworthiness'.[3] He points out that in modern English translations of the Bible the word 'inspired' occurs only once, in 2 Timothy 3:16: 'All scripture is inspired by God and profitable for teaching, for reproof, for correction, and for training in righteousness ...' (RSV). Warfield, in discussing the meaning of the word translated 'inspired', suggests that it is not a good translation. He writes,

> *theopneustos* very distinctly does not mean 'inspired of God'. [It] has nothing to say of *in*spiring or of

*in*spiration: it speaks only of a 'spiring' or 'spiration'. What it says of Scripture is, not that it is 'breathed into by God' or is the production of the divine 'inbreathing' into its human authors, but that it is breathed out by God, 'God-breathed', the product of the creative breath of God. In a word, what is declared by this fundamental passage is simply that the Scriptures are a divine product, without any indication of how God has operated in producing them. No term could have been chosen, however, which would have more emphatically asserted the divine production of Scripture than that which is here employed. The 'breath of God' is in Scripture just the symbol of his almighty power, the bearer of his creative word. 'By the word of Jehovah', we read in the significant parallel of Ps. xxxiii.6, 'were the heavens made, and all the host of them by the breath of his mouth.' And it is particularly where the operations of God are energetic that this term ... is employed to designate them. God's breath is the irresistible outflow of his power. Where Paul declares, then, that 'every scripture,' or 'all scripture' is the product of the divine breath, is 'God-breathed', he asserts with as much energy as he could employ that Scripture is the product of a specifically divine operation.[4]

The reader may be referred to Warfield, and to more recent works such as J. I. Packer's *Fundamentalism and the Word of God* for the further defence of this historic Christian position. Our purpose is to clarify the basis in Scripture for doing Christian theology. The text Warfield discusses in this passage, though alone in employing the word *theopneustos*, is but one of hundreds which speak of the divine origin of all or part of the Bible. To speak of its *origin* in the mind and breath of God is not to speak of the method by which it came to be written. It is a common fallacy, especially among critics of this view of the Bible, to see it as involving the by-passing of the personality and mind of the human authors of the Bible. But evangelicals do not claim this, as we shall see.

The Bible is *inspired*, that is, the product of the divine creative breath. As we turn to consider other relevant concepts it will be seen that they are all derived from this the primary concept. They arise as questions are asked concerning the implications of inspiration and its significance.

Plenary, or verbal, inspiration

The first question raised in many minds by the ascription of 'inspiration' to the Bible is that of the *extent* of inspiration. Granted that the Scriptures are *inspired* in the sense defined above, need this involve the belief that inspiration – the divine superintendence of their composition – extends right down to the form of words used by the human author? Might it not be that, while God superintended the general approach and subject-matter, the literary form and all the detail he left to the human writer? This is a frequent argument, and a plausible one. In fact, as writers such as Warfield have seen clearly, these objections do not hold, and essentially for two reasons: the first logical, the second biblical. To begin with, if we agree that the Bible is inspired, breathed out by God, we must ask ourselves, What is the Bible? Whether we like it or not, the Bible is a book; and like every other book it is composed of chapters, paragraphs, sentences and words. Any claim we make about the book as a whole must hold good of its parts. If it is not the *parts* of the Bible that are inspired, then what is left? The inspiration must be *full*, or *plenary*, as earlier scholars put it; it must, if the question is raised, extend to the very words employed. The older, positive designation 'plenary' in fact is the better one. Inspiration is not limited in extent, and any attempt so to limit it must be arbitrary and depend ultimately on some authority outside the Bible.

This *logical* point is paralleled by the fashion in which Scripture explicates its view of itself. There is widespread scholarly agreement that, for instance, the New Testament writers held much the same view of the inspiration of the Old Testament as did their Jewish contemporaries; and, in their view, inspiration extended down to the last 'jot and tittle' (Matt. 5:18, AV; a reference not to words but to the smallest letter and a tiny part of a letter!). The New Testament, and in particular the teaching of Jesus, is full of arguments and expositions which depend for their force upon individual words and phrases in the Old Testament Scriptures. This should serve as a powerful corrective to the widespread assumption today that it is not the text of the Bible but the events to which it witnesses that really count. Of course, events such as the exodus were seen by the Bible writers as of great revelatory significance. But so were details of the text of Scripture, as we find exemplified in Jesus' devastating use of Psalm 110 against the Pharisees (Matt. 22:41–46). The hand of God is present in the great facts of Israel's history; but it is there also in the details of the *record* of that history, which becomes itself a vital element, and not the least element, in the very redemptive process.

Infallibility

A further question arises: given that all the Bible is inspired, is it all true? To attribute infallibility to Scripture, it is said, will seriously detract from the 'human' side of its divine–human character. If this objection has force, a serious problem is raised. How may a book containing errors be the starting-point for our knowledge of God?

In fact, two separate issues are raised. First, a matter we have not discussed so far, the question of the production of the Scripture documents. We have said that the highest claims may be made for the *inspiration* of Scripture without there being any implications for the method of composition employed; and, in particular, without any need for it to have been 'dictated', as we understand the term. The idea of 'dictation' involves two elements – the result achieved (which is identical with that intended by the originator of the message), and the means by which this result is achieved (the passive attitude of the writer, who is simply a scribe, a human typewriter, and whose mind is not engaged in the operation except in listening to the message and reproducing it on paper). The scribe contributes nothing to the content or form of the message. Handwriting is the only distinctive feature that is added. It is possible to write a dictated message without the ability to apprehend its meaning at all; even to write a message dictated in a foreign tongue, provided rules of pronunciation and spelling are known. There need be no understanding, and there can be no contribution, on the part of the scribe.

It is clear that, thus understood, such a concept of the *method* of biblical composition does violence to the Christian view of the Bible as a book both divine and human. But the former element, the achieved result, is not open to objection. Indeed, that the end product should be identical with that intended in the mind of God as if he had simply dictated it is implicit in the idea of inspiration itself. But that is the limit of the analogy, and while it has been used (by Calvin, for instance, and by the influential nineteenth-century scholar Gaussen), it is less than helpful because of the misunderstanding it provokes.

But its value to us now is that this discussion shows the limits between which we must understand the composition of Scripture to have taken place. The human authors were consciously involved in the process, but at the same time what they actually wrote down was precisely what God had intended that they should. Is this conception coherent? Some would say that it contradicts itself, and that only by over-riding their individuality and personality could God have ensured that the product of their labour would accord precisely with his intentions. Not only so, but they would assert that the idea of infallibility is inimical to the fact of the sinful human nature of the writers of Scripture. The first of these objections – relating to personality and authorship – derives from our discussion of the actual process of composition; the second, dealing with sin and fallibility, takes us on to a separate question.

The defenders of the orthodox Christian doctrine of Scripture have seen the process of inspiration from one angle, as simply a special case of the doctrine of God's providence. Warfield writes of the preparation of the men to write these books:

> ... a preparation physical, intellectual, spiritual, which must have attended them throughout their whole lives, and, indeed, must have had its beginning in their remote ancestors ... to bring the right men to the right places at the right times, with the right endowments, impulses, acquirements, to write just

the books which were designed for them ... If God
wished to give his people a series of letters like Paul's,
he prepared a Paul to write them, and the Paul he
brought to the task was a Paul who spontaneously
would write just such letters.[5]

There is no over-riding here of the personality of the human
author. On the contrary, that very personality is the product of the
careful preparation of the sovereign God. Not that the Scripture
accounts are without direct evidences of the miraculous, of
prophetic trances and dreams and special communications, but the
general testimony of the biblical books that they were the product
of the normal operation of human minds is in no way set aside by
the belief that the human minds worked as the unerring creatures
of the providence of God.

The second issue is then reached. Must not an infallible book,
however produced, be a less than human work – because it is more
than human? If this were true, it would logically rule out the
possibility of infallibility, whatever other evidence might say. The
real, personal involvement of the human authors of Scripture
precludes the possibility of its being without error.

This objection was examined in the nineteenth century by
Edward Garbett, and we can do no better than quote him in
response. Scripture, he writes,

is the product of two constituent elements, the
Divine and the human ... both the elements are to be
maintained complete. This can only be done by
retaining what is essential on either side, all, without
reserve, necessary to the existence of the authority of
God on the one side, and the intelligent instrumentality of man upon the other ... the human
element does not derogate from the absolute truth of
Scripture. When the words 'human element' are used
in the sense of necessarily involving ... the mistakes
characteristic of secular compositions ... their use
involves not only ambiguity of language, but a fallacy
... Man is as clearly fallible as God is clearly infallible.

> But to be fallible, or capable of making mistakes, is
> not the same as making mistakes; the liability must
> not be confounded with the act. To be wrong is a
> separable accident, not an inseparable property of
> human nature. If it were of the essence of humanity,
> then man could never be right, but must be univer-
> sally and invariably wrong; but man is sometimes
> right, sometimes wrong. Many human narratives are
> wholly true, a thing may be wholly human, and yet
> not untrue ... the fact that the Scriptures were
> written by human instruments does not prove the
> existence of mistakes in them; all it proves is, that in
> the absence of any other influence to prevent it, there
> might be mistakes in them. But this corrective
> influence is supplied by the Divine element ... [6]

In short, it is quite possible for an unaided human being to write
a narrative which is wholly true and contains no mistakes. Many
human narratives are, therefore, infallible. The mystique that
attaches itself to the idea of infallibility is out of place. The full
'humanity' of the Bible is in no way compromised by assent to its
complete reliability.

Revelation

If we grant that the Bible is inspired and, consequently, without
error, the question is raised of its purpose – and we have come full
circle. God 'breathed out' this collection of books, by the
instrumentality of human authors, in order to reveal himself. It was
necessary that that revelation should be trustworthy and without
error. An unreliable, erroneous revelation would give a distorted
picture of God. It would not be suitable as the ground for human
knowledge of God, for theology.

Some further comments may be made. First, the revelatory
significance of the Bible is soteriological; it relates to salvation. We
may see this from two angles. On the one hand, the role of the
Bible is limited to the period between the fall and the eschaton.
Before the fall, humanity had uninterrupted communion with

God. There was no need of a special revelation; but with the coming of sin the prior revelation of God in nature and conscience no longer availed to bring knowledge of God to humanity. Some new revelation was required to mediate that knowledge, and the special revelation to humanity in the primeval world (Gen. 4 – 11) and then to Abraham and his descendants (Gen. 11ff.) culminated and was deposited in the Scriptures of the two Testaments. When the sin which thus necessitated a special revelation is no more, that revelation, which we have in the Bible, will no more be needed. We shall see God face to face.

On the other hand, it is important to see the role of the Bible *in* salvation. Not only does it tell us of the mighty works of God, wrought for us and for our salvation, but in itself it is one of them. The extensive and concentrated work of the Holy Spirit, preparing the writers of Scripture from before they were born, and indwelling them and guiding them in their task, was itself a major act of God in history. We must not underestimate the importance of the role played by the Holy Scriptures down the ages, in the nation of Israel, in the life of Jesus Christ, and in the church.

This moves us on to the directly related question of *authority*. Three elements are necessary for an act of revelation to take place. There must be a revealer, something revealed, and finally someone to receive the revelation. Revelation cannot take place in a vaccuum: it must have a recipient. That is, of course, the aim of God in revealing himself in Scripture; and it is this that gives authority to the biblical revelation. God has inspired it so that it may tell of him, and consequently to receive the revelation one must place oneself under its authority.

The authority of the Bible here draws together the various strands of our discussion. The purpose of Scripture is revelation, its underlying quality is that of inspiration, its function is that of authority for theology – for mediating knowledge of God. The method of theology, in accepting the authority of Scripture, places itself at the end of the process of revelation as its recipient. The correct interpretation of Scripture is the reception of revelation, the trusting acceptance of what God has chosen to disclose of himself. Theology, then, the study of God, is the end and goal of all revelation, whether it is attempted by learned people or simple; but their labours can provide but a fractured reflection of that beatific vision which one day both simple and learned will share.

Theology and the Bible

'You can use the Bible to prove anything.' How often have we heard that statement, whether on doorsteps or from liberal theologians, in response to a quotation from Scripture? The strength of the objection lies in the fact that it is largely true. A plethora of pseudo-Christian sects has flooded the world since the mid-nineteenth century, all eagerly adducing Scripture to substantiate their claims. Must it be true that the Bible is open to such a variety of interpretations that we can gain from it no certain knowledge of God? We have already drawn attention to the variety of 'theologies' which surround us at the present day, and suggested that this pluralism witnesses to the use of different methods in theology; for all 'Christian' theology seeks to validate its proposals by reference to Scripture. The distinctive evangelical doctrine of Scripture, outlined above, is clearly insufficient in itself to distinguish between proper and improper interpretation, since most of the sects claim a high view of Scripture (though frequently they play down its humanness), and, for all they may say to the contrary, most theologians use the Bible as if it were inspired and authoritative. How may Scripture be properly interpreted?

The belief is widespread that the evangelical method of interpreting Scripture for theology is naïve and rather crude. A century ago Abraham Kuyper, the Dutch statesman and theologian, wrote as follows:

> The legend is still current that the Reformers intended to represent the Holy Scripture as a sort of code, in which certain articles were set down in ready form, some as things to be believed, and some as rules for practice (credenda and agenda). According to this representation the Holy Scripture consists of four parts: (1) a notarially prepared official report of certain facts; (2) an exposition of certain doctrines drawn up by way of articles; (3) an instituted law in

the form of rules; and (4) an official program of things to come.[7]

Kuyper suggests that some 'simple believers' do see things in this way. He continues: 'Scripture-proof seemed to them to be presented only by the quotation of some Bible verse that literally and fully expressed the given assertion.'[8]

What is significant is that while exegesis and interpretation of this sort masquerade as piously biblical, they are in fact nothing of the sort: they are quite arbitrary. That of course is the criticism of the 'you-can-prove-anything-from-the-Bible' school, which believes that that is how evangelical theology uses the Bible. The criticism is more than justified, but finds its target elsewhere, not in the theology of the Reformers and their best evangelical successors today, but in some popular preaching and, especially, in the sects. For these, such a method is a charter to total liberty, freeing them from any real biblical control, and enabling them to impose on Scripture interpretations which do not arise out of it.

That such an approach is fundamentally mistaken is evident not only from the pseudo-theologies of the sects (Jehovah's Witnesses, Unification Church, Mormons, etc.), but indeed from the character of the Bible itself. It is plainly not what Kuyper humorously suggests that this method assumes it to be. Had the Holy Spirit intended that it should be employed in this fashion, it would be a radically different document. As it is,

> The task imposed on us is much more difficult and intricate; and so far from consisting of a mechanical quotation with the help of the concordance, the production of what Scripture contains demands gigantic labour ... The special revelation does not encourage idleness, neither does it intend to offer you the knowledge of God as bread baked and cut, but it is so constructed and it is presented in such a form, that utmost effort is required to reach the desired result ... We do not imply that this whole task must be performed by every believer personally ... But the subject of the science of theology is not the individual

believer, but the consciousness of our regenerated race.[9]

The theological task must begin with an awareness of the precise nature of Scripture as we are presented with it. We have spoken at length of the Christian belief in its inspired origin, and consequently in its infallibility. We must turn now to the actual human character of the documents which compose it, for if its origins are indeed as we have suggested, the details of its literary and historical form must also be seen as the products of inspiration. They are keys, given to us with the inspired text itself, with which we may open its truth. The unity of Scripture will emerge only upon examination of the very evident diversity in which that unity consists.

Unity in diversity

There is a tendency for the student of Scripture, having confessed a high doctrine of its nature, to shy away from its actual form. C. J. Ellicott, Anglican Bishop and eminent scholar of the later nineteenth century, writes:

> It may be safely asserted that half of the misconceptions and perverse systems of interpretation which have darkened the true light of God's Holy Word may be traced up to a neglect, or want of due recognition, of the multiform character of Holy Scripture, and the 'divers portions' and 'divers manners' (Heb. 1.1 [Revised Version]) in which God has vouchsafed to speak through His appointed media to the children of men ... What, however, can be more patent, when we allow the thought to rest on it for a moment, than this – that we have in the Old Testament a literature extending over at least 1100 years, and including History, Poetry, Ethics, and Prophecy, each department requiring its own form of preparatory study ... Nor can it be less clear, with reference to the New Testament, that ... the forms in which Christian

doctrine is presented by the inspired writers have many differing features, and can never be properly appreciated without an independent study of the system consciously or unconsciously adopted by the individual writer.[10]

He offers the following advice to the student of Scripture: 'Cultivate the habit of regarding the Old Testament and the New Testament as each the aggregate of the productions of independent writers, and in passing from the study of one writer to the study of another make distinct preparation accordingly.'[11]

Yet that is not, we may hasten to add, all that there is to say. If it were, and here is the problem at the heart of so much modern theological writing, it would surely be impossible to do coherent theology at all. If we have in Scripture real, irreducible, pluriformity, as many writers would have us believe, then the task of reaching a unified theology and real knowledge of God must be frustrated. An authority that speaks with more than one voice must cease to be an authority – authority removes to the man who chooses which voice he will hear.

The diversity in the Bible is not of that kind, however. It comprises two Testaments, the records of two covenants, and they must first be separately examined, in their mutual distinctiveness and contrast. When that has been done, they may be examined together, and their integrated structure will emerge – the Old Testament restlessly striving forward to the New, the New rooted and grounded in the Old. In all this, two principles remain clear: that God planned and breathed out all that we have as Scripture (and that therefore it finds its unity in his all-knowing mind); and that it was this collection of historically conditioned books, from the pens of human writers, which was the form chosen and indeed specially devised by God as the medium for his self-revelation.

We have, therefore, a charter for the most detailed labours to discover the teaching of each book, each chapter, each verse, and indeed the precise meaning of every word that the Book contains; but we have also an assurance which becomes, for our study, a presupposition that because Scripture reveals one God it is an organic whole.

Theology and tradition

It is a vexed question to what extent church tradition has a part to play in the formulation of theology. In reaction against the Roman Catholic emphasis on unwritten tradition, which supplements and guides the interpretation of Scripture, many Protestants assume that the tradition of the church can have no part to play. They assume that every person may, or must, start afresh from Scripture, and formulate his or her own theology anew. But, even if that were possible, it would be misleading. It is not what the Reformers did, for there was then, as there is now, a very broad area of fundamental agreement on basic theological questions which were settled early in the life of the church. These include the doctrines of God, the Trinity, the incarnation, and so on. Further, as Kuyper points out, 'no single person, but thinking, regenerate humanity, is the *subject* of theology'.[12] That is to say, it is the (true) church, not the individual, to which the total revelation in Scripture is addressed. In actual experience this is borne out. Kuyper writes,

> No theologian, following the direction of his own compass, would ever have found by himself what he now confesses and defends on the ground of the Holy Scripture. By far the largest part of his results is adopted by him from theological *tradition*, and even the proofs, which he cites from the Scripture, at least as a rule, have not been discovered by himself, but have been suggested to him by his predecessors.[13]

The theologian stands in a tradition, particularly when he is a member of a church with a confession of faith at its root. He may not lightly set it on one side, especially when he remembers that creeds and confessions of faith represent, not the insights of an individual, but the consensus of all the theologians of the church of the day, a day of great spiritual and intellectual power. In consequence, Kuyper argues,

> One should not begin by doubting everything, and by experimenting to see whether on the ground of his

own investigation he arrives at the same point where
the confession of his Church stands; but, on the
contrary, he should start out from the assumption
that his Church is right, while at the same time he
should investigate it, and only oppose it when he
finds himself compelled to do so by the Word of
God.[14]

This is a wise and most practical piece of advice, and may readily
be adapted to the present ecclesiastical situation, in which churches
are departing from historic confessional standards. Clearly,
submission to such a standard will depend on its being framed in
accordance with the principle of authority set out above, that
knowledge of God comes solely through the revelation in
Scripture. Such confessional standards as the Westminster
Confession of Faith and the Thirty-Nine Articles of Religion of the
Church of England fall comfortably into that category. Kuyper is
careful to qualify his position by emphasizing that it can never be
simply because the church has decreed an article of faith that it is
to be accepted: 'The point of support for theology may never be
looked for in the Church. It only finds that point of support when
it shows that what the Church has offered it as acquired treasures,
were really taken *from* the Scripture and *after the rule* of the
scripture.'[15]

The tradition, therefore, of evangelical theology of the churches
of the Reformation is one that should command the deepest
respect of all who stand within it, not because it is the tradition of
the church, but because it is biblical, quarried from Scripture by
people of exceptional spiritual and intellectual gifts. Theologians
today do not set out across untrodden ground. They follow in the
steps of others, whose goal and whose aids have been their own,
using their paths until they can find out better for themselves.

Revelation and salvation

From what has been said so far, it might have seemed possible to
pursue theological study in a purely intellectual fashion. But
theologians, though they may be academics, are no *mere*

academics. Theology is the study of God, the reception of the knowledge of God; and the knowledge of God is not *simply* academic. God is no object in the creation that he might be known with the mind alone. He is the creator and sustainer of all things, who is personal and who works toward moral purposes. The God revealed in the Bible is no abstraction. He has 'metaphysical' existence, but he reveals himself in holiness and redemption. People who would know him must open to him not merely their minds, but their wills and all their being. Only thus will God be known.

For the God who reveals himself in words in the Holy Scriptures, has culminated his self-revelation in the one to whom all the Scriptures bear witness: the Incarnate Son, Jesus Christ, in whom all the fullness of the Godhead was manifest. We have said that the special revelation in Scripture is soteriological. This is the case partly in order that revelation might be comprehensible to sinners, so that their sin does not prevent their receiving it. But it is soteriological also in a deeper sense: it mediates and is inseparable from salvation itself. Knowledge of God is no mere knowledge of facts: it is knowledge of the one whom to know is life eternal. Knowledge of God *is* salvation. It is no more possible to know God apart from his revelation than it is to know the revelation apart from God. That is not to say that God may not reveal himself to some who reject or ignore him, or that one day he will not be revealed to all people, including those whom he will tell to depart from him. But it does mean that the revealed knowledge of God may not be received in any but the most superficial sense by those who do not know salvation in Jesus Christ. Christian theology, as the enterprise of knowing God, is for Christians.

This casts some light on the question raised earlier about the place of Jesus Christ in revelation. Some would say that because, as we have seen, knowledge of God is ultimately personal knowledge, the propositional, 'factual' knowledge we find in Scripture must be subordinated to the personal knowledge of Jesus Christ. But this is to set up a false antithesis. Personal and propositional knowledge need not be mutually opposed. Propositional knowledge *per se*, a mere intellectual exercise, is not in view here. Personal knowledge *per se*, experience without content, is not in view either, as surely it is an absurdity. Reflection on our own knowledge of persons will reveal that, while it is by no means simply 'propositional', it cannot – and we have no wish that it should – avoid propositional elements. Our knowledge of loved ones is built up of elements of both, and even the personal experience of meeting and greeting those we love is itself not devoid of content that either is, or could be, expressed in words. What we know *about* people plays a vital part in our knowledge *of* them. The attempt to construct an imaginary, purely 'personal' relationship, or encounter, devoid of any propositional or factual knowledge, will convince that this is the case.

What we find in our human relationships is exactly what we find in our divine relationship: that personal and propositional intermingle and integrate to build up our knowledge. The two hang together and reveal Christian theology as a discipline that involves not simply the head, but the whole person. The place of Scripture is to supply all the elements in the relationship which, in the analogy of a merely human relationship, are reducible to propositional statements. When we meet a person for the first time, how does the relationship take up? The present writer met two schoolgirls for the first time after a church service. The context of the meeting immediately told him various things about them. They introduced themselves and explained their family background, spoke of their school, their plans for university and the future, and they discussed a concert which both they and he had attended. Numerous elements in this encounter were either expressed directly in statements or could be so expressed, recording visual impressions, inferences, assumpions based on analogy with other relationships, and so on. Not that the encounter could be entirely *reduced* to such propositions: it was irreducibly personal, the meeting together of human persons. But neither could there have been a personal encounter *without* these elements, each of which made the meeting more, and certainly not less, personal.

The purpose of this discussion is to parallel the relation of personal and propositional elements in the knowledge of God with the elements of a human encounter. In the meeting with God, the propositional elements are provided by the Scriptures. God's special revelation of himself in the words of the book give introduction, content and enrichment to the personal relationship which he establishes with man in Jesus Christ.

The work of the Spirit

A further illustration may aid the understanding of the relationship of God himself to his revelation in Scripture. The Bible is no more God than is a colour transparency the Colosseum in Rome. But the transparency faithfully bears the image of the Colosseum, and enables it to be seen by people who are unable to visit Italy. Moreover, the transparency is dark and indistinct, if not completely black, unless it is held up to the light. The revelation of God in the Bible, though it is ever present (as the image of the Colosseum never leaves the slide), is not there for all to see. It requires the action of the same Spirit who inspired the Scripture to illumine it, and in so doing to reveal the God behind it. If light streams through the transparency and throws its image onto a screen, although the viewers will know that they are not in Rome, what they will *see* will be identical in every respect with the Colosseum. God in himself we do not know: what the Bible spreads before us is God as he has revealed himself, his image as it were photographed, inscripturated for sinful men and women.

In fact, the activity of the Holy Spirit is twofold: not only does he shine through the words of Scripture to illumine them in the eyes of believers, but he works in believers themselves, opening their eyes and granting them the sight that is needed to interpret what they read. This is, of course, well known; but it needs to be borne in mind as we consider the work of the theologian. Far from being able to interpret Scripture for theology without the aid of the Spirit, theologians of all people most need the Spirit's help. The interpretation of Scripture can never be divorced from the spiritual life and made a merely intellectual study. It is, indeed, intellectual, and there is no need for Christians to disparage or be embarrassed by their intellect. The intellect is a supreme gift of God, as it is by means of the activity of the intellect that knowledge of God is assimilated. The intellect may not be highly developed, and the fundamental truths of salvation may be grasped by the simplest of minds. But the mind of Paul, a towering intellect of his day, was unable to exhaust the riches of God's self-revelation. The intellect of the spiritual person is the instrument with which he or she appropriates Scripture and learns theology. At the same time, the intellect of an unspiritual person, however brilliant, is simply unfitted for the task. It is beyond him or her, and we should not be surprised that, when he or she attempts to theologize, what he or she produces is a travesty of the knowledge of God. 'The Spirit breathes upon the Word / And to the Word gives light.' The one who inspired Scripture must interpret it.

Yet the work of the Spirit is not confined to the mind and heart of the individual believer. The Spirit also indwells the church, and since theology is a task for the church as well as the individual, we may expect to see the leading of the Spirit in the theological development of the church down the ages. Perhaps some eyebrows will be raised by such a reference to the work of the Spirit in this context. But as we survey the progress of theology from the days of the apostles onwards, we see how, gradually but definitely, the church has been guided by the Spirit to formulate one doctrine after another. The first explosion of doctrine in the apostolic writings, the deliberations of councils of the universal church, the confessions of the Reformation – in all these we witness the Spirit's gentle leading into further truth; yet all hewn from the same scriptural quarry. As we look back to the high-points of theological activity in the sixteenth and seventeenth centuries, we should not assume that the quarry has been fully worked. The Spirit is still leading the church onto fresh discovery, but always in the same Bible. As Kuyper has put it, 'The exegesis of Holy Scripture is correct and complete only when the Holy Spirit interprets the Scripture in the Church of God.'[16]

Theological studies and theological study

We have suggested that, because the revelation of God to men lies principally in the holy Scriptures, the study of theology – the study of God's self-disclosure – is properly carried on by the interpretation of Scripture. To that extent, all simple believers who seek to know God by the Scriptures are theologians. The person of great learning differs from them only by degree. Theological students, though in the throes of essays, seminars and examinations, are theologians too. Their object is not simply to learn the opinions of great and influential thinkers; it is to learn of God. There need be no contradiction, and there will be none if they bear their goal ever in mind.

But to study theology at a university today – or, for that matter, at many denominational colleges – is to be faced with a bewildering array of disciplines, apparently bearing little or no connection with each other. G. Ebeling has put it well:

> The organization of academic theology suggests the conception of an isolated existence of the disciplines. The bond that unites theology seemingly exists only in the external form of being organized as a faculty or as a department within the university as well as in the pragmatic purpose of educating people for ecclesiastical vocations.[17]

In fact, this is not merely an appearance of diversity. In many institutions different teachers and departments pursue different objectives by radically divergent methods. There may be an Old Testament lecturer who believes it to be unscholarly to study the Old Testament in a Christian manner, a dogmatician wearing Barthian spectacles who frankly attacks the scepticism of his colleagues (and the credulity of his conservative evangelical students), and perhaps an evangelical who looks – and maybe feels – rather a fish out of water. One must candidly recognize that the century or more that has passed since the rise of the 'critical' view of Scripture, and the failure of confidence in Scripture as the rule of all thought about God, has witnessed the fragmentation of Christian theology. There is now no single 'theological method': there are a hundred such methods. Indeed, it is the mark of an up-and-coming theologian that he develops his own, different from the rest! C. S. Lewis wrote an essay with the title, *Is Theology Poetry?*[18] It is very hard to see how a great deal that passes by the name 'theology' today can have any more claim on our faith.

But theology is not poetry, an imaginative fancy seeking to interpret life. It is a scientific discipline – scientific in the sense that it is controlled by its object, and is ever open to justification and correction by comparison with that object. How then may that object – the knowledge of God in Scripture – relate to the diverse disciplines of academic theology? As it happens, although these departments of study may now appear to conflict with one another and be unrelated to the knowledge of God, most of the usual theological disciplines have their origins in days when matters were different. If the Bible is the ruling principle of theology, its close exegesis must be the basis of theological study. So the biblical languages of *Hebrew* and *Greek* still have an important place in the theological curriculum, and here is an area where, whatever the standpoint of their teachers, evangelical students can benefit greatly from their studies. Closely related is the detailed study of biblical texts in departments of *Old* and *New Testament*. All further theological enquiry rests upon the accuracy of such study.

The meaning of the text emerges as it is questioned and as the intentions and objectives of the original human authors of the text are brought into the open. In this task, the discoveries of the last hundred years have helped immeasurably. We have now far more detailed information about the societies in which the biblical books were written: Mesopotamia, the Eastern Mediterranean, and Egypt, and, later, the Graeco-Roman world. Hoards of clay tablets have been unearthed from the libraries of ancient civilizations to bring their daily lives, their religious beliefs and practices, and their national histories before our eyes. Languages cognate with biblical Hebrew have been discovered and deciphered, with considerable advantage to our interpretation of many difficult texts. The Dead Sea Scrolls and other finds have, in their turn, illumined the world of the New Testament and its religions. All this wealth of knowledge must be laid under tribute by the theologian as he seeks to ascertain the precise meaning of the biblical text as its authors intended it to be interpreted.

The discipline of *biblical theology* then comes into play, building up from the exegesis of the text a comprehensive picture of the overall teaching of the individual books of Scripture. Then the canvas is broadened, and the books of each Testament are placed in perspective as the story of the Old Testament is unfolded in law, prophecy and wisdom, and the New Testament in gospels and epistles. This is perhaps the most difficult task of the theologian: the relation of books and testaments, and, above all, principles and teaching derived from them, one to another. Is this instruction of lasting significance, or is it limited in application? Is this prophecy fulfilled in that event, or is that event but a prefiguring of its final realization in Christ, or in the eschaton? How do the Testaments relate to one another?

The next task is that of *dogmatic* or *systematic theology* (the terms are used variously). The theologian now begins to stand still further back from Scripture, and continues the process of analysis and synthesis begun in biblical theology. He or she builds upon it, and is ever sensitive to the contextual exegesis that must govern all his or her use of Scripture. The statements of Scripture may indeed be quoted to justify or illustrate his or her propositions, but only with the highest attention to the meaning they have carried in the lower levels of study, to the biblical scholar and the biblical theologian. It is a faithful saying that 'a text without a context is a pretext'. The 'proof-text' method of which Kuyper makes fun in the passage we have quoted is not in use here. It is the Bible itself that must be left to determine its interpretation.

So the dogmatician synthesizes and collates the teaching of Scripture, paying careful attention to the relation of the Testaments and their several parts. Gradually an edifice is built up, the ever-incomplete structure of Christian theology. But even as this happens, other disciplines come into play. Theology is the task of the church, not simply of the individual, and of the church down the centuries. Brick is added to brick, and each generation confirms anew that the structure is sound, or it may effect alterations and improvements. The disciplines of *ecclesiastical history* and *historical theology* serve as a powerful corrective to the dogmatician: the past errors and excesses of the church, and its achievements, are laid bare.

Practical theology (which may go by some other name) has the task of interpreting those same Scriptures for the life of the church today, in its structure, its practice, its ethics and its pastoral care. This discipline is often omitted from a modern university or treated as a Cinderella while in fact it represents the crown of all the rest and the goal of Scripture itself, for the aim of God's self-disclosure is the creation of a regenerate community in response to his word. This is no intellectualistic religion, but a religion directed to the end of converting men and women to God and nurturing them in a redeemed community. Practical theology is the *application* of God's revelation to the individual and the church. It represents the climax, and the final point of theological endeavour.

A word must finally be said of the discipline of *apologetics*. This covers a wide area of study where Christian theology interrelates with the world outside, particularly with philosophy and with rival world-views. It is not, properly speaking, a component part of theology itself, as it should not be allowed to determine of our knowledge of God. On the other hand, it performs the vital task of preparing theologians for the world in which they live, and in front of which they must seek to justify their theological conclusions. It tests and tries these conclusions, and forces them to explain them in language and in concepts that are comprehensible in the world at large. It is both a reflective discipline and an essential preparation for evangelism and mission. It is really a component part of practical theology, broadly conceived.

So theological *studies* need not be the enemy of theological *study*. It is ironical that university departments and colleges, established to run on much the lines indicated above, still reflect this structure while playing host to individuals and ideologies at odds with any coherent and unified view of theology. The departments of religious studies which have been set up in some of the newer universities, and the religious studies courses being integrated into theology faculties in some older institutions, reflect much more truly the state of theology today. In abandoning its principle and rule in the holy Scriptures, it has abandoned not only its unity and integrity as a discipline, and its scientific character, but also any hope of regaining them. The pluralism is becoming ever more diverse, and increasingly it is recognized that it is in religious studies, the attempt to assess man as a religious animal, that there lies the only kind of 'theological study' that can make sense today in a secular intellectual climate.

Theological study, as a discipline with a distinct method and a definite goal, is an exercise to be attempted only within the Christian church. When evangelical Christians find themselves in a mixed college or a university department there will be tension and ambiguity, though it need not prevent their pursuit of real theology – real knowledge of God. Their need is to see the priority, amidst all the demands on time and energy and the competing claims on loyalty, of developing their own knowledge, personal and propositional, of God.

Kuyper eloquently sums this all up:

> Knowledge of God is the crown of all that can be known. Knowledge of God is inconceivable, except it is imparted to us by God himself. This knowledge, given us by nature in our creation, has been veiled *from* and darkened in us by the results of our sin. Consequently it now comes to us in the form of a *special revelation*, and we have received *divine illumination* by which we can assimilate the content of that revelation. And *science* is called in, to introduce this knowledge of God, thus revealed, into our human thought.[19]

Notes

[1] A. S. Peake, *The Bible: its Origin, its Significance and its Abiding Worth* (1913).
[2] See J. W. Wenham, *Christ and the Bible* (IVP, 1984).
[3] 'The Biblical Idea of Inspiration', in *The Inspiration and Authority of the Bible* (Presbyterian and Reformed Publishing Co., 1948), p. 131.
[4] Ibid., pp. 132–133.
[5] Ibid., p. 155. Cf. Gal. 1:15.
[6] E. Garbett, *God's Word Written: the doctrine of the Inspiration of Holy Scripture explained and enforced* (London, n.d.), pp. 141–142.
[7] A. Kuyper, *Encyclopaedia of Sacred Theology* (ET: Hodder and Stoughton, 1899), p. 564.
[8] Ibid., p. 565.
[9] Ibid., p. 567.

[10] *Foundations of Sacred Study* (SPCK, 1893), pp. 47–49.
[11] Ibid., p. 49.
[12] Kuyper, *Encylopaedia of Sacred Theology*, p. 574 (my emphasis).
[13] Ibid., p. 575.
[14] Ibid., p. 577.
[15] Ibid.
[16] Ibid., p. 585.
[17] G. Ebeling, *The Study of Theology* (ET: Collins, 1979), p. 157.
[18] In *Screwtape Proposes a Toast, and other pieces* (Collins, 1968).
[19] Kuyper, *Encyclopaedia of Sacred Theology*, p. 327.

4. Faith and certainty
Stephen Williams

Stephen Williams is Professor of Systematic Theology at Union Theological College, Belfast.

Preface

It is tempting for anyone involved in intellectual or academic work to exaggerate the significance of the problems with which they wrestle. Good, sound immersion in life and in the needs of others is an excellent way of conquering the temptation. But the traffic is not all one way. Good, sound immersion in life and in the needs of others will also convince us of the need for our intellectual labours. These may or may not be in an academic context and it should not be taken for granted that our academic institutions always provide a helpful or necessary context for the pursuit of some important intellectual questions. Those questions arise all the same. And while it seems hard to figure out just how important questions of faith and certainty are in comparison with other things we might think about, it seems clear that they are important questions.

This extended essay on faith and certainty was written seven years ago. Seven years on, I should write it rather differently but it has been allowed to stand. It contains consistent warnings that short-cuts were being taken for the sake of brevity. In light of these, it is as well to take this opportunity to summarize what is going on in this piece and to clarify some points.

'Faith and certainty' really consists of some ruminations on the grounds of Christian belief and the way in which we might justify our claims to be sure of that which we believe. The governing mood is that of the apologia. It is not straighforwardly apologetic, in that it is aimed to get Christians to think about epistemological issues and not to offer to non-Christians directly a case for Christianity. It is really about the logic of certain aspects of believing and the logic of claims to certainty. Yet it is clearly some sort of exercise in persuasion as well. So it attempts both to clarifiy the logic of belief and certainty from within a Christian framework and to suggest a commendation of Christianity to those not committed to it. But it may be asked whether these are not two separate enterprises. This is best addressed by sketching out the argument of the essay or we shall be debating in the dark.

The biblical witness evinces tremendous confidence in the truth and certainty of its claims. On what is such confidence based? Apparently, principally on religious experience and the evidence of the senses. The decisive example of the latter, as far as Christians are concerned, is the resurrection of Jesus Christ. It is true that the story is told against the background of Israelite belief in God, and assumptions about the Creator's power to effect this or that in his universe. But it is permissible to examine the accounts of the resurrection without insisting on forming beforehand our own definite judgments about those background beliefs, just to see what kind of phenomenon they bring before us. And we emerge from such an examination convinced that the early Christian community believed, declared and sought to give empirical grounds for the belief that Jesus was risen from the tomb. The alleged resurrection is of universal significance. Is the deity presupposed in and revealed by that account really credible?

Many arguments have been offered to demonstrate the existence of God. But in the end, if one pursues these, demonstration is difficult in practice, whether or not appropriate in principle, and one is left at best with the need to form a personal 'intuitive' sort of judgment on a number of features of the world, which we try to integrate in our thought and into that judgment. It is not a personal judgment that is purely intellectual, where talk of God is concerned. For to talk of God is to talk of one who is personal, and personal beings are known by disposing the heart in certain ways in our relationships, not by approaching them as one might a mathematical theorem. If God is known supremely through Jesus, then we approach the knowledge of God by approaching Jesus.

When we do so, it is clear that the religious issue (the issue of knowing God) is a profoundly moral or spiritual issue, forcing the head to attend to those things that are matters of the heart – sin and guilt, holiness and forgiveness. Further, however much the head may wish to suspend belief, life involves commitment to action, no matter how uncertain we are of our convictions. The model of action with which we are presented in the witness to Jesus is the model of compassionate and serving action, one wherein people find perfect freedom. This portrayal of Jesus, whose basic historical truth we need not doubt, reveals the inner fragmentation of our lives. It simultaneously reveals that religious or spiritual understanding is impossible unless the will is engaged, and disposed to understand and to learn. Acquiring faith and certainty, that is, if they are obtainable, cannot be a merely intellectual exercise in the light of the witness to Jesus. This is crucial.

Still, from an intellectual point of view, can we pass beyond possibility, opinion and scepticism with regard to claims to religious knowledge? In principle we can. There is no need to extend scepticism to the moral domain in the sense that we are entitled to affirm a moral certainty of, for example, the evil of torture. Why, then, dismiss the possibility of religious knowledge and religious certainty in matters of the heart? Ultimately, certainty is the gift of the Holy Spirit, but since we are willing to give grounds for our beliefs – since we are willing to defend the rationality of belief in the resurrection, for example – the appeal to the Holy Spirit is not an escape from reason. Ask me why I believe what I do, and I point to the record of Jesus; ask me why I am certain in my belief, and I must bring in the self-testimony of the Spirit of God. God's special action in a particular space and time, far from being designed to bestow religious knowledge on the very few, occluding the universal knowability of his revelation, exhibits an important logic which we should outline. God, wishing to identify himself with humanity, becomes one of us; but that inevitably means that he is confined by that incarnation to a particular space and time, since humans are creatures of particular space and time. Every step is taken, including the writing of translatable Scriptures and creation of a missionary community, to ensure that knowledge of God is not limited to that particular space and time in which he became incarnate in Jesus Christ.

So what is going on in 'Faith and certainty'? It might be read as an attempt to demonstrate by reason the plausibility of Christian belief. If so, does it not tumble into an obvious snare? For surely there is no such thing as 'reason', something which is common to all, something we can pretend is neutrally deployed without any presuppositions by believer and unbeliever alike. The production of rational evidences of supposed universal validity is surely a thing of the past at best. At worst, that kind of apologetics was always egregiously wrong anyway.

Stated in that form, I agree with the objection. But it is still possible from within Christian faith to describe and analyse the logic of one's own position; to work out why it is reasonable for me. And that enterprise can involve giving the kind of reason that others may be urged to consider. It is possible to grant that there is no such thing as one 'reason' common to all, and to grant that no-one approaches issues without presuppositions, and yet lay out what we regard as reasonable in a way that challenges others. While I should not concur in everything he says, I might draw attention here to the way forward on this matter provided by John Frame in his work *Apologetics to the Glory of God.*[1] Speaking personally, as I examine the grounds on which I believe in Jesus Christ, I cannot easily separate them from the grounds on which I think anyone should believe in Jesus Christ. Much more could be said about the relationship between what is reasonable from a believing point of view and what is reasonable from another point of view. And there is much to be learned from a figure such as the medieval thinker, Anselm of Canterbury, as we think about the connections between believing thought and theological method, on the one hand, and unbelieving thought and apologetic method, on the other. These points could be expounded further, but I hope that enough has been said to indicate how the following essay should be read.

This is not the place to do much more than reiterate yet again what I said above and what I say throughout – that often brevity has been purchased at the cost of adequacy. What is said, for example, about the meaning and significance of Jesus' proclamation of forgiveness or about the possibilities of moral knowledge and of moral scepticism, really need expansion and modification. Reasons could have been set out to explain why the essay has been written in this form in a postmodern culture, whatever that means. And throughout it all, I have not forgotten that the witness of the life of the Christian community is the vital context for all that is said in words or thought in arguments. All this is said more in the mode of excuse than repentance, however, for I stand substantially on the ground of what I argue in this piece. If and where I am wrong, my hope is that the readers who correct my thinking will do so in a way that strengthens faith and deepens certainty.

Introduction

Many Christians seem quite sure that what they believe is true. Many non-Christians seem equally sure that what Christians believe is not true. But a large number of people, which includes some who call themselves Christians and some who do not, believe both sides to be mistaken. They do not exactly cry 'a plague on both your houses', because such an attitude would display the wrong spirit in such matters. In these matters, they say, we must avoid dogmatism and practise tolerance. And that is why Christians and non-Christians alike, if they say they are sure, are in the wrong. The proper stock-in-trade in matters of religious belief is opinion and possibility, not dogmatism and certainty, so the argument goes.

Such a position is obviously attractive and strong reasons can be given in its favour. Some have detected its roots in the late seventeenth century and since then the tree of tolerance has blossomed into the largest of growths, with enough room for us twenty-first-century birds of pluralistic culture to make our nests in its branches. It is the fact of pluralism that makes tolerance seem so important. We live in a world and society of fundamental religious and moral differences and the situation is practically irreversible. In such a situation, religious certainty is socially dangerous, let alone intellectually unwarranted. For those who are certain will try to impose their views on others and that makes for arrogance and conflict.

'Epistemology' concerns matters of knowledge and of belief. How do we know what we know, or why do we believe what we believe? In this essay, we shall not pursue the social implications of epistemological questions. But we are indicating the social context which gives importance to such questions. Epistemology is a wide and rich field for exploration which has been ploughed for centuries and long before the coming of Christianity. Our study, although it draws on some of this wealth and engages some of the historical issues, is neither a scholarly nor a rigorous treatment of the questions involved. An appended guide for further reading makes suggestions for any who want to go into things more deeply. But we shall, within severe limits, outline an approach to the issue which we are describing as the question of 'faith and certainty'. Our exercise is preliminary but, it is hoped, worthwhile.

Terminology

A colleague of mine was once told that a clear desk was a sign of insecurity. That should give most of us enough confidence to keep us going for a good while. The definition of terms can likewise look like a bit of insecurity; in the presence of an awesomely large subject we spend our time putting our terms in order. But, as a matter of fact, we do need to say something about our terms and concepts at this stage and to signal some distinctions to keep in mind.

The word 'faith' is used in many senses. It has a non-religious as well as a religious use, although sometimes the uses overlap, as they might well do when I say that I have faith in the mechanic who is attending to my car. Our concern, however, is with religious faith. Here again the word is used in different senses. One distinction that is often made is between faith as an internal something lodged in my heart and faith as an external something – that which is believed. When we talk about 'Christian faith' we might mean either. On the one hand, we may speak of people who are weak or strong in faith. Their Christian faith grows, changes, is lost or gained. On the other hand, we may speak of someone who subscribes to the Christian faith, meaning that the content of what they believe is Jesus Christ, God in man, risen from the dead or however we spell it out. We might make exactly the same distinction with regard to the word 'belief'. However, some also want to distinguish 'faith' from 'belief'. They think of faith as being wider than belief for belief is an intellectual matter, but faith involves not just giving intellectual assent to something but actively trusting as well. So it may be said that we should have not only a belief that Jesus is risen but also faith in the risen Jesus. 'Belief that ...' may just be a matter of the head; 'faith in ...' a trust of the whole person.

With the word 'certainty' we need to distinguish at this point not different notions of certainty but the difference between 'certainty' and 'knowledge'. (Some have indeed talked about the difference between 'certitude' and 'certainty', but I shall not be using the former word at all, so the distinction does not concern us. And others have been happier to speak of 'assurance' than 'certainty' in phrases like 'assurance of faith', but I shall be using 'assurance' and 'certainty' or 'sure' and 'certain' interchangeably.)

Let us consider an example. Supposing I say that I am certain that the First World War was caused by troops from Luxembourg burning down farms in West Wales. Perhaps my father had told me that as a child. Confidently, I tell you that 'I am sure; I know that was how it was caused.' Then you convince me that I am wrong and that my father, one sincerely hopes, had his tongue well lodged in his cheek. What should I say? I could certainly say that I was certain, because I was certain. And everyone might agree on that. But could I say 'I knew'? No, we should not normally allow that. Why not? Because I got it wrong. Really to know something is to get it right, whereas I can be certain about things which turn out to be wrong. What I should say is: 'I *thought* I knew'; that is, I could not have known really, because I got it wrong. But I need not say: 'I thought I was sure.' I was sure, but certainly wrong. When I say I am certain, I seem to be making a comment about my psychological state: 'This is how I feel about this or that.' But if I *correctly* say that 'I know' something, I seem to be making a comment about the item I am talking about, and not just my psychological state. You can only really know what is true.

These distinctions made, we should make clear what we are aiming to do here. A Christian has faith in Jesus Christ, meaning that he or she trusts in Jesus Christ and has certain beliefs about

Jesus Christ. Doubtless, faith arises in different ways, but trust implies certain beliefs that we have, and mature faith seeks to advance by understanding ever better the truth about Jesus Christ. We shall be concerned with the truth about Christ, or the truth of Christianity. But how should we regard what we think is the truth? If we have faith, is that something which falls short of knowledge? And if it falls short of knowledge, are we ever justified in saying that we are certain? These are the kinds of questions that will exercise us. They are practical and not just intellectual. If I try to go about sharing my faith, I may be accused of false dogmatism, of being certain of things which cannot really be known. And I do not want to be dogmatic where I should not be. If the alternative, however, is to advance faith as a possibility, to be tentative and not assured about it, I have an opposite worry. Am I guilty of failing to trust and believe in God and Jesus Christ properly and doing faith, religion or Christianity an injustice? At the end of the day, what we are trying to do is to find intellectual integrity in relation to Christianity. This is no trivial pursuit.

The biblical picture

When some Christians say that they are sure that what they believe is true or that they know that what they believe is true, they may be doing so for a variety of reasons. We are often unprepared to admit these reasons. Sometimes, we are insecure. We do not like this wild world with its innumerable options for thought and action. So we seal ourselves off and refuse to admit doubt. Sometimes, we are arrogant. Some of us are temperamentally unable to be tentative about anything. Dogmatism in all things, doubt in nothing; that is our method in religion. And in fact, the above things often go together. Some of the most strident and dogmatic Christians are secretly insecure.

There is, however, another reason for being certain or maintaining that we know. The Old and New Testaments bear witness to a faith which is assured and believes itself justified in being so assured. We can know the truth of those things which we believe with assurance. We cannot study the ins and outs of biblical terms here, just as we cannot engage in an historical exploration of epistemological discussions. The attempt to relate biblical to philosophical vocabulary, which is an important theological task, is a large exercise in itself. But a wide variety of phrases in our English Bibles rightly convey a connection between the notions of faith, certainty and knowledge. Examples are Luke's 'so that you may know the certainty of the things you have been taught' (Luke 1:4); Peter's 'We believe and know that you are the Holy One of God' (John 6:69); the famous connection of faith with certainty in Hebrews 11:1 and the exposition of knowledge and revelation by Paul in 1 Corinthians 1 and 2. If we cannot pursue biblical semantics, at least we must comment on some broad lines of biblical religious epistemology.

It is often said that the Bible introduces God without question. There is no investigation of what we mean by the word 'God' nor a preliminary attempt to prove his existence. That does not imply that these questions are entirely ignored throughout the Scriptures, simply that talk of God gets under way as a pure assumption. From an epistemological point of view, the most impressive fact about God in relation to us is that God is *heard*. We are thinking here primarily of the Old Testament. He speaks; there is a word of God and words from God. As we read the account, centuries later, we may be puzzled by this. What exactly was it like to hear God? At times, it appears to be a literal hearing of the ear and we might scrutinize the accounts of the revelation on Mount Sinai, for example, whether to Moses or to the people, in that connection. More often, however, it seems to be an inward hearing, a sense every bit as clear as the outward sense, a clear sense that God is saying or communicating something. We get this impression in the case of Abraham, for example. Clearly, what we have is something which we can label 'religious experience', whereby people are sure of God and of what he is saying. I use the phrase 'are sure'. It is an interesting question and well worth considering whether there are hints in the Old and New Testaments that the coming of Jesus Christ meant the dispersal of doubts that might have lingered in the Israelite mind about God. We must consign this to the growing list of subjects we have no space to treat! At all events, the account of faith in the Old Testament, though tried and tentative and striving, often unconsciously conveys to us a sense of a confidence people typically had that God has spoken and that we may know what we are supposed to do in obedience to him.

The New Testament scene is dominated, of course, by Jesus Christ. A visible person is now centre stage. The Old Testament had already emphasized the importance of what is seen. Hence extraordinary events and visible phenomena attest to the fact that the Lord really has spoken. The word interprets the events and the events attest the word. But God himself is almost always an unseen presence and those incidents that talk of people seeing God witness to the very exceptional nature of such experience. They also invite consideration of what exactly 'seeing God' means in such a context, for in the New Testament it is stated, in the spirit of the Old, that 'no-one has ever seen God' (John 1:18). This is very striking, since it is stated at a point where the contrast between the old and the new is described: 'For the law was given through Moses; grace and truth came through Jesus Christ' (John 1:17). Even bearing Moses' experience and Jesus Christ in mind, John goes on to say: 'No-one has ever seen God', but he immediately emphasizes that something has happened now to our knowledge of God: '... God the only [Son], who is at the Father's side, has made him known' (John 1:18; translations vary). In his first letter, John says that the person 'who does not love his brother, whom he has seen, cannot love God, whom he has not seen' (1 John 4:20). So the invisibility of God is reasserted in the Johannine witness.

Yet, there is a sense in which, according to that very same witness, we can talk of seeing God, and this in a different way from the old. This is where Jesus Christ makes the difference. The most explicit and deliberate statement of this is the one recorded in John 14:9: 'Anyone who has seen me has seen the Father.' God as he is himself cannot be seen with the physical eye because he is not a physical being; God is 'spirit' (John 4:24). Jesus, like any other human being, possessed both visible characteristics (a body) and those characteristics we discern spiritually (goodness, gentleness, and so on). The New Testament testifies to Jesus as one whose spiritual being was not like that of any other human being, for he was uniquely related to God. Indeed, he is sometimes explicitly called 'God'.[2] One cannot see the deity of Jesus, in one sense, more that one can see God. However his personal appearance in particular space and time obviously has deep consequences for religious epistemology. Faith, certainty and knowledge of God are now focused on Jesus Christ.

What accounts for the confidence with which religious claims are voiced in the New Testament? We should distinguish here between two things. The first is the confidence that God exists, that he can speak and has spoken, as we found in the Old Testament. The second is the confidence concerning Jesus that we meet in the New. The first confidence was shared by the disciples and opponents of Jesus alike. No-one tries to prove to the Jewish opponents of Jesus that there is a God and that he spoke in the Old Testament. Christianity is often described as a form of theism, belief in one God, and Judaism, Islam and perhaps some Hindu traditions, are its alternative forms. The New Testament account, to all appearances, presupposes a theistic framework. How we can be confident of that framework is a question it seems not to address. It is a confidence born not of Jesus but of the Old Testament witness. At least, so it seems on the surface and we shall not try to penetrate beneath it here. But there is the 'second confidence'.

Confidence about Jesus comes about in slightly different ways. According to the reports, at least some of those who saw and heard Jesus during his earthly life were convinced by what they saw and heard. Conviction varied amongst his disciples during that period of earthly life, but took solid hold of them as witnesses to the resurrection. On the other hand, the majority in the early churches had neither seen nor heard. They were convinced by the witness to what was seen and heard. No doubt this witness took various forms, but we should not minimize the importance of the words and deeds of Jesus. The gospel writers who set out to portray Jesus report the words and deeds, and, in particular, Luke and John deliberately draw attention to their importance.[3] The words 'Blessed are those who have not seen and yet have believed' (John 20:29) must not be misunderstood. Clearly, if faith in Jesus was to survive the first generation of disciples, it could not depend on people seeing and hearing Jesus as he was seen and heard on earth. But it might none the less depend on the fact that *others* had seen things, and this is implied by the overall thrust of John's Gospel.

So much for faith and certainty centuries ago, but what has it to do with us? Can our faith be formed in the same way? Is certainty available to us? Can we know? It is tempting to think that the logical order for starting our investigation is to enquire first about the God of Israel and then about Jesus Christ. Doubtless there is more than one way of doing these things and although I am setting out things in a deliberate order, there is no suggestion that this is *the* order in which to look at the matters before us. There is, however, something to be said for starting with Jesus Christ. For although those who first believed him did so presupposing belief in God, it does not follow that all other times and places must first ask about God apart from Jesus before enquiring about Jesus himself. Possibly those of us who have not come up through Hebrew religion will be convinced about God by Jesus. As the four evangelists speak of Jesus in the light of the resurrection, perhaps we should speak of God in the light of Jesus. If we start with Jesus, we at least start with a concrete, historical phenomenon, a datum of history which we almost all agree to be given. We shall not argue here with those who maintain that Jesus never existed; but we shall start with the witness to Jesus and everyone agrees that we have that, even if the witness really had no object! So what are we to make of this?

The hinge

Whenever we consider the witness to some event or other and find ourselves needing to assess it, we do two things. We ponder the nature of the witness and we ponder the character of the witnesses. If an alleged event is an ordinary event and a witness reliable, we normally assume the truth of the report. If an alleged event is an ordinary event and a witness unreliable, we suspend judgment. If an alleged event is highly unusual and a witness unreliable, we are inclined to disbelieve. If an alleged event is highly unusual and a witness reliable, we might find ourselves in a quandary. We believe in accordance with both the nature of what is said and the character of whoever says it and we weigh both to reach a verdict. Assessment can be quite a painstaking business and we admit that in what follows we must take some short-cuts.

What is clear in the case of the witness to Jesus is that it is in its nature highly unusual. That is so from almost any angle, religious as well as non-religious. It is presented not as an ordinary but as an extraordinary story. Biblical critics often argue that we must not naïvely believe that the evangelists were trying to record historical facts. It is not even a case of historical facts in a theological framework. Rather, gospel writers employ a rich and sometimes sophisticated method of weaving together story, rhetoric, event, symbol and theology in a literary way to present us with a whole, powerfully rendered world generated from their religious understanding. Now there are debatable matters here which we must leave aside, as is now our unfailing custom! What is indisputable, however, is that, whatever else is intended, we are intended to believe that an extraordinary person spoke extraordinary words and performed extraordinary deeds. If this witness comes to its climactic point anywhere, it is in the witness to the resurrection. The witness to the resurrection is the hinge on which the New Testament account turns. It launches the *kerygma* and is pivotal for the four evangelists who write their accounts in its light. In fact, the four gospels are preaching *kerygma*. If we start to consider the witness to Jesus anywhere, then, this is a logical place to begin.

The resurrection of Jesus Christ

We are on the trail of faith and certainty, and the resurrection seems an obvious place to start. 'If Christ has not been raised, our preaching is useless and so is your faith', and '... if Christ has not been raised, your faith is futile ...' (1 Cor. 15:14, 17). However, it may seem, at the same time, that we have landed ourselves in a difficult dilemma. If we are enquiring into the credibility of the witness to the resurrection, we surely cannot get too far without making certain assumptions about God, the laws of nature, and the possibility of miracles. Should we not have started by examining these assumptions?

It is, of course, true that most of those who try to evaluate the witness to the resurrection will come to it with preconceptions about its possibility, preconceptions which themselves need to be tested, if possible, and preconceptions which influence the investigation. Yet, it is quite in order to see how far one can go with the investigation of the data without depending on the aforesaid, often called 'metaphysical', assumptions. We must not be too ready to prescribe in advance just how far we can get. Let us think of it from an historian's point of view. Whatever we say about historical method, the historian deals with the unique. It is difficult to generalize about what the historian may or may not investigate or conclude, because in order to generalize successfully one would have to investigate the whole of history, to see what kind of phenomena crop up in it. Faced with a set of reports about the resurrection of a dead man, the historian may plausibly assume from the outset that he or she cannot settle the matter. But we are not asking anyone to settle the matter at the moment. Just what will emerge from the investigation awaits the investigation itself. We have a religious investigation afoot, but, as a matter of historical fact, a set of reports have played a decisive part in the formation of Christianity, so we simply want to cast a preliminary eye over the reports. Certainly, some will want to lay down a stronger line here: our belief in the possibility of miracles or our beliefs about the laws of nature must be derived from a study of supposed miracles or apparent violations of a law of nature, it may be said. So we *should* start with reports. That may or may not be the case. We simply want to pause with an historical phenomenon to see what, if anything, we can make of it.

The first thing on which we must insist is that the gospels intentionally convey as a matter of historical fact that the tomb was empty and that it could not have been otherwise if the risen Jesus truly was identical with the crucified Jesus. This may seem obvious but it is often obscured. Thus, when he made public pronouncements on this some years ago, the Bishop of Durham made much of the fact that the resurrection was about much more than empty tombs or the fate of bones. In saying that the resurrection was 'much more' than this, he and others are quite right. In fact it would be interesting to discover anyone who had ever denied it. The resurrection has to do with our justification before God, the present lordship of Christ and our future hope. The question is whether it also has to do with an empty tomb; whether it is 'less than' that, not more than that. Literary and religious wealth in the gospels there may be, but quite obviously they also embody the intention to state certain facts.

A great deal hangs on this. One reason that people either despise or deny the religious importance we should accord to an empty tomb is that they are captivated by the realm of ideas. What is a bundle of reports about women and tombs compared with weighty ideas of sublime divine and human realities? They sound intellectually dull and religiously impoverished. This outlook has elements of truth but far greater elements of error. Christian faith is and always has been more than intellectual acceptance of the claim that certain events have taken place. And if we have been guilty of impoverishing its content, we must put our 'facts' into perspective. But Christianity is not a religion out to generate intellectual excitement. The facts of life are too serious to strive for that *per se*. It is interested rather in our humble acquiescence in the truth. And if the truth be a matter of receiving testimony to event, so be it. The gospels witness not to ideas but to that 'which we have heard, which we have seen with our eyes, which we have looked at and our hands have touched ...' (1 John 1:1)

We should keep in mind the contrast between testimony and idea when we consider the exact form which the witness to the resurrection takes. 'Witness to the resurrection' is not strictly witness to the event of resurrection, for no-one witnessed that. It is nevertheless witness to its fact, by experience of the appearance of the risen Jesus in conjunction with the fact of the empty tomb. There are plenty of conceptual problems that arise here. What is the supposed relation between the continued and the transformed elements in the risen body of Christ? What properties does it supposedly possess after resurrection and what is their relation to any properties which his supposedly ascended body possesses? Some believe that once you begin to ask those questions you get into inextricable difficulties and wish you had not started to talk about 'facts' at all. Conscientious theology will accept that such questions as these may be perfectly valid and take responsibility for responding to them one way or another. But the scriptural testimony stems not from the philosophically or the theologically educated, but from what ordinary people say that they saw. 'We speak of what we know' (John 3:11), and it is facts, and not concepts, that are presented to the world as the foundation of faith and assurance.

We stress the importance of the fact that the gospel intends to bear witness in this particular way, because it confronts any reader with a question that is scarcely avoidable. It is true that we must be sensitive to literary genre, cultural particularities and world-views very different from our own when we try to understand an ancient text. But having worked through all these and any other considerations, the stubborn fact remains. If it is clear that the gospels mean to communicate the fact of an empty tomb and a risen Jesus identical with the crucified Jesus, what is one to make of it? If all this is seriously intended, we are bound to give it a serious response. As a first step we need to recall the text itself.

Even a cursory reading of the texts stumbles upon an irony here. If, indeed, we speak of the evangelists' interest in historical report and the centrality of the resurrection in their witness, we should expect that report to be as clear as anything we can find in the gospels. If facts matter, we may say, they matter here; but if ever facts are confused, it may be retorted, it is here. When we compare the resurrection narratives in the four gospels, we find a rather bewildering conflict. One does not need to be a nasty-minded semi-pagan sceptic to discover that; it is apparent to anyone reading the accounts in an English, or any other, text. And the conflicts surround what happened at the tomb and the appearances of Jesus, the very things, unfortunately, we have highlighted. So if people suspect that behind this investigation is a barely hidden agenda, a desire to rest faith and certainty on the reliability of the biblical reports, they will say that we have blundered into a swamp. We have sown our own destruction and the destruction of faith. I shall not rehearse here the familiar account of the conflicts which appear in the text.[4] But do they help to discredit belief in the historicity of the resurrection and force us to abandon at least this path to faith or certainty?

A 'conservative' approach to the biblical material can take many forms at this point. It may be argued that while the resurrection narratives appear to contain discrepancies, they do not in fact do so. Then alternative positions can be taken. It may be urged that although we have reason to believe that there is no conflict (on the basis of a particular view of Scripture), we cannot actually demonstrate that there is no conflict. The harmony of the accounts is a matter of faith and not of demonstration. Alternatively, one can proceed to essay a demonstration that there is no conflict. On a rather different view of Scripture, it can still be maintained that there are no conflicts, but this time it is not that one believes this on principle; rather, one thinks that a thorough investigation of the data actually reveals that there are no conflicts where we thought there were. Another line is that there are no *significant* discrepancies between the accounts, only minor ones. We could ring many changes on these defences, but it is impossible to trawl through all these options. Their assessment would involve us in a discussion of the nature of Scripture which is theologically important but unmanageable within the limits of our project.

Here let us assume, just for the sake of argument, that there are discrepancies. We need to keep in mind the fact that discrepancies as such do not entail the overall falsity of an account which contains them. We are all perfectly familiar with examples of reports that differ on some things but agree on their main point and are credible at that point. Traffic accidents will be described differently by different witnesses and they will sometimes clash in their descriptions. This clash might be important if one wants to assign blame aright, but the fact of the accident will not be in dispute. Discrepancies can be severe or slight; they can concern things of importance or things of relative unimportance. The weight we attach to them depends on the particular case in point. In relation to the question of the resurrection, the question must be whether any alleged discrepancies are of such a kind as to cast doubt on an empty tomb and make the witness to the appearances of Jesus fundamentally incoherent.

This subject has been discussed for a very long time and predictably we cannot pursue it. What is clear is that the accounts do not collide on the two points at the heart of their witness. They agree on the fact of an empty tomb and a risen Jesus identical with the crucified Jesus. These are the things they want to establish by their witness. Those who wanted to overthrow their testimony would have had to address the two vital issues concerning the allegedly empty tomb and the alleged appearances of Jesus. And it is the persistence of these very beliefs as we find them in the New Testament documents that is intriguing.

We can indicate this by turning to the familiar evidence contained in Paul's first letter to the Corinthians. When Paul wrote to the Corinthian church in the fifties, he was entirely confident of the witness to the resurrection of Jesus and virtually invited doubters to check the stories for themselves (1 Cor. 15:3–8). Many to whom Jesus had appeared were still alive. Paul, at any rate, was probably thoroughly familiar with these testimonies and felt no qualms in referring people to the witnesses. He all but provided questioners with contact numbers and addresses. Although he refers specifically to the appearances and not to an empty tomb, there is no hint that he could conceive of the one without the other, any more than we find them separated in the gospel accounts, and he explicitly speaks of something that happened 'on the third day', which strongly suggests the empty-tomb traditions.

The Pauline testimony is intriguing because it confirms one's convictions that the gospels contain claims that, as far as we can tell, should have been quite vulnerable to refutation. Gospel criticism over the last decades has thrown up a variety of purported reconstructions of the formation of the resurrection narratives. People differ, for example, on whether the accounts of an empty tomb and the appearances of Jesus, conjoined in the gospels that we have, were always associated and both very early. But although we must be tentative in any reconstructions, one is forced to ponder the significance of the emergence of these traditions. It is hard to work out how an empty-tomb tradition could come into being unless the tomb was empty. Even many years on, there should have been no trouble in discovering the burial place. So there should have been no trouble in scotching the story if it were false, and the references to names and places that powder the gospel accounts are most extraordinary if the tomb was occupied. Of course, an empty tomb does not indicate resurrection; according to Matthew, Jews of his day were satisfied that the tomb was empty, but they attributed that fact to theft on the part of the disciples (Matt. 28:15). And, of course, when bodies disappear from tombs it is far more likely that they do so by some natural causality of that kind than because of resurrection.

Such a general likelihood, however, does not count for very much in this particular context. As the gospel writers saw things, what they reported certainly was unlikely when viewed in terms of general likelihood but compelling in the context it was made, namely that this was a unique, divine intervention in human history. Theology aside, the problem with the theft idea is the widespread claim amongst disciples that Jesus was seen, not in the form of a vision which required no bodily continuity with the crucified Jesus, but in a form which did evidence some bodily continuity.

Now widespread delusions are possible, as are planned conspiracies to proclaim dastardly lies. Strange and sinister things happen in religion, as everywhere else. Furthermore, we are not in a good position to elaborate all the options, let alone assess them, as we speak of an event so long ago and documented in such a way as this. But as far as anyone can judge, if we concede the intention of the gospel witness, we are bound by certain alternatives. The alternative to the truth of the witness really seems to be either deceit or delusion in the case of a considerable number of early disciples. This would of course be a sorry outcome of the life-work of Jesus, who sought to teach the difference between delusion and truth in religion and hypocrisy and sincerity in speech. In fact, Jesus would probably turn out to be the least successful founder of any religion we can think of. Yet the early Christian communities exalted truth-telling in their midst and exuded humble confidence before the God to whom they prayed and to whom they gave such thanks for Jesus Christ. Still, tragedy is the human condition, and there is plenty amiss in religion, to say the least. So we must suspend a positive verdict on this witness.

Now I warned from the outset that we were taking short-cuts. Nevertheless, I hope we have said enough to show that we are confronted with evidence which demands a verdict. If the nature of the biblical witness makes it difficult to accept, the idea we get of the nature of the witnesses, if they were so thoroughly unreliable, is also surely difficult to accept. As a casually interested general reader or as an *historian* one may leave the matter unconcluded. But *personally*, if one is religiously serious, one cannot. According to the gospels, we are dealing with matters of universal significance here. If Jesus really rose from the dead, then the whole affair seems to impinge dramatically on my existence. The crucial question is whether or not it is plausible to believe in the sort of God supposedly responsible for the sending and raising of Jesus. To this question we now turn.

The existence of God

As we said earlier, it would have been possible to begin our enquiry into faith and certainty by starting with God rather than Jesus. And over the centuries, argument over the existence of God has gone on without reference to Jesus. A number of arguments for the existence of God have been proposed. The topic is still a lively one in contemporary philosophy of religion. These arguments usually deal with theism in general, that is a belief in God shared by many Jews, Christians and Muslims and some others. They include arguments that take their departure from the world about us. How can this universe exist at all without a Creator? Or how can this universe be so orderly unless it has a Designer? Again, there are arguments that take their point of departure not from the world about us but from an examination of our experience. Can religious experience, in all its historical length and cultural breadth, really be illusory? Can our moral sense be explained unless there is one who gave us a moral law? Many people will accept the importance of trying to answer these questions, but there are other arguments which can look very much like the plaything of professional philosophers. Such are the 'ontological' arguments for the existence of God which try to show that the very idea of God leads us to affirm his existence.

Among the traditional arguments for the existence of God, however, there have also been 'historical' arguments and these have had reference to Jesus. Historical arguments, or the arguments from history, purport to show that some phenomena in human history constitute evidence for the existence of God. In the past, the argument from miracles was particularly important here; how can you explain the occurrence of miracles unless God was behind them? The resurrection is a crucial example of a miracle. So an argument is possible to the effect that (a) the resurrection of Jesus occurred and (b) its occurrence is evidence for the existence of God. Now perhaps we think that it is clearly implied in our discussion so far that this can never work. For it seems that we can believe in the resurrection of Jesus only on the assumption that God exists. If so, we cannot use the resurrection as evidence for God's existence, for we should need to assume the existence of God to believe in the resurrection in the first place.

But we must pause for a moment to notice how our arguments sometimes work. Consider a heavy case that was moved from one spot in my house to another. I am a little baffled because I thought I was the only one strong enough to lift the case. However, the best explanation I can come up with is that my ten-year-old son shifted it. On the assumption that he is strong enough to shift the case, my problem is solved. But why should I make that assumption? Well, actually I make that assumption only because the case has been shifted! I need the assumption to explain the facts, but it is the presence of those facts that generate my assumption. This is logically a perfectly proper procedure.

Our example is not meant to be analogous to the case of resurrection. In our example we are dealing with an indisputable datum: the case was moved. In the case of the resurrection, it is precisely the datum which is at issue. Nevertheless, the example interestingly displays the logic of certain arguments. When I say that I can believe that 'x' occurred only if I assume 'y', that does not stop me from using 'x' as evidence for 'y'. So I may grant that I can never believe in the resurrection unless I make the assumption that there is a God, but studying the witness to resurrection may press me towards that very assumption.[5]

What study of the resurrection reports forces me to do is to consider rather seriously the question of God. To be sure, plenty of other things may force me to do that as well, but the very specificity of Jesus and of resurrection claims sharply focuses the belief that there is a God at work in the world. It may be right to press for explanations of 'the world', 'order', 'morality' and 'religious experience', but these are big and even rather unwieldy sorts of ideas; they are important but it is difficult to get a handle on them because they are in one way more complex and indeed more abstract than a person and a report about an event. The data is rather harder to hold in one's head while one is trying to think it through. Nevertheless, the attempts have been made. And it is usually conceded that none of the so-called arguments for the existence of God actually offer proof of his existence. Indeed, some thinkers aver that, to the contrary, we can disprove the existence of God or at any rate show that it is highly improbable. What, then, about probability rather than proof? Will the arguments take us some of the way if not all the way to affirming the existence of God? Will they give us some evidence, if not conclusive proof? Or will they not even get us that far?

To repeat our refrain: it is impossible to survey this long-standing debate, still being prosecuted. Some will consider some arguments for God's existence to be stronger than others; likewise, some will consider some arguments against God's existence to be stronger than others. In contemporary philosophy of religion, the arguments offered on different sides of the debate have become technically very rigorous. For example, there has been a celebrated attempt to weigh probabilities in a rather mathematically exact fashion, emerging with the conclusion that the balance of probability is in favour of the existence of God. The problem with this is one common to the debate as a whole. It all calls for logical calculations which most of us cannot make and even for those who can make them, so much weight is put on getting the exact arguments right that if one step in the argument is logically faulty, one has to work out another way of getting to one's conclusions or give up those conclusions. The whole enterprise, almost by its definition, is precarious and unlikely to yield anything conclusive, certainly not for the unphilosophical.

This is not to say that the whole exercise is completely valueless either for the religious believer or for the unbeliever. For arguments are very often attempts to turn intuitions into demonstrations. You may well show me that an argument I produce for the moral superiority of socialism over capitalism is false. I agree that my argument does not hold water, but I think that although my argument is wrong, my conclusion is right. So I look for a better argument. Now perhaps I am pig-headed and should give up my conclusion, but perhaps I am not really pig-headed and quite rightly keep my conclusion but admit that I am not very good at arguing for it. What I show in such a case is that my belief does not really depend on my ability to argue well for it. And this happens in technical philosophy as well as at a humbler level. Arguments are reformulated, showing that the belief is not the result of an argument. Indeed, if important religious beliefs were the result of argument, we should be in a sorry state, since very few are expert in argument and those that are know how inconclusive arguments are. The underlying 'intuitions', then, or whatever we may want to call them, often precede and survive arguments. These 'intuitions' about the connection between the ideas of God and morality, or God and created order may still be worth investigation.

However, if, as a matter of fact, we are inclined to the existence or non-existence of God less by logical exactness than by a rather more intuitive method, it is also frequently the case that it is not one feature, but an accumulation of features that impress us. What many people have, when they think about it, amounts to an overall impression: the fact of a material world; the elements of order in it; the religious experience of humankind; the mysteries of conscience; the phenomenon of Jesus Christ and perhaps even the puzzles of the ontological argument – together they suggest God to us. We do not make a logical deduction about each item, but a kind of judgment about the whole, though we shall probably give more weight to some things than to others. Our reason is fully involved in that judgment. Our judgment is formed on the basis of pondering different ways of explaining the world, morality or religion, and is formed as we try to think through the implications of these things. However, it is not really a formal and logical deduction.

Now the way we put things together in judgments may be very hard to describe philosophically but it is a very familiar experience. It is as though we often find some intuition working away, not apart from our normal reasoning process but not something we can identify either with just the correct logical steps. 'Intuition' is potentially a dangerous word. It may be used as a cloak for resigning from argument and retreating into the recesses of subjective judgment. This kind of 'subjective judgment' may be difficult to commend to people who simply do not share that intuition. So perhaps we should use the word 'insight' instead of 'intuition', although they can mean different things. But whether we prefer insight to intuition or want a sharp distinction between them, we are pointed to an interesting and crucial reality in our 'epistemic' functioning – jargon for the way we function when it comes to knowing and believing. Things certainly work that way in that most important area, our perceptions of and dealing with other people. Much that rightly passes for wisdom in life is a sort of intuition or insight. We greatly prize the wisdom which understands people and people's motivations. Blessed are we who digest the book of Proverbs! Our insights or intuitions about people can be frighteningly near the mark and are certainly not irrational, but they cannot be explained easily by analysing logical processes. When we think of religion, then, we must make room for intuitive judgments or insights, and when we think in general, we must observe that these function very importantly in our assessment of people. From considering the fact that there are intuitive factors and judgments that play a role when people think about the existence of God, we have moved to the related reminder that insight and wisdom play a decisive role when we are trying to understand other people.

It is important that we connect the two things. The problem with some of the arguments for the existence of God is that they treat God as though he were not a living, personal being to whom we are personally related, but as an object whose existence and nature is subject to disinterested scrutiny. Now certainly there is nothing wrong with treating a person as an object of thought. For certain purposes that is exactly what we must do when we try to understand them. But we do so, or should do so, within a certain context of relationships. We enter into relationships of respect, kindness, service and love or their tragic perversions – heedlessness, cruelty, domination and hatred. It is possible to have wisdom and insight born of bitterness and there is effective witness to this in literature. But we have plenty of reason to believe, too, that the wisdom and insight that best enables us to understand and relate most fruitfully to other people comes in a different context, a context of willingness to learn and to serve, of humility and of love. Understanding in personal relationships, therefore, is neither a merely logical exercise nor something which develops quite irrespective of our personal attitudes. On the contrary, personal attitudes make all the difference in the world. They can cloud or they can advance our understanding. Understanding is a matter of my attitudes, what we shall term the disposition of the heart, as well as something of the mind.

It is no different in the case of God. *If* there is a personal God, why should we believe that we can advance far in knowledge and understanding by purely intellectual processes? We are assuming here that knowledge of God may have parallels to our knowledge of other people. But, it will be protested, it is all very well to say this if we assume that there is a personal God. Our problem at the moment is that we can make no assumptions either way. The question of the existence of God is an open question. So what is the use of talking about attitudes of humility and so on in relation to the knowledge of God?

The answer is that there is a great deal of use; indeed, that it is vital. According to the Christian witness, if the reality of God's personal being comes into view at any point, it is with the person of Jesus. We have talked about resurrection and about general belief in God. But it is the resurrection *of Jesus* that has been proclaimed, and in the coming of Jesus it is said that God has appeared in his world, no longer a theme of thought that is beyond, above or apart from it, but now personally within it. As we have said, the record of Jesus presupposes the existence of God. Jesus, however, was to be proclaimed, and was proclaimed, to the whole world, including those ignorant of the God of Abraham, Isaac and Jacob.

According to this proclamation, our attitude to God is brought to light in our attitude to Jesus. Jesus was a person. He can be understood, if at all, only in the mode of personal knowledge. We have found that this is bound to require a certain disposition of heart. It follows that if our enquiry about God takes the form of an enquiry about Jesus, it requires a certain disposition of the heart to conduct it aright. This is not to prejudge the result of the investigation. The candour with which we try to approach the witness to Jesus may lead us to say that Jesus gives us no special reason for us to believe in the existence of God. But this is certainly the direction in which we must now turn.

Approaching Jesus

Although a consideration of Jesus promises to focus our question about God, we may wonder whether the gain in specificity is offset by loss in accessibility. Ideas about God can be entertained, shared and discussed, but understanding a person requires knowing something about a person. And that, it may be said, is our problem here. Jesus as he was is hidden from view, available only according to the impression he made on disciples and believers who do not pretend to be dispassionate. The problem that faces us is often called the problem of the historical Jesus, and the dilemma it causes for faith is accordingly labelled 'the problem of faith and history'. However, since the issues were first formulated in those terms, the biblical and theological scene has changed so much that the formulation can sound dated. Many things contribute to this, whether we think of 'literary' or 'narrative' approaches or the entry of post-modernist or feminist critiques of the entire theological enterprise. If 'faith and history' was once something of a minefield, it is now either much more of a minefield or it is a field falling into disuse, depending on the way one looks at things.

There is no substitute for the need to work through the various options here; neither religious epistemology, nor any other important religious subject, yields its secrets quickly on the academic plane. Nevertheless, we must not be tempted to think that because there is an array of options, we must be plunged into greater uncertainty. A range of proposals indicates that a subject is lively; it does not necessarily mean an increase in the number of plausible proposals compared to a situation where there are fewer options. Furthermore, certain presuppositions can be common to an otherwise varied assortment, or certain explicit contentions always advanced. In rejecting these for any reason, one may be rejecting a great number of options.

What one needs to underline positively here is that, whatever else we say, there is no getting away from the historical element in the biblical testimony. It is obviously found in the gospels. It is all but impossible to read the introduction to Luke's Gospel in any way other than as a declaration of intent to take an interest in historical fact. Luke bears sufficient resemblance to Matthew and

Mark for us to make the same judgment about Matthew and Mark, a judgment we might in any case make if we considered then apart from Luke. Because of its distinctive features and its interpretation over the years, we must leave aside comment on John's Gospel here. But the distinction between the synoptic gospels as more 'historical' and John as more 'theological' is widely recognized as simplistic, to say the least; one can argue either for the 'theological' in the synoptics or the 'historical' in John. Here we should just observe that John presents the material in terms of the historical causes of controversy over Jesus Christ; what was seen and heard of him generated this or that response. And, as hinted earlier, the Johannine literature (specifically John and 1 John) is perhaps the most epistemologically self-conscious literature in the New Testament.

It is important to hold stubbornly to the internal evidence that the evangelists were interested in historical report. (If John causes people problems, one should read 'synoptists' for 'evangelists' from now on.) One should certainly attend to the literary devices of the evangelists, the differences in their reports and the distinct forms which 'historical report' may take. Doubtless we are capable of imposing views of 'history' or 'historical' on the evangelists in a way that obscures what they were doing and which presumes false notions of 'accuracy', 'report' and, indeed, 'fact'. But here, as we found when we touched on the resurrection, if we pursued all this in more detail, we should drift in the direction of discussion of our notion of Scripture. Nor can we ask to what extent the rest of the New Testament bears witness to an historical interest. Opinion differs, for instance, on the place Paul may have allocated to the earthly Jesus in his missionary preaching. What is clear, however, as the emergence of the canon reflects, is that the story of Jesus is an integral part of the witness of the church. For our particular purposes, we isolated the matter of the resurrection, but one cannot do that for long without seeming curiously abstract, despite our talk of historicity. The gospel narratives which report the resurrection are credible only in conjunction with the whole witness to Jesus. If this man really was as he is reported there, the resurrection is, in retrospect, 'fitting' and credible in a way it would not be if we were simply told about a man who lived, died and rose again.

At this juncture, it is enough to draw attention to one singular feature of the evangelists' account. The evangelists wish to present Jesus not only as good, remarkable, authoritative, humble, active in healing and trenchant in teaching. Also they wish to present Jesus as one who proclaimed the forgiveness of sin. And they wish to present Jesus, implicitly but clearly, as himself without sin. We must explore the significance of this for the question of approaching Jesus.

Forgiveness and sin

There are two things that are distinctive about the reports of Jesus' forgiveness. The first is that usually Jesus does not forgive sins directed against himself. It is sometimes rather casually stated that Jews believed that only God could forgive sins; Jesus forgave sins; therefore, Jesus implied his deity. But it is not true that only God could forgive sins. I am supposed to forgive my brother or sister who sins against me, as the Lord's Prayer assumed. What is marked about Jesus is his forgiveness of sins directed against God. And that, of course, is the truth of the point about his claim to deity.

The second distinctive is related to this. Jesus forgives rather than just pronouncing forgiveness. One could modify the claim that Jesus was distinctive if he pronounced the forgiveness of sins directed against God, as the spokesman of God, in prophetic style. He would not then be doing the forgiving; he would be pronouncing the forgiveness of another. But in the case of prophets, as of priests, the last thing a reader of the Old Testament is tempted to do is to accuse prophet or priest of blurring the distinction between God and themselves. In fact, their very presence, which has a mediating function, just underlines the gulf between God and humans. But all the gospels record how Jesus drew attention to himself in a way foreign to prophet and priest. He was quite naturally and quite rightly viewed as a prophet, according to the gospel evidence, but according to that very same evidence, he did not fit the mould. This appears all the way from the contrast with John the Baptist to the eucharistic words in the upper room. In this context, quite apart from the records of the stories themselves, the forgiveness of Jesus is utterly distinctive.

One might be sceptical about the historicity of these reports, but on what grounds? How does one explain their invention? If, as a matter of fact, Jesus said anything at all about sin, and if he had even a fraction of the prophetic consciousness of its gravity, one would have expected an entirely different report of things from what the gospels offer. We should not get the impression that he himself was always free from sin. Yet the evangelists are implicitly committed to the sinlessness of Jesus. They do not say that in so many words, but their belief in it can be inferred in two ways.

Firstly, while arguments from silence are often dangerous, they are often telling as well. In this case they are. While Jesus talks of others' sins, he does not confess his own. There is no sign of sorrowful penitence or repentance for what he himself has said, thought, done or failed to do from the time of his baptism in the Jordan to his death on the cross. He seems weighed down, yet one cannot find any trace of his being weighed down by his own guilt. Such is the clear presentation of Jesus.

Secondly, the kind of goodness positively portrayed is singularly incompatible with sin. A kind of holiness is manifest, neither an ostentatious separation from the mass nor one that is interwoven with sharp consciousness at one's own ethical distance from a holy God. It is not that the memory of all others always shows traces of their shortcomings. Gautama the Buddha is a striking example. What distinguishes Jesus from Gautama in this respect is not some moral superiority which appears on the surface of the literature. It is that Gautama does not appear in a tradition where the distinction between a holy God and a defiled humanity constitutes the cardinal issue in religion. Where it does, as both Old and New Testaments alike indicate, the appearance of an apparently sinless Jesus is rather extraordinary.

Of course, it can be maintained that the evangelists were deeply confused or seriously misunderstood Jesus or that they wilfully turned on its head the message of the one whom they claim led them into God's presence. The only reason for taking this line seems to be the difficulty of believing that Jesus forgave as he did. For if he did, what are we to make of him? Are we prepared to shift from the evangelists on to Jesus the accusation of a confusion or deceit so radical as to destroy his religious credibility altogether? Even many of those professing no adherence to Christianity will baulk at that. The ministry of forgiveness, no less than the resurrection, demands an explanation.

Now this intensely sharpens the situation in which we find ourselves when confronted with any morally impressive person. Even if we will not swallow sinlessness, we should acknowledge that the portrayal of Jesus is a standing judgment on all manner of dispositions: selfishness, greed, hypocrisy, dissimulation, to mention but a few things. But at least we may offer ourselves the somewhat spurious comfort that we are all in the same boat, though widely different in degrees of moral achievement. Still, we can live with our imperfection. Not so when it comes to the portrayal of Jesus. He places the whole question of the relationship between God and ourselves in the most serious conceivable moral context. Indeed, the words 'moral', 'moral achievements' or 'moral superiority' begin to sound rather thin to describe human lives, conditions and relationships exposed to the searchlight of the person of Jesus.

The message is clear. The supreme religious difficulty is not epistemological but moral or, if we have abandoned that word, spiritual. There *is* an epistemological difficulty, there is a problem of religious knowledge, but it is generated by a spiritual condition. That is why we are back with a vengeance to the question of the disposition of the heart. If there is a God to be known through knowing Jesus, God cannot be known without a certain attitude to Jesus. We must press on now to say more about that attitude.

Conditions of understanding

During his imprisonment after being caught in a conspiracy to assassinate Hitler, Dietrich Bonhoeffer tried to finish a study which eventually came out under the title *Ethics*.[6] Bonhoeffer had long been reflecting on the nature of Christianity in a world where people thought they could manage without God and certainly where you could explain the world and events within it without recourse to the idea of God. Bonhoeffer was persuaded that a proper presentation of Jesus Christ was the key theological response to the needs of the day, and in *Ethics* he began by trying to show how two things went together in Jesus Christ: freedom and action. Jesus' freedom lies in his complete unity with the will and word of God. That unity impels him into sustained action whose quality Bonhoeffer captured in a comparison between Jesus, the man of action, and the Pharisee, the man of judgment. It is very strikingly effected.

In delineating the action of Jesus, Bonhoeffer convinces us of the importance of action, not by imparting a conviction to the head, but by impressing its significance on the heart. Here is human life as it is meant to be, entirely oriented to action. And of action, we must say two things.

The first is that it is in some sense inevitable. One may contrast 'action' with 'inaction' or 'contemplation', but we can also rightly think of both inaction and contemplation as forms of action. That is, we are always doing something with our time, however 'inactive' or however 'contemplative'. In this sense, action is not an option; it is the given of human life.

The second is that it is in some sense committed. Judgments and opinions can be suspended; action cannot. I may have reservations about whether I should go to London or not, but the moment I am on the train I have committed myself as fully as the person who goes confidently to London, at least until the next stop. I may be in a moral dilemma about whether I should have an abortion or not, but the moment I have it, it is an entirely committed action. What must happen is that I either do or do not have an abortion and no amount of suspended judgment on its rights and wrongs alters the imperative to act in one way or another. Action is imperative whether or not I can change my mind or do something about consequences.

However much, then, we protest our inability to conclude on weighty matters of religion, we are forced to act. Jesus' action, as Bonhoeffer presents it, is the judge of ours. It judges ours not because Jesus is sniffing out the weaknesses of inferior spirits, but because he is bound to act, as we are, and by the nature of his action he seems both to parade the high vocation of humanity and to convict us of our own failure. One does not have to agree on either of these points. Jesus' action is designed entirely in the service of his neighbour, but we can say that even if this has some laudable aspects, we disagree with the principle of loving our neighbour as ourselves. And while we admit imperfection, we are certainly not going to get caught calling ourselves failures. So we are not bound to assent to and to live by the light of Jesus' action. But we are bound to action.

This casts in a different light the business of defending or of justifying Christianity. Where positive world-views, religious or otherwise, are propounded in contrast to Christianity, their adherents are in the same position as Christians. They must justify or defend their positions if they require justification or defence from Christians. Where people eschew dogmatism, however, the onus seems to be on Christians to prove their case or at least to show its strength. But that is never the true situation. All are committed in action. Those who would suspend judgment and cannot suspend action may be asked to justify why they act in one way rather than another. If they offer a justification, certain beliefs bound up with the actions will come to light; actions are generally not performed in some entirely beliefless vacuum. And so the people in question are in the same position as the others: if they require a justification from Christians, they must be called to account themselves. Alternatively, they can offer no kind of account or justification or defence of why this and not that action was performed, why they did do this (regarded as morally wrong by others) or did not do this (regarded as morally right by others). But if people refuse to give any sort of account here, it is impossible to demand some sort of justification for Christian belief either, since justifications apparently do not matter.

The kind of vision of action, then, that Jesus offers is a vision of life in the service of others. We are of course making a minimal claim here, neither examining whether Jesus performed miracles nor propounding a doctrine of unique self-giving action in atonement. Are there any reasons for commending this vision rather than other visions?

The answer is that we cannot give decisive reasons, but we can and should draw attention to the importance of compassion. Interestingly enough, one of the most striking expositions of the moral status and nature of compassion comes in the work of one of the first atheistic philosophers of the West, and one of the first to turn East for inspiration, Arthur Schopenhauer.[7] Schopenhauer argued that compassion alone has moral worth. And he took compassion to be a very powerful phenomenon. In compassion I mysteriously identify myself with the sufferings of the other. The mystery is that, whereas I seem to experience the sufferings of the other not as mine but as his or hers, I genuinely do experience them myself. There is profound identification. Schopenhauer went on to conclude that the best explanation for this was that, in some way, I am actually one with the other person in my being, and he drew on oriental religious philosophy to expound this point. Here he exalted the superiority of the East over Christianity, although he granted that the discovery of *agape* does indicate one meritorious feature in Christianity.

Schopenhauer argued that the moral life was a matter of advancing the well-being and alleviating the pain of the other. He was shortly thereafter attacked on this point by a far more virulent anti-Christian, namely Nietzsche. But in public life and public pronouncements in the West, an implicitly Schopenhauerian line is taken, independent of any belief in God and to that extent practically, if not theoretically, atheist. Let us, then, take this position seriously. Supposing I grant compassion high, if not highest, moral worth. My life should be suffused with it. Should I not perhaps dedicate my life to the well-being of my neighbour, in every act seeking the good of the other, identifying with the pain of the other not only to empathize but to be empowered in the struggle to alleviate pain?

If I have even struck out in the direction of this conclusion, the portrayal of Jesus indicates the deep fragmentation of my life. Bonhoeffer wrote of the simplicity or integrity of the action of Jesus. He was struck by the fact that knowledge of good and evil, which some people think is a sign of our moral dignity, is a sign of our moral disunity. For we were not created to know good and evil. Knowledge of good and evil is the result of the fall. We were created only to know the good, only to know God, who is the good. Jesus did not live a life choosing between good and evil. This is how Bonhoeffer expresses it:

The freedom of Jesus is not the arbitrary choice of one amongst innumerable possibilities; it consists on the contrary precisely in the complete simplicity of His action, which is never confronted by a plurality of possibilities, conflicts or alternatives, but always only by one thing. This one thing Jesus calls the will of God. He says that to do that will is His meat. This will of God is His life. He lives and acts not by the knowledge of good and evil but by the will of God. There is only one will of God. In it the origin is recovered; in it there is established the freedom and the simplicity of all action.[8]

We, on the other hand, cannot successfully harmonize action and knowledge. What we morally ought to do or to be, we find ourselves unable to do or to be. If I discern some sort of moral pull to do or to be something, then I ought to be able to do or to be that thing. But for whatever reason, I fail. I can bring action and knowledge into line by saying that if I cannot do something, then I was never really obligated to do it anyway. Serious exposure to Jesus shatters that way of thinking. Jesus does not possess a humanity that has nothing to do with my own; I feel demands made upon *my* humanity, confronted with the self-giving service of Jesus. Jesus does not act in a way unrelated to my actions; I feel demands made upon *my* actions, confronted with the self-sacrificial actions of Jesus. True, the early Christians proclaimed the distinction of Jesus and the uniqueness of a sacrificial death. But they summoned believers to live as ones now participating in his risen humanity. His humanity was to be expressed in theirs. For anyone willing to exalt compassion and face the facts, it appears that Jesus possesses an integrity, in the sense of a unity of conviction, will, intention and action, that we do not have.

In Jesus, sinlessness and integrity come together, as we realize that our disunity is not there in him. There is no moral restlessness, excuse or anxiety, no regret at action undertaken or action omitted. While we talk the language of sinlessness we may seem to be talking of an entirely different humanity to our own. Why make out that anyone should feel badly about not being like that? Surely you cannot have a guilty conscience just because you are not perfect. However, when we think not in terms of sinlessness but in terms of the concrete integrity of conviction and action, it is different. We feel not only something amiss, but something deeply fragmented in our humanity, something that needs healing.

We could say that Jesus is portrayed as an ideal, but that does not ring true. The least we can say is that the biblical witness intends to present us with the singular humanity of Jesus. St Paul and the other converts or disciples sought to integrate in their own humanity faith and love, truth and humility. The proclaimed source of the new creation, as they now regarded themselves, was the risen Jesus. It was the power of personal influence, personal moulding, not the power of an idea that they believed they were experiencing. Ideas as such do not play a large role in biblical Christianity. They are not the source of change. But did Paul and the others, then, *baselessly* suppose there was in Jesus an integrity and influence that moulded them according to his perfection? One can say so. But is it plausible?

So we have arrived at this point. The witness to the resurrection is evidence that demands a verdict. Hence we enquire about God. We find that we will learn of him only if he exists as Christianity thinks he does, if we approach him personally. That entails a disposition of the heart. Jesus is the point of approach. As one who forgives, he identifies the fundamental religious condition as one of spiritual alienation as the root cause of any intellectual perplexity. As one who acts, he brings our actions to judgment. And all along we insist that what we ascribe to Jesus we ascribe to an historical person and not to an idea. Of course, some will remain sceptical. We have not yet tackled the matter of certainty. But one thing surely has become clear. We are incapable of understanding religious faith, certainty or claims to knowledge if we disregard the question of our personal, spiritual disposition.

It is at this point that we must remark on the human will. We are quite used to thinking of the contrast between faith and reason when we reflect on religious belief. There is another contrast, less familiar to many but equally familiar in the history of thought, and that is the contrast between will and intellect or will and understanding. When we act, we often do so after thinking about it. Both understanding and will are components of action. I may decide that I ought to act in a certain way, but although I may understand that, it does not guarantee the action. Action requires an act of the will. So much is plain enough, but we need to draw attention to other ways in which the will is related to the understanding.

Supposing, for example, you ask me about the effects on the environment of the use of leaded petroleum. I might say to you honestly that I don't exactly know. But I may choose not to know. I may suspect that it is detrimental to the environment but that means the bother of converting my car or changing my life-style, so I don't want to know too much about petrol and the environment. I have a sneaking suspicion that I am causing some damage and I might admit to you quietly that I *ought* to find out and know what there is to know. But I can say quite honestly that I have not looked even casually at the evidence or tried to check the reliability of those statements that tell me that I might be doing damage. So I have chosen ignorance. This is akin to the process we call 'turning a blind eye'. We can genuinely profess ignorance or uncertainty but we might have opted to be in that position. Of course, we might investigate a matter assiduously and remain ignorant or uncertain at the end, but that is a different matter from the ignorance of unwillingness or unconcern. In this case, I have a desire not to find out, so the will has directed the intellect to go and think about something else instead.

Or supposing you are arguing with me about my responsibility to give away more of my money. I am pretty reluctant to do so, but this time I cannot avoid the issue in the middle of an argument with you. Because I wish to come to certain conclusions rather than others, I shall look for arguments. Just how far I can genuinely persuade myself in these things is a matter for separate discussion, but I can certainly advance arguments for a position I wish to hold. Further, if I am sufficiently skilled in argument, I might get the better of you. Possibly you could have come up with an argument that forced me to agree with you, but I am very glad you did not. Here, again, the will affects the intellect. Whatever is going on inside me, the external presentation of my case to the outside world is not the result of a dispassionate consideration of the arguments for and against. It is the result of selecting a line of argument which gets me to my desired end: that of hanging on to my money. The will has driven the intellect to look for good intellectual moves in the argument.

Or supposing, finally, that I hold a certain business practice to be ethically wrong. Other people may defend it, but I am sure it is wrong. One day, still acknowledging its wrong, I yield to the temptation. My yielding becomes occasional and finally habitual. The more I yield, the less the conscience protests. The less the conscience protests, the more open I am to the intellectual persuasion that, after all, it may not be unethical. Five years down the road, you ask me whether this conduct of mine is ethically in order. I answer that whereas I was once certain it was wrong, now I am not so sure; it is an open question on which one should not be dogmatic; personally, I see nothing wrong with it. Again, whether there is some suspicion deep down that I am doing wrong, I do not know. As far as I and other people can judge, I have honestly changed my mind. But note how it happened. It happened when the will to act according to what I understood to be right was weakened. The failure of my will has led to a clouding or changing of my understanding. It does not matter for a moment whether I was right or wrong in the first place. Maybe I was over-scrupulous, legalistic and wrong in the first place. What is interesting is the process by which I have changed.

Now the will is vitally involved in our assessment of the claims of and about Jesus. To follow our first example, I may suspect that Jesus preaches pacifism when I should rather go to war, so I choose not to look into that. To follow our second example, I know that Jesus calls for sexual self-control, but I don't want to exercise it, so I look for arguments against that proposition. To follow the third example, I used to believe that Jesus taught the renunciation of wealth but I have gradually found it hard to obey and now I am really unclear as to whether he taught it or not. We are not concerned here with what Jesus did teach on violence, sex or possessions. We are deliberately choosing areas of vital personal or political concern for many people. The fact is that on the terms that they are presented, Jesus calls for a personal revolution that transforms my practices and my allegiance. If I admit his moral authority, let alone his claims to be speaking for God, I am bound to change my life or at any rate stop justifying my failure to change my life. In other words, I cannot approach the question of Jesus in a disinterested way. And we may say that more broadly of God. The possibility of God's existence is one of vital existential interest. So while we may profess uncertainty about God or Jesus, we can have our motives, too. We do not want to be sure either of God's existence or of Jesus' authority. Uncertainty, in this case, is the symptom of moral or spiritual fault, not the product of genuine intellectual grappling.

Let us be clear about what is being said. The point is *not* that all lack of faith or certainty is the product of unsound motivation. Indeed, we should remember that the argument cuts both ways: people believe or profess belief as well in order to satisfy certain wishes in a way that is no more 'honest' than those who are religiously evasive. We are making two points. The first is that we must not assume that epistemological issues are just intellectual issues. The second is that where Jesus is concerned, the issue at stake is profoundly existential and not dispassionately cerebral. Yet one may think that if this is true, we are intellectually swamped. If most, if not all, of us approach these issues with our hidden agenda, can we settle arguments on the objective level at all? Are we not all doomed to scepticism? And does that not serve the purposes of irreligion rather than religion? These are questions we must now face.

Scepticism

Loosely, we can characterize scepticism as the claim that nothing can be known by us. It featured long before the coming of Christianity and enjoyed a renaissance around the time of the Reformation and afterwards with the republication of classical sceptical texts. So when rival religious positions sundered the social unity of Europe, scepticism began to come into its own. It is to all appearances an ideal and attractive position to hold in our irreversibly pluralistic culture.

Scepticism, however, is varied, and its alternative forms are interesting. We spoke of the belief that nothing can be known by us but admitted this was a loose way of speaking. The reason is this. Again, long before the coming of Christianity, some sceptics denied the claim that we can know nothing. They denied it because it was not a piece of consistent scepticism. For to say that we know nothing is to utter a dogmatic proposition. A dogmatic proposition is not a proposition spoken by a dogmatic person or in a dogmatic mood. It is an assertion about something. There is a definite or determinate claim involved. Now if we truly know nothing, how can we claim dogmatically that we know nothing? We are saying that we know that nothing can be known by us. If we were truly sceptical, we should not say dogmatically that nothing can be known by us. We should say that we cannot even know whether or not anything can be known by us.

Life gets rather complicated at this point. For on the one hand, all this may not get us very far; we may deny that we can know that nothing can be known, but every time someone claims to know anything, we shall deny that this thing can be known as well. So perhaps we are back with the original scepticism. On the other hand, the exercise draws attention to the fact that those who deny on principle that anything can be known are being as dogmatic as any religious or other person who insists on the possibility of genuine knowledge. There are two routes we may take in considering the challenge of scepticism. In the first case, we may ask whether quite generally, our scepticism is warranted. In the second, we may ask whether religion has the resources to respond to scepticism. Let us take these in turn.

Is scepticism warranted?

Scepticism can extend to the material world, as when we say we do not know if there is a chair in front of us. We leave aside this kind of scepticism. It can also extend to the world of ideas. Take our moral notions. It is wrong to torture, right to alleviate pain. Can we say we know this? Some will hesitate to extend the realm of knowledge from the realm of 'facts' (the chair over there) to the realms of 'values' (this action is right or wrong). 'Facts' have to do with our five senses. 'Values' are different. We shall linger with this world of values, or this moral world, because it is rather more helpful for our interest in religion than is the discussion of an external world.

Let us take a tragic case, not in the spirit of clinical analysis, but in order to see if it helps us in our thinking. One reads a report of a two-year-old child beaten or tortured to death. Was that action morally wrong? The majority of people in Britain today would say it was. Every single public comment on such a case either states or assumes it. It is not argued. Why not? Is moral right and wrong not entirely subjective? So it may be said that we should not say: 'this *is* morally wrong', as we might say 'this is 2001', but we should say: 'this is morally wrong for me or for us, as far as I or we are concerned'? Most people would want to say 'this *is* morally wrong', but they might be puzzled all the same, for 'values' are not quite the same as 'facts' about the world. So they are attracted to the case for moral relativism. This is the belief that there are no moral absolutes which we should all accept and which are binding on us whether we like them or not.

According to this view, moral standards are of our devising and not the expression of some universal or absolute truth, not grounded in some given order apart from what we devise. There are some complex questions here about the meaning of 'objective' and 'subjective'. We must avoid them. Only two things can be said here. Firstly, if we say that all moral truths are relative, we seem to be propounding a dogma, and (as with scepticism) why should we accept a dogmatic assertion that all moral truths are relative? Secondly, although people might turn a sympathetic ear to the case for moral relativism in general, they do not adhere to moral relativism in practice. Hear them on the environment, the Tory party, homosexuality, women's liberties, child abuse and they are certainly not relativists. They believe that certain conduct is morally wrong and certain action morally obligatory. And if certain persons or whole cultures think otherwise, it is a sign not of acceptable differences, but of corruption. They should change.

Now in accordance with the practical convictions of the majority, I think we should maintain that some moral certainties are justified and that we have moral knowledge. There is no reason to believe that we should call our understanding anything less than knowledge. I am thinking of the kind of brutality and cruelty in our torture example. I am not asking things like: should you cause slightly painful torture to a prisoner because if you do, that is the only way to get him to admit where the bomb is planted which will kill several innocent people? And I am not claiming we should be morally certain and can have moral knowledge of everything. But it seems to be that the denial of any moral knowledge whatsoever rests on two false notions.

The first is an unduly restrictive notion of what counts as knowledge. 'Knowledge', for some people, is something within the province of scientific investigation or something which is immediately given in our sense experience or perhaps it is of a mathematical type. The world of moral values has to do with our judgments about things outside the realm of the five senses. So we cannot 'know' here. But why not? What justifies our reservation of the term 'knowledge' just to the realm of mathematics, logic, sense-experience or science? For many people, what justifies this is that for something to be 'knowledge' it must be capable of proof of some kind or it is just evident to our senses. But humans are not constituted so that knowledge is restricted to these things. Sensory experience or truths of logic or mathematics have to do with just one area of human knowing. Moral apprehension is a different area where scientific proofs do not apply but where there can be knowledge all the same. Nor need we discover some moral perceptions that are common to all people. If people at certain times and places do not seem to regard the cruel abuse of children as morally wrong, it does not mean that we must surrender the claim to knowledge any more than we doubt our knowledge that the world is spherical just because some people believe the earth is flat. In both cases, we lament the ignorance involved. The ignorance is sadder if it is moral than if it is scientific.

The second is that some think that knowledge is the kind of thing we need to justify intellectually, whereas doubt is always intellectually respectable unless we can argue someone out of it. The contribution of Descartes is very well known in this respect. Descartes, in the seventeenth century, set out as a matter of intellectual integrity to doubt everything he could, so that anything he claimed to know, he knew after overcoming the doubt. Whether or not this exercise had merit, the fact is that we must ask why doubt is more fundamental than knowledge, in the sense that I have to justify the latter but not the former. I can express a doubt that this world exists, but that is not to say that there is any good reason for seriously doubting it. Reasons can be offered for seriously doubting it. But why should those reasons strike me as more convincing than my conviction, in common with that of every other sane adult, that this world does exist? Let us put it this way: what justifies our doubting? We should apply this to the moral realm also. The reasons for seriously doubting the wrongness of torture are far weaker than the reasons for accepting the correctness of our moral apprehension, if 'reasons' can take us very far either way.

Does religion have the resources to respond to scepticism?

There are also specifically religious or theological reasons for challenging scepticism. Supposing it is said that nothing can be known by us. From a Christian point of view, that is not just a restriction on human abilities. It places restrictions upon God, as well. If God exists, God may have the capacity to communicate truth to me. If we say 'We can know nothing', what we are saying is really 'There is no God with a capacity for communicating anything to us so that we can know it.' So scepticism turns out to be dogmatic not just in general (when someone says that nothing can be known) but in religion in particular (there is no God of this kind). The issue, then, turns on the question of whether we have grounds for supposing that there is such a God. That is precisely what we have tried to indicate. We have added to this the suggestion that at least in the moral sphere, we have an example of knowledge of things invisible. We cannot rule out such knowledge in religion, then, just because it trades in things not provable by the senses. More than this, we have spoken about moral knowledge without really asking where it comes from. In Christianity, however, the source of our conviction is God himself. There can be no higher authority, if there is a God, and what we apprehend when God communicates something has every entitlement to be labelled 'knowledge'. Here we must speak of the Holy Spirit.

It is said of a preacher that he had scrawled in the margin of a sermon: 'Shout here: argument weak.' One suspects that this sort of thing happens with the doctrine of the Holy Spirit in religious epistemology. Unable to justify our certainties, we appeal to the witness of the Holy Spirit. What is regrettable here is not only the taking of the name of the Lord in vain, but also that it obscures a perfectly proper and important appeal to the epistemological relevance of the Holy Spirit. According to the broad biblical witness, it is the Spirit that enlightens our minds to understand, receive and embrace the truth of the gospel of Jesus Christ. Assurance and knowledge come from God himself by the Spirit. As God created, spoke through the prophets, became incarnate and effects our salvation by grace, so certainty is the gift of God.

The obvious objection to an appeal to the Spirit is that it seems to open the door to all manner of weird and irresponsible claims and it seems to be a strategy open also to more respectable and more credible, non-Christian, religious adherents. That is precisely why we have spent time on grounds for Christian believing. There are grounds to which one can appeal. So it is not a matter of irrational or supra-rational 'anything goes'. But here we meet a vital distinction. *It is the distinction between the logical grounds for our belief and the existential cause of our certainty.* We can give reasons why we believe something, but they do not account for our certainty. We can appeal to the Spirit for certainty, but we can give grounds for what we believe.

An aspect of this process can be explained by observing how debate and persuasion sometimes proceed. Think how much harder it can be to explain how our certainty comes about than to give reasons for our beliefs. Supposing, for example, we are perplexed about the question of abortion. We hear someone argue the case against abortion and find ourselves drawn to it. We think it is quite a strong case, but we lack certainty. The person who argues it, however, is certain, and we find it hard to account for that certainty. So does the other person. She can repeat to us the reasons why she is against abortion and we see the point. For her, however, it is a matter of certainty, for us no more than a plausible position, persuasive on balance, but not entirely convincing. Yet we are examining the same data. We seem to agree on the same things. It is just that where I find that there is still a chance that she is wrong, she really thinks not. We put it down to a number of factors, one being temperamental difference, perhaps. But over the next months, the more we go over the argument, the more convinced we become. Finally, we share the other's certainty. How did that happen? We do not know. All we know is that the same argument has impressed us more every time. Nothing new has been added. It is just that what once made for probability now makes for certainty.

In such a case, there are no *separate reasons* for being certain added on to the reason for believing something to be likely. There is some parallel to this in the case of religious belief. We admit that when we consider the arguments for the resurrection, the possibility of God's existence and the person of Jesus, we can show up to a point why we believe what we believe and therefore show that our beliefs are not groundless. What we cannot do is to show how we can pass beyond merely believing in the sense of deeming something likely. That is because the reason for being certain is the action of the Holy Spirit on us.

It is instructive here to recall the efforts John Locke made in the late seventeenth century to work out the principles of religious epistemology.[9] Locke first set about outlining the principles of epistemology in general, without reference to religion. Here faith and knowledge stood in contrast and both were the product of reason. When we work something out from our reason and think something is probable but we cannot be sure, we end up with faith. When we work something out from our reason and demonstrate the certainty of something, we end up with knowledge. All this happens when reason is trying to work its own way to conclusions. But what happens when someone claims a different source of knowledge, a source in revelation? Locke agrees that if something comes from God, we may be assured of its truth. We can use the word 'faith' in its peculiarly religious sense now to describe our response to God's revelation. The problem is: how do we assess claims that revelation occurred? By reason, says Locke. Reason makes sure that we understand what is being said; that what is said does not contradict anything known to itself; that there are good grounds for believing, like miracles or reliable witnesses. But Locke's difficulty was this: the most that could be shown by reason was that a claim to revelation was *probably* true. And yet, if God has revealed something it is *certainly* true. Locke had some difficulty in showing how certainty could emerge from probability.

What he did not do was to speak of the witness of the Holy Spirit. His reason for this was his great fear of what he called 'enthusiasm' – groundless, wild and irresponsible claims that we should believe all manner of things with assurance because the Spirit told us so. Had Locke given room to the Spirit, he would have improved his account of things. We must be careful here. We are not suggesting that *first*, we get as far as we can by something called reason and *then*, having reached possibility or probability by reason, speak of the Spirit as giving us certainty. How people become certain varies. 'The wind blows wherever it pleases' (John 3:8). We are saying simply that reasons or grounds can be given for what we believe. Whether or not it brings us to high probability is a point I shall leave aside; 'probability', whatever its uses, is too large an area for us here. The point is that when it comes to laying out the logic of our epistemology, we should hold together the grounds and reasons on the one hand and the certainty on the other.

The memorable description of Christian assurance in this connection comes from the pen of John Calvin.[10] Calvin asked how it was that we knew the Bible was the word of God. We know it by a kind of intuition on our part, as we know the difference between bitter and sweet, or black and white. But we can come to such conviction only by the Spirit and the 'internal witness of the Holy Spirit', where 'internal' (in all probability) means 'within us'. Calvin went on to say that there were, however, evidences that the Bible was the word of God. Commentators have long argued about how important these were to Calvin. Some maintain that they are important in his scheme; others that they can be omitted. But however we interpret Calvin, pride of place goes to the witness of the Spirit. 'Evidences' may support or show that we are intellectually responsible when we believe, but they do not convince. That is the work of God the Spirit.

We need not go all the way with Calvin to appreciate that he was right in pinpointing the importance of the Spirit. Some will want to deny Calvin's equation of the Bible with the word of God;

others will accept it, but refuse the suggestion, if Calvin meant it, that it all becomes *clearly* the word of God in the light of the Spirit. Not for the first time, we steer clear here of the wider questions of Scripture. We have concentrated on Christian faith understood as the witness to Jesus, perfect, divine and risen. We conclude simply this. It is through the Spirit that we may be assured and know the truth of what we believe as we reflect on the biblical witness. We can have faith and certainty.

The logic of Christology

Does that make sense? If there is a God who wants people to know of his existence, nature and purposes, would he not have made himself clear? Would not religious certainty be our common experience? There are a variety of ways in which people have tried to answer this question. We cannot cover all aspects of it, but it deserves some consideration.

Supposing, then, that there is a God of the kind that Christians believe in. If no-one anywhere at any time could justifiably say 'I know there is such a God' or 'I am sure there is such a God', then, indeed, we might well doubt the likelihood of such a God. A God universally hidden would not be personal in the sense that Christians have had in mind: personally concerned, able to communicate, with purposes to fulfil. That, indeed, is one reason why notions of God which describe him just as 'the Real', whose nature is unknowable by us, who might be personal or impersonal, are quite unsatisfactory from a Christian point of view. For if we never have very good reason to believe that there is a personal God, then God, if he exists, is either unable or unwilling to communicate with us. Neither divine inability nor divine unwillingness fit in with a Christian view of God as personal. So universal hiddenness implies that this 'Reality' is not personal in any sense Christians have believed him to be. But is the alternative this: if there is a personal God, he should be universally known?

Now of course, people may hold beliefs or know things that they never disclose to us. To that extent, the breadth or nature of religious conviction is not easily amenable to empirical proof. Some knowledge, though unconfessed, is involuntary. That applies in the non-religious realm. You may have told me that you were once imprisoned for theft. I wish I had never known, but now that you have told me, I don't have much choice in the matter. I am stuck with that knowledge or, if you prefer, that belief. I may never tell anyone and may seem to know nothing. I can deny that I was told anything when it is put to me. I can do something else, too: I can 'suppress' the knowledge. I can tell myself not to believe it; talk myself into disbelieving it. How far I can get with that I do not know, but people can go a startlingly long way in these things. They persuade themselves of something so thoroughly that as far as they are consciously aware, they really do believe it, and it takes some unusual confrontation, trauma or therapy to reveal something suppressed. This is obviously relevant in the case of religious conviction. It is logically possible (to put it at no more than that) that many suppress unwanted beliefs or convictions.

This is related, of course, to what we said earlier about 'disposition'. Pascal, whose *Pensées* is required reading for any concerned with the issues in this essay, emphasized that God's disclosure of himself was congruous with the fact that humans can be closed as well as open to God in their spirit.[11] Several times, he drives home the fittingness of the fact that God can be hidden as well as revealed: there is enough light for those who really seek God to find him, but God does not reveal himself to everyone, being hidden from those who do not seek him. And Calvin, whom we cited earlier, himself emphasizes the way humans have suppressed the knowledge of God so that while they cannot get it out of their system entirely, they can certainly obscure that knowledge effectively.

Now it will seem absolutely preposterous to many people if it is suggested that this is universally the case with the knowledge of God. However, my purpose here is not to explore this position, but rather to draw attention to the way moral and dispositional factors can affect our knowing or claiming to know. The line I wish to take here is rather different, consistent with an acceptance or rejection of Pascal and Calvin on the terms that we have presented them. I want to think rather of the logic of special disclosure in particular space and time.

One of the most common and surely the weightiest of

objections to Christian belief stems from the fact of suffering or the manifestation of evil. In my view this is so important that it merits a few words in connection with the theme of this essay, for what we say of faith and certainty may lack much force while that issue is before us. So I have included a short appendix in relation to it. At this point, we introduce it in the context of thinking about revelation and the knowledge of God. For many people, suffering or evil is hard enough to reconcile with the existence of God, but if God himself is immune from suffering, the situation becomes intolerable. If God is credible, he must suffer.

Different views have been held on the question of God and suffering in Christian theology. So let us ask two questions at the same time. Supposing God is personal and wants to show himself and suppose God is concerned to share in human suffering. What is the best indication that could be given of this? Well, God might communicate with everyone telling them that he is both personal and that he suffers. But then we might say 'Prove it!'

So what is the highest proof? Presumably the highest proof is to make a personal entry into his own world in human form, if that is possible, to show through humanity his own being and nature and to suffer as a human being. But to be human in our world and to suffer as a human in our world is to be restricted to particular space and time. So if God is personal and suffers, it must be as a human in particular space and time. It does not help to suggest that he ought to do it several times over, in several particular spaces and times. What about the fact that you can be in only one place at one time, so that you could not in any case, during your earthly life, be in more than one place? Is it harder to believe in the incarnation in one place and time than to believe in successive reincarnations, so that the same person is a first-century Palestinian Jew, a second-century Egyptian, a third-century Irishman, and so on? And we are not even touching on the question of an atoning act in human history. We are concerned simply to note that what seems arbitrary for God, namely special revelation in particular space and time, turns out to be quite the opposite: it is the condition of revealing his nature and sharing human suffering.

Let us press it further. If God is eager for people to know him, you would expect him to find a way of telling us about this historical appearance. And how better than by someone writing about it? If you write, you write in a particular language. If humans write, they write as humans write, with all their cultural distinctives. Any piece of writing is subject to our problems of translating, interpreting, understanding, and so on. Yet we are still talking about the importance of a personal appearance and personal communication on the part of God. We are outlining its logic. Our procedure must not be misunderstood here. We are not really starting from an idea of a personal God and trying to work out the likelihood of an incarnation and a Scripture. What we are saying is that when people believe in an incarnation and in its testimony in Scripture, it has a logic to it which we can describe in response to those who say that if there is a personal God, everyone would be sure of it. Faith is the conviction of things not seen (Heb. 11:1). Since it trades in unseen things, it is faith rather than sight, but since it deals with an invisible God, it can be certain, not subject to perpetual uncertainty. It is pinned on Christ and the comprehension of Christ is its strength.

Conclusion

When one is writing an essay on a huge subject, one is almost certain to do two things. The first is to leave questions open which in another context one may want to be decisive about. So one often appears more tentative than one really is. The other is to be dogmatic on issues which in another context require cautious and painstaking elaboration rather than definite assertion. Please bear in mind!

Doubt is common in Christian experience. It has many roots and takes many forms. Sometimes we seem to experience a mixture of faith and of doubt. There may be doubt in cases where we, as far as we can judge, are trying honestly to understand or get at the truth of something. There is nothing whatsoever to fear in that. It is far better than one-eyed dogmatism. Openness of heart and of mind is what God requires of us in all things, and those who patiently seek, living according to the light given to them, are rewarded, although it is not always ours to know how or in what form the reward comes along. Why some and not others are certain is a question we do not need to answer comprehensively, because it is part of an even wider question of why some believe while others do not, a question which we need not feel that we must be able to answer.

There are doubts of other kinds. No-one writes more plainly and straightforwardly in the New Testament than James, but we may be tempted to think that bluntness has given way to harshness when he writes as follows:

> If any of you lacks wisdom, he should ask God, who gives generously to all without finding fault, and it will be given to him. But when he asks, he must believe and not doubt, because he who doubts is like a wave of the sea, blown and tossed by the wind. That man should not think he will receive anything from the Lord; he is a double-minded man, unstable in all he does (Jas. 1:5–8).

James is talking specifically about 'wisdom'. Whatever the scope of that concept, we must heed his words in our broader context. The doubt that James has in mind is not what we may label 'honest doubt'. We do well to read his words here in connection with what is written later in the epistle about asking and not receiving, because one asks with wrong motives (Jas. 4:2–3). James is concerned with doubts that stem from 'double-mindedness'. Most of us are drawn by a variety of things and in a variety of directions that are very attractive and although these are at odds with our religious or our moral convictions, we compromise. We often try to acknowledge God but are rather selective in our obedience. We are not single-hearted and single-minded. It is no wonder that when we ask and pray we doubt, and even less wonder that we do not receive the wisdom which is from above. It is ours to search as diligently as we can and when we find, to obey; it is God's to reveal himself and to assure. Yet such is his concern that he is the fount of our searching and strength of our obedience.

'There are only three sorts of people', said Pascal: 'those who have found God and serve him; those who are busy seeking him and have not found him; those who live without either seeking or finding him'.[12] Of course, there is no point in seeking if we are quite sure he is not there to be found. Those who profess atheism must be persuaded of the genuine possibility of their error. Those so persuaded must in all integrity seek. And those who seek must come finally to a conscientious resolution of the question 'Who do you say I am?' (Mark 8:29). Life is busy and short, so there is no time to ask questions merely to satisfy intellectual curiosity. While searching, we act. But while acting we meet Jesus again. 'I am the light of the world. Whoever follows me will never walk in darkness, but will have the light of life' (John 8:12). The man or woman of faith believes that if there is such a thing as truth, Jesus is its embodiment. Where there is certainty, we should express it less by saying 'We have the truth', than by saying 'He is the truth.' The truth about God, Jesus and ourselves awaits its public, evident and outward demonstration. Such knowledge as we have is fragmentary, partial and open to the charge of being mere opinion. But that should not make us insecure. Christian faith appropriates a promise that the world will be filled with the knowledge of the glory of God as the waters cover the sea. Until then, said the prophet who wrote those words, we live by faith (Hab. 2:4, 14).

Appendix: The problem of suffering

This is a question of such importance that although we cannot treat it, we must refer to it. In the light of it, it is easy to imagine people thinking of the argument in this essay as a resounding gong or a clanging cymbal.

The problem in the form it takes for Christians lies in the difficulties of reconciling three claims. The first is that God is sufficiently powerful to prevent suffering. The second is that God is perfect in goodness. The third is that suffering exists. If we take for granted the third of these, how can we possibly believe both the others? It seems that we must surrender either the power of God or the goodness of God or both, and to many people this last alternative is best, to the point of surrendering belief in God's existence altogether.

The problem of suffering impinges on the account I have given of faith and certainty in at least two ways. The first stems from belief in the resurrection of Jesus. If God raised Jesus from the dead, he is capable of working miracles in history. If he is capable of doing that, why is his intervention rare, if not completely absent, when it comes to alleviating suffering? The second is broader, but very important. It may be said that we arrive at positive conclusions about religious faith and assurance only by concentrating on certain issues and turning a blind eye to that which stands in the way of faith, namely the fact of suffering. Walking by faith and not by sight turns out to be a matter of closing our eyes altogether to the human condition.

These are serious objections which deserve a response that we shall not attempt here. I shall make, however, three preliminary points.

Firstly, the facts of suffering reinforce the emphasis we place on action in the argument of this essay. If there is any insight available on these matters, we are not entitled to think that it will come to us just when we sit down and think about it. We can hope for it only if we act to do what we can in relation to suffering. Love, which means action, is a pathway to understanding.

Secondly, many of those who deny the existence of God in light of the facts of suffering seem deep down to be questioning his goodness rather than his existence. Deep bitterness and profound anger are often signs that there is an underlying suspicion that God does exist, for you cannot get bitter or angry at a being who does not exist. So it may be that what suffering really induces in people is frequently not refusal to believe in God's existence but a sense that God couldn't care less about what the rest of us go through.

Thirdly, the problem of suffering for religious belief surely lies not in the quantity but in the quality of suffering. Even if all the human race had to suffer in minor ways, we might not hold that it disrupted belief in God. When we think of it, we might conclude that it is not the sheer number who suffer that generates the theological problem, say 70% as opposed to 8% of the world population. Rather, our problem is the *kind* of suffering, its quality and intensity, that is often found. An individual case, such as that of little James Bulger, causes the problem, though tragically we know there are cases of equal cruelty.

Of course, a variety of answers are offered. One line that is taken is that if humans are to attain the highest good, they can do so only if they are given a measure of freedom, but if they have a measure of freedom, there is the risk of its terrible abuse in an evil way. Again, a world in which there are possibilities of moral good and moral evil must have possibilities of natural good and natural evil too; the only way you can have a world in which one has the moral freedom to break another's arm is if arms are frail and subject to damage in natural ways. Further, the eschatological element is often introduced; there is an order that is yet to come where the evils, injustices and sufferings of this life will be remedied.

Certainly one can ask of all these things whether they contain some truth. Even if they do, however, they do not necessarily contain the answers. Perhaps humans do have some freedom and that is why moral evil is sometimes perpetrated. But did God have to create a world this way? If this is the only possible world, would it not have been better not to have created it? If God can sometimes intervene, why so rarely? The same may be said in relation to natural evil. The eschatological perspective raises in one of its many forms the whole question of faith and reason. If one believes that there is an after-life, it certainly puts a perspective on suffering which we need to take into account as we try to reconcile divine goodness and power with the fact of suffering. Yet, if one asks without presupposing religious truth 'Is it *possible* that the future could at all "compensate" for the suffering of the present?', we might have to remain agnostic. How could we know what amounts to 'compensation', which sounds a very crude word? How could *anything*, we may say, justify misery of *this* intensity? Further, our initial set of questions, asked in relation to human freedom, remain.

I do not think there is an easy answer to the question 'If God can feed, heal or convert hearts, and so on in one case, why does he not do it in many more, if not every case?' What we do need to ponder is this: what exactly are we asking for? Are we committed to believing that the *only* world of people consistent with the existence of God is a world where *all* evil actions were thwarted and *no* suffering permitted? Some people are so committed, quite understandably. Or one can try to envisage a reduction in the intensity or kinds of suffering, though in such a world its inhabitants might ask exactly the questions we ask. While there are no easy answers and perhaps no answers at all, it is important to recall that our problem is not placed before Christianity and introduced from outside it. The biblical vision of new heavens and a new earth remind us that the only world ultimately tolerable to God is one where he cast out sin, with all the evil and suffering that comes in its train. Further, the more one considers the account of the fall in the early chapters of Genesis, the more one realizes that it is the Bible itself which presents us with the mystery of evil with suffering in its train. The serpent in the garden, however we understand the narrative, has a character and contact with humans whose origin is quite unfathomable. The book of Revelation, in which the serpent is identified with the devil, reminds us that there are dimensions to the human condition that are beyond our power to comprehend. It also reminds us of the battle Christ fought. He was indeed raised from the dead by a mighty act, but it was he too who suffered most intensely. If we hold that God suffers not only in Jesus Christ but in all suffering, this will not 'answer' our problem, but it will alter our mood and make us more ready to believe in the compatibility of the existence of God with the fact of suffering, though we do not understand how.

We said that the problem of suffering impinges on our theme not just because we refer to an act of God in history (resurrection as an instance of miracle), but because we can be accused of pursuing faith and certainty by turning a blind eye to the most significant facts about the human condition. The point is a fair one, but it cuts both ways and this is vital for us to understand in relation to this problem. Let us take an example which risks trivializing the issue, but need not do so if we keep its purpose in mind. Supposing I insist that my son is the best footballer in his village team. You then pick on one of the most vital features of the game, namely his ability to score goals. You point out that he lags far behind in this respect and there are several ahead of him. So how can he be the best footballer in the team? I agree that his goal-scoring performance is actually pretty feeble. But I then speak about his defensive ability; his ability to read the game; his ability to head the ball. I then run through a comparison with all the other players in all significant features of the game and conclude that overall he must be deemed the best player in the team.

There is nothing wrong with that procedure. As long as I concentrate on one phase, my claims seem to come unstuck, but while I look at the overall picture they are upheld. Now this is *not* an analogy. It just makes a point. From a Christian standpoint, one may well conclude that as long as we simply concentrate on suffering, the case against God looks strong. But we cannot possibly arrive at general conclusions about God by selecting one significant feature of the human condition. Against the fact of suffering we place other facts: the fact of Jesus, the fact of the existence of a cosmos, for example. We may say that we cannot believe in God because of suffering; but we may also say that we cannot explain the mystery of the goodness of Jesus unless there is a God.

This essay has looked at only one side of things. That side of things remains even if we consider suffering and evil. As we are concerned with the question of faith and certainty, strictly speaking, it has been impossible to take on the problem of human suffering, a suffering which is at the very heart of our concern as disciples. Spending time considering the nature of faith in Christ should not lead us away from the problem of suffering. On the contrary, it should guarantee as nothing else that we shall not evade it.

This edition © Stephen Williams, 2001

Notes

[1] J. Frame, *Apologetics to the Glory of God* (Presbyterian and Reformed, 1994).
[2] For a swift note on the main candidate passages, see Christoper B. Kaiser, *The Doctrine of God* (Marshall, Morgan & Scott, 1982), pp. 29–32.
[3] Luke 1:1–4 is, of course, an important text, whereas John, throughout his gospel, is conscious of the empirical bases of faith.
[4] These range from the number of angels or messengers at the tomb to the location of Jesus' manifestations.
[5] This example is adapted from the work of William Abraham,

whose book on *Divine Revelation and the Limits of Historical Criticism* can be commended as a whole (OUP, 1982).

[6] D. Bonhoeffer, *Ethics* (Macmillan, 1965).
[7] *On the Basis of Morality* (Bobbs-Merrill, 1965).
[8] Bonoeffer, *Ethics*, p. 30.
[9] See details in 'Guide to further reading' below.
[10] *Institutes of the Christian Religion*, edited by F. L. Battles (SCM, 1961), vol. i, starting at Book 1.1.
[11] B. Pascal, *Pensées*; see details in 'Guide to further reading' below.
[12] Ibid., p. 82, para. 160.

Guide to further reading

Although it is not specifically about epistemology, Colin Brown's *Philosophy and the Christian Faith* (IVP, 1968) is a good general historical introduction to themes and thinkers that helps us set epistemological questions against their wider background. Brown has rewritten and considerably expanded this account in *Christianity and Western Thought*, Vol. 1 (Apollos, 1990).

Although his theological conclusions on several points need to be challenged, Hans Küng always introduces his material clearly and the sections of *Does God Exist?* (Collins, 1980) which describe different thinkers, including their epistemological contributions, are well worth reading.

Standard introductions to the philosophy of religion are usually the best place to go for someone who wishes to get to grips with the contemporary debates in religious epistemology. There are several of these, including a number of good ones, and they continue to be produced. Two are selected here for special mention. One is that of William Abraham, *An Introduction to the Philosophy of Religion* (Prentice-Hall, 1985); the other is chosen because it is both very recent and readable: M. Petersen et al, *Reason and Religious Belief* (OUP, 1991; 2nd edn, 1998). Both devote a decent amount of coverage to epistemological issues. Peterson et al. have also edited *Philosophy of Religion: Selected Readings* (OUP, 1996). See too Paul Helm (ed.), *Faith and Reason* (OUP, 1999).

A general introduction, extending beyond the bounds of

religion, is that of D. L. Wolfe, *Epistemology: the Justification of Belief* (IVP, 1982). But if one wants to delve further into contributions specifically in philosophy of religion, there is a vast and still growing literature. Despite the way that the debate has moved on to some extent (on which the introductions report), two works produced some years ago may be mentioned. The first is Basil Mitchell, *The Justification of Religious Belief* (Macmillan, 1973), whose approach is judicious and whose argument is still widely discussed. The kind of painstaking and careful investigation of a range of concepts that must take place in any serious study of our issues is well-illustrated in the second work, that of H. P. Owen, *The Christian Knowledge of God* (Athlone, 1969).

Epistemology is of interest to theologians as well as philosophers. Particularly lively contributions have come from the pen of Lesslie Newbigin in recent years and these have two merits. First, they are oriented to the needs of the church and not to the academy. Secondly, they are part of a vigorous attempt at a 'missionary encounter with modern culture'. Although the historical judgments are sketchy and questionable at points, and although I believe Newbigin is insufficiently critical of 'narrative' approaches to the Bible stemming from the Yale school, it is important to digest his contributions. They are: *The Other Side of 1984* (World Council of Churches, 1984); *Foolishness to the Greeks* (SPCK, 1986); *The Gospel in a Pluralist Society* (SPCK, 1989); *Truth to Tell: the Gospel as Public Truth* (SPCK, 1991). Epistemological issues are discussed mainly in the earlier sections of these books.

It is often the case that pithy or substantial contributions of great usefulness are tucked away in works which do not appear on a standard reading list. Two examples are mentioned here. The first is that of Karl Barth in chapter 11 ('Doubt') of *Evangelical Theology* (Fontana, 1965). The value of this brief treatment lies in its pastoral sensitivity. The second is an older work, probably little read today though its author is still well respected. I refer to John Baillie's work, *The Interpretation of Religion* (T. & T. Clark, 1929), whose seventh chapter, 'The Foundations of Belief', rewards attention.

And of course one should dip into some of the great classical treatments. I have referred to the contributions of Locke and of Pascal. Locke was one of the most formative thinkers England ever produced and his *Essay Concerning Human Understanding* (Clarendon, 1975), which appeared in 1690, inaugurated a new era. His discussion of religious epistemology is brief but very important and appears towards the end of Book IV in chapters 18 and 19. However, one will miss the deeper significance of these discussions unless one ploughs through the whole work; possibly the argument can be picked up to some extent at IV.xiv.

Pascal's *Pensées*, which emerged earlier in the seventeenth century, is in a class of its own (Penguin, 1966). Whether or not Pascal appeals, much of his literature hits on its head the nail of modernity today as it did in his own day. His discussions of issues in religious epistemology appear at intervals throughout the work, including both his classified and his unclassified papers.

Finally, some regard Wittgenstein's *On Certainty* (Blackwell, 1969) as a modern classic. The literature surrounding Wittgenstein, one of the most influential philosophers of our century, is voluminous. It is impossible to comment on his book *On Certainty* in this space; equally, one hardly dares to neglect mentioning it in an essay bearing the title: 'Faith and certainty'.

Finally, as the text touches on the question of the historical Jesus and the resurrection, it is well just to refer readers to one or two books in this area. Generally, despite the bewildering twists and turns of the 'historical Jesus' debate, one should consult both Howard Marshall, *I Believe in the Historical Jesus* (Hodder, 1977) and Craig Blomberg's more recent book, *The Historical Reliability of the Gospels* (IVP, 1987). On the resurrection in particular, there is the enormously detailed investigation by William Lane Craig, *Assessing the New Testament Evidence for the Historicity of the Resurrection of Jesus* (Edwin Mellen Press, 1989). We should also refer to the unexpectedly 'conservative' conclusions on this matter that emerged in the treatment of one of the leading German theologians of our day, Wolfhart Pannenberg, in *Jesus – God and Man* (SCM, 1968), chapter 3, section IV.

5. Maintaining an integrated devotional life
David Cupples

David Cupples studied Greek and Philosophy at Queens University, Belfast, and Divinity at St Patrick's College, Maynooth, Republic of Ireland – only the second Protestant ever to study Theology there. In September 1987 he was ordained minister of Enniskillen Presbyterian Church, Northern Ireland and was formerly assistant minister of First Bangor Presbyterian Church from 1983 to 1987. He is currently also Chairman of the Board of IFES Ireland.

Introduction

Here is a question for you, an important one. Ponder it for a moment. What has been the effect upon your spiritual life of studying theology? Here is the answer of one twenty-year-old:

> The highest science, the loftiest speculation, the mightiest philosophy which can ever engage the attention of a child of God, is the name, the nature, the person, the work, the doings and the existence of the great God whom he calls his Father ... The most excellent study for expanding the soul is the science of Christ and him crucified, and the knowledge of the Godhead in the glorious Trinity. Nothing will so enlarge the intellect, nothing so magnify the whole soul of man as a devout, earnest, continued investigation of the great subject of the Deity.[1]

With these words, the young Baptist preacher C. H. Spurgeon opened his morning sermon on 7 January 1855, in New Park Street Chapel, Southwark.

Victorian language apart, I wonder if your answer to our question would be anything like Spurgeon's. Certainly for some students it is. They have found the study of theology an immensely beneficial experience; their understanding has been advanced, their faith deepened, their relationship with God enriched. Yet for many others Spurgeon's words will appear only to highlight, even to mock, their present doubts and spiritual struggles. Almost everyone who comes to the study of theology with a living faith and who gets seriously involved with the subject faces problems. If theological study has led you into what is sometimes called 'the dark night of the soul', take heart immediately. You are not alone: and help is at hand. Quite apart from anything else, your spiritual anxiety is evidence that your faith is important and real enough to you to worry about when it is threatened. Your very struggle is the sign that you are alive.

This essay has a positive aim. It is not just to help you handle some of your spiritual problems; it is not even solely to help you adopt a consistent approach to your study of God's Word both in and out of the classroom (though I hope it will do both these things). Its real aim is to convince you that Spurgeon is not hopelessly idealistic. None of us would doubt that he is right, but then he wasn't studying in our faculty, or our department! None the less, all of us wish our studies would lead us into a deeper experience of God. I believe they can if we approach them in the right way. True theology is always a prelude to doxology: it is the best fuel for devotion. Surely it is not unrealistic to expect that theological study will enrich our devotional life and bring blessing to our whole Christian life? It would seem not: and that is where we shall begin.

Most students of theology begin their course in the expectation that it will benefit their faith. They believe that on a daily basis they will be engaging with topics of study which will uplift and nourish their soul. Before long many are totally disillusioned. Their evangelical faith is not so much questioned as dismissed. The lecturers are learned, their manner detached, their approach sceptical. The emphasis in the course may turn out to be more on human religious experience than on the things which God has said and done for our salvation.[2] In particular the authority and trustworthiness of the Bible is rejected under pressure from 'the assured results of modern scholarship'. This strikes at the very heart of the spiritual life, for it leads to a loss of confidence in the Bible as the Word of God. Previously we had sought to know God through hearing and obeying his Word as it came to us through Scripture. Scripture spoke a word to us that bore the stamp of divine authority. Now a thousand questions undermine its authority; a bewildering variety of interpretations rob it of any clear meaning. We feel we can no longer either trust or understand it. It is deprived of all power to teach, rebuke, correct and train in righteousness (2 Tim. 3:16). Once the Scripture judged us: now we judge it.

For the young Christian this is traumatic; the great reversal is totally disorientating. He or she faces a challenge. The 'Sunday-school faith' will no longer do. It will have to be replaced, but with what? With an adult faith? Agnosticism? Or no faith at all?

While in one sense this challenge is a problem, it is also an opportunity. There is no growth in faith without questioning, heart-searching exposure to objections to our position. It can lead us to discover the foundations that are there which others have built on and which can become the support for our belief, 'the reason for the hope that you have' (1 Pet. 3:15).

Faced with this kind of challenge people make a variety of responses. Before we try to set out an integrated view of faith and study, we need to examine some of the alternative and inadequate reactions.

Differing responses to the challenge

Submission

Some are persuaded by radical views. They either abandon their former faith completely or change it into something quite different. Os Guinness describes the painful process: 'What happens then is that faith runs up against an awkward question or a scornful dismissal, and suddenly everything that had seemed so unmistakably certain, meaningful, true, collapses like a balloon leaving the remnants of faith limp and deflated.' He diagnoses the cause as being that the believer had no sure and sufficient reasons for what he or she believed. Faith had 'no reason why'. He continues,

> As the flaw is exposed and the doubt sweeps in with
> its impressive academic credentials and powerful,
> emotional threat, the doubt is unanswerable because
> there is no reason why not ... Caught with neither a
> foundation, nor a thought-through framework for
> their faith, they find university-level questions
> puncturing their Sunday-school level faith.
> Overtaxed by questions they are discouraged from
> facing, they escape the impossible tension by
> 'graduating' from such a faith.[3]

We are not suggesting here that the ideal is for no change to
occur in our faith as a result of our studies. We are thinking of that
basic loss of confidence in the message of the Scripture and with it
the rejection of the cardinal doctrines of the Christian faith.
Within the spectrum of theological opinion there is a clear
difference between those who accept Scripture as the Word of God
and those who think that 'Word' must be dug out from layers of
merely human opinion.[4] It is a real tragedy when the study of
Scripture leads to spiritual deadness and loss of faith.

Repression

If some students give in to radical views, others try to ignore them.
Fearing the perceived threat to their cherished beliefs they try to
suppress the problem by dismissing all unwelcome questions from
their minds. This response is understandable: nothing is more
important to the Christian than his or her relationship to God and
it can be devastating to feel it coming under threat from questions
for which we have no answer. This response, however, cannot be
condoned. It is emotionally dangerous since secret fears are being
repressed; it is intellectually indefensible in that it suggests there are
questions or truths that Christians cannot come to terms with; it is
spiritually inadequate because a faith never exposed to trials,
whether practical or intellectual, will be weak and artificial. Our
faith needs to be strong, genuine and growing. This will never

happen if we dodge the awkward questions thrown at us by life or by study (1 Pet. 1:6–8). Above all, this response is morally dishonest: it is pretence, hypocrisy, a plain refusal to face up to real questions. All these objections apply with particular force to those who are training to be preachers of God's Word and pastors of his flock. How can you call on others to develop a Christian mind if you have not tried to do so yourself?

Segregation

The difference between this and the last response is that this time students not only fail to attempt to integrate their faith and their studies, but do not even perceive the need to do so. Their faith is such that it appears to be immune from and unrelated to the views expressed in their courses. 'Scripture is just a description of people's religious experience'; 'God is not personal'; 'Jesus is neither divine nor uniquely the Saviour of the world' – these views do not worry such students unduly for they relate only to their academic life. They engage in their studies in isolation from their life-commitment to Jesus Christ. In private and in their fellowship their beliefs are orthodox, their religion supernatural, their Bible trustworthy. In class, the basis of all this is questioned but their faith is not disturbed. It is sheltered and not awake to the issues at stake.

In practice there may be few students who display such a polarization of academic and spiritual life, but it can happen in varying degrees, and it does raise a very important issue: what is the nature of true spirituality, authentic Christian experience? This is a vital question both for the study of theology and the discipline of a devotional life.

We can lead into this matter by showing the full implications of this response. How is it that Christians, consciously or unconsciously, can segregate their faith from their theological studies to the extent that they do not see how they ought to relate to each other? It is surely because their Christianity is orientated around experience and emotion. The mystical element predominates. Their hearts are involved rather than their heads. We might term it a kind of 'religious existentialism' in its preoccupation with immediate experience. Commenting on this kind of spirituality Francis Schaeffer says,

> Everything is experience: emotion (or emotionalism) is the base. We must of course be careful here, because we are not saying there shouldn't be any experience or emotion. There is and there should be. But neither experience or emotion is the basis for our faith. The basis for our faith is that certain things are true. That of course will lead to an experiential relationship with God, but the basis is content not experience.[5]

The appeal here is not for any dry intellectualism, but rather that we should realize that genuine experience is generated by living on the basis of what is true. The link between truth and experience is formed by faith and understanding; the intellect is involved.

Consider the implications of a spirituality where the mind is partly disengaged, or even despised.

Firstly, it is *dishonouring to God* who created our minds that we might use them for our good and his glory. Rationality is his gift; to use it to understand both the created world and the revealed Word is our privilege and responsibility.[6]

Secondly, it is *disobedient to Christ* who gave us as the first and greatest commandment that we should love God with heart, soul, mind and strength and whose whole life and teaching demonstrate thinking governed and illumined by the Word of God.

Thirdly, it is *dehumanizing for men and women* whose ability to reason is an aspect of the image of God in them, and something which distinguishes them from the animal creation (Ps. 32:9).

Fourthly, it is *destructive of a Christian world-view*. This we must deal with at some length, but we are at every point still involved with the question of what is true spirituality. What does it mean to love God with our mind?

A world-view seeks to unite all the phenomena of experience into a coherent and consistent overall interpretation of reality.[7] Such an enterprise assumes that truth is a unity, that all the different fields of knowledge can be inter-related and seen as aspects of a whole. It does not deny the presence of mystery: we are not suggesting we can know everything in an exhaustive way. But it is the alternative to absurdity, the presence of final and absolute contradictions in the universe. The response of segregation implicitly denies rationality. It is inherently dualistic in that it allows a set of beliefs to be valid and meaningful in the religious realm while being false in the scientific and historical realm. There are now spheres of experience and what may be true in one may not be true in another. Truth has been split into two unrelated fields.[8] This is manifest in various ways:

Reality divided. If the realms of reason, science and all the critical disciplines are divorced from the realm of religion then we have a dualistic position, two aspects of reality completely unrelated. The spiritual is cut off from everything else. This denies the doctrine of creation which demands that all things must be related to God their Maker and therefore to each other, and must be known fully to the mind of God. The inevitable conclusion is this: 'The Christian who thinks cannot keep God in his soul and leave him out of his world.'[9]

Faith and reason divided. Faith goes beyond reason, but if Christianity is true it must also be reasonable. Faith is not contrary to reason: reason is not hostile to faith. The task is to find their proper relation. Faith is not credulity, believing something when there is no basis for it. It is a commitment of the whole person to a life based on God's revelation, which is true to the way things are and therefore eminently reasonable. Indeed it follows that reason and faith are closely linked. Both are meant to be part of our response to revelation. Segregation of the two makes faith an irrational leap into a religious experience, a step into the dark rather than into the light.

Faith and history divided. Christianity claims to rest on certain historical events, principally the life, death and resurrection of Jesus of Nazareth. The record and interpretation of these events is given in the Bible. Our religion is at heart a story with an explanation. This makes it vulnerable and open at one level to historical enquiry.[10] The very foundations of our faith are open to attack and to doubt. There is a risk. Take away the historical events and the faith goes too. They are inseparably bound together.

To try to retain the message without the facts which gave rise to it is like building a castle in mid-air. Existentialism cuts faith loose from the moorings of history; the history can go but the experience will remain. This seems to protect Christian experience from being open to doubt through historical enquiry, but what it really does is to deprive faith of its very basis. It also means that the gospel has nothing to say about the meaning of history, when in fact there is nothing more central in the whole biblical message. Our faith is in God, the Lord of history, who has acted in history to save his people and will one day bring the historical process to an end.

Language divided. Religious terms must now bear a different meaning. They do not have any objective content: they just describe the experience of the speaker. For example, if Jesus did not in fact rise from the dead, yet someone were to say, 'Jesus is risen and lives in my heart', what could this mean? According to the normal use of language it would simply be a false statement, but when religious experience is divorced from our other experience, it can be meaningful as expressing the subjective experience of the speaker. This does violence to language in that it purports to be stating something which is objectively true, when in fact it is nothing more than a label for a subjective experience. In a way it is 'true' for the speaker, but not for anyone else. But this is not what we really claim for our Christian confession. We believe we are speaking of God's mighty acts, events with an objective meaning, true and meaningful for all people everywhere. The response of segregation devalues and demeans language itself and our Christian confession in particular.

What we have been trying to show in dealing with the response of segregation is simply this: that if we isolate entirely our devotional life from our academic life as students of theology, if we think we can keep the experience when the intellectual challenge is not faced, then in practice we have adopted a mindless Christianity, which carries with it all the consequences outlined above, and is therefore totally discredited.

Those who do react in this way are being conformed to the world in that they reflect the current emphasis on experience. It is a form of escapism, a flight from the harsh, real world of stiff challenges into a fantasy world of warm, pleasant feelings. The wonderful experience of knowing God is being looked on in the same way as any mystical experience or even a trip on drugs.

In contrast to this unbalanced, mystical view of Christian experience, we need to see that knowing God involves us in a relationship to God's work in history and to the truth revealed about life in God's Word. The message of the Scriptures is that God is re-establishing his rule over all creation through Jesus Christ our Lord (Eph. 1:9–10; Phil. 2:9–11). The gospel calls all people to believe this, to repent and be born again into a new life in God's kingdom. To be a Christian, then, is not just to find inner peace and joy (though we do find that), but to begin to live the life of the age to come. All things become new because we are living on an entirely new basis, the basis of the reality of God's kingdom and rule in history.[11] We now seek to bring all of life into conformity with the Word and will of God. His rule over us as Creator and Redeemer becomes the principle of integration for the whole of our lives. We learn then that 'true spirituality covers all of reality ... the Lordship of Christ covers all of life ... and it covers all parts of the spectrum of life equally. In this sense there is nothing concerning reality that is not spiritual'.[12] Personal salvation and love for God, are rightly understood only in this wider setting of Christ's Lordship over all aspects of life. Let us reject the way of segregation.

Integration

Having rejected three responses as inadequate, we now present a more excellent way – the way of integration. This response seeks to find a way of harmonizing our academic and devotional reading of Scripture. It offers a perspective in which they are complementary aspects of a consistent attitude toward Scripture as the Word of God. It aims to unite mind and heart, theology and experience, life and learning in a vision of the commitment of the whole person to Christ. Calling us to such a vision, Trevor Morrow writes,

> If the purpose of studying theology is the knowledge of God, then our believing (with all that this means for our prayer and worship and devotion) must become inseparably integrated with our theologising.

> The need of this hour is for theologians who will not
> just be academically informed, but men of God who
> will be transformed by the renewal of their mind in
> order to be conformed to the image of his Son.[13]

This is the only response to the challenge of theological study
that is biblically based, intellectually honest and spiritually healthy.

In the remainder of this essay, in the course of expounding the
way of integration, we will attempt to do four things. First, to place
'devotional' and 'academic' study of the Bible in a perspective
which allows us to see both of them as contributing towards the
same ultimate purpose. Second, to deal with some of the peculiar
problems theological students may face in maintaining their
spiritual life and vigour. Third, to provide incentives for following
this way of integration: and finally, to remind us that our studies
are an opportunity for us to equip ourselves for service to Christ.

The purpose of the Bible

The primary purpose of the Bible is that we might be brought to
that knowledge of God and of his Son Jesus Christ which is eternal
life. It was not given to be a textbook of theology, but to show us
how we might glorify God and live in a right way before him. In
Paul's words, the Scripture was given by God 'to make you wise for
salvation through faith in Christ Jesus ... for teaching, rebuking,
correcting and training in righteousness, so that the man of God
may be thoroughly equipped for every good work' (2 Tim.
3:15–17). Chris Sugden draws the conclusion: 'The goal of Bible
study is not to produce abstract theological truths and fit together
a jigsaw of biblical doctrines. The goal is to seek by word and deed
to incarnate in our context the words and works of Jesus.'[14]

Jesus himself endorsed this view of Scripture as essentially a
witness to him not only in direct claims (John 5:39), but also in his
use of Scripture with the disciples after the resurrection (Luke
24:25–27, 44–45). He included within this view the writings of
the New Testament in advance when he taught that the Spirit
would bear witness to him in and through the witness of the
apostles (John 14:25–26; 15:26–27; 16:12–15). Therefore the

purpose of Scripture should be seen in the divine economy as being included in the work of the Holy Spirit. The ministry of the Spirit is to universalize the presence of Jesus, to glorify him and reveal him to his disciples. The Spirit does this primarily (some would say exclusively) through the inspiration, preservation and present illumination of the Scriptures, the written witness of prophets and apostles to Christ (1 Cor. 2:6–16; Heb. 2:3–4; 1 Pet. 1:12). The Spirit leads us to the Living Word through the written Word. This is how God in his wisdom has chosen to make his revelation universally available: he has caused the record of his mighty saving acts, and their meaning, to be written down.

If this account of the purpose and place of the Bible is correct, there are certain implications which are important for Christian living and which I shall outline below.

Scripture is central in our faith and devotion. This is not bibliolatry. It is the outcome of the fact that there is no other witness. We have no other Christ than the one the apostles gave us.[15] R. T. France stresses this:

> God's special definitive revelation of himself to man
> is thus through the Word, the word spoken and
> written and the word incarnate. The two are
> inextricably woven together: they are interdependent.
> And both come down to us in the pages of the Bible.
> Thus it is not strictly correct to say that God's special
> revelation comes through Scripture and through
> Christ. More exactly it may be said to come through
> Scripture, and particularly through Christ as we find
> him in Scripture.[16]

Scripture is sufficient for its purpose. If God was fully revealed in Christ, and if Scripture is a faithful witness to Christ, then it is able to bring us a true knowledge of God. This is not meant to deny the need for the church to construct theological syntheses to set forth more fully the teaching of the Bible. Nor is it meant to deny the need for the written Word to be contextualized today. It is simply stating that there is no other source of revealed, authoritative knowledge.

Scripture is clear in its main message.[17] In spite of the countless difficulties of interpretation and the many obscure texts, the main doctrines of the Bible are clear. This is only what we would expect since the Bible is given to reveal to us the way of salvation. The periods of difficulty and spiritual dryness through which we all pass do not invalidate the great weight of Christian testimony to the clarity of Scripture. But, above all, what this view is stressing is that for us God's Word is inseparable from God himself. Through his Word God reveals and gives himself. It is God's personal address; what Scripture says, God says.

This is not to say that we do not encounter God in worship and prayer, in the sacraments, in fellowship with other Christians, in the experiences of life. Of course we do. God wants to walk in communion with us every minute of every day. He does not meet us only when we are reading the Bible. The point we are making is that the Scripture is the place where God has told us about himself, and the rest of life becomes an experience of God only insofar as we see and live life in the light of what Scripture teaches. The biblical teaching is like a pair of spectacles which, when we look through them, transforms our view and our experience of life and enables us to see God and glorify him in every part of life.

Scripture, then, is central to the Christian faith because it is the vehicle of the divine revelation. What does this imply for our study of it? It means that we can never rightly use the Bible for any purpose other than that for which it was given and intended by God. In every setting, public and private, church or lecture hall, we must come on the basis that God speaks to us in the Bible to bring us to know him. Precisely because in Scripture God himself meets us and meets us for a specific purpose, to approach the study of Scripture on any other terms is to come to God in the wrong attitude.[18] Without faith it is impossible to please God (Heb. 11:6). God cannot deny himself. He can never allow us to treat him as if he were merely an object of study or curiosity. He is neither of these; he is the living God ever to be worshipped, trusted and adored.

Likewise, he can never allow us to come to his Word except on the terms that we accept it as his Word. We can never treat it as if it were just like any other book. We cannot be neutral here. To scrutinize the Bible at arm's length, in a detached, academic manner is to treat God in the same way. The principles of our Bible study must then be as consistent as the principles which govern our whole relationship with God. In practical terms this means there is not and cannot be an absolute distinction between 'academic' and 'devotional' Bible study. All our reading of Scripture should be both academic and devotional, always involving both mind and heart, always seeking to uncover the true meaning of the text and also to receive and reverence its message as the Word of God.

Someone may immediately object that this is both idealistic and contrary to experience, which reveals a stark difference between how we treat Scripture in class and in our private devotions. This objection does not refute the argument above, but it does bring before us a fact of experience: there are real differences in approach to Bible reading. The distinction between 'academic' and 'devotional' Bible study may not be absolute, but it is valid and meaningful. How can we explain this relative difference? How can we distinguish the two emphases yet insist that in practice they ought to be inseparable? This is the question we now try to answer.

Distinguishing between academic and devotional Bible study

In the minds of many the difference between academic and devotional Bible study lies in the method or principles of interpreting the text. Academic study uses the scientific method, that is, the various forms of literary criticism, discovering the historical background, careful exegesis and analysis of the text. Devotional reading instead adopts a kind of 'intuitive' approach,[19] gleaning helpful insights and making immediate personal applications. It is often implied that only the latter has any spiritual value.

This does not seem, however, to be the best explanation of the distinction. It places them in too sharp an opposition and makes them both dangerous: for the academic carries with it no application to life and becomes dead, while the devotional without sound principles of interpretation can ignore the original meaning of a passage and read into it all sorts of fanciful ideas. The difference cannot lie in the principles of interpretation which must be the same at all times; nor does it lie in the ultimate purpose of Bible study which must also be the same at all times, as was pointed out earlier. It seems best, in our view, to state the distinction between academic and devotional study in terms of their immediate purpose, their intended effect. They both build up our knowledge of God but at different levels. Broadly speaking, in academic study the main emphasis falls upon deepening our understanding, renewing our mind; in devotional study the main emphasis is on maintaining and restoring our daily fellowship with the Lord. But in both we engage mind and faith: in both we seek to 'correctly [handle] the word of truth' (2 Tim. 2:15) and respond to it as the Word of God. The renewal of the mind and the transformation of life are part of the one work of the Spirit in our lives (Rom. 12:2).

We can make the distinction clearer by looking now at the variable factors which determine the character of a particular Bible study. This will help us to appreciate the different intended effects and value of different types of Bible reading.

There seem to be four main differences, each of which we will seek to look at below.

Setting

We read the Bible in a great variety of situations – in time alone with God, in church, in discussion groups, in counselling, in lecture hall and library. In each of these the needs of people are different and so is the purpose of the gathering. This affects our handling of Scripture. In class we may be defending our view of Scripture, in church we assume it. In the library we may compare the views of Paul and James on justification, in counselling we may be helping some guilt-ridden Christian appreciate his standing as one justified by faith. In a discussion we may debate the political implications of the gospel, in private we may consider what it means to be a good citizen. In all of these contexts the immediate purpose of our study differs, but the ultimate purpose of seeking to live by the teaching of the Bible remains the same.

Passage of Scripture

All Scripture is equally inspired, but it is not all equally inspiring. There is a great variety of material and some of it has a much less direct bearing on our lives than others: for example, Exodus 34 – 48, 1 Chronicles 1 – 10, Ezekiel 40 – 48. The presence of passages like these in God's Word highlights the fact that there is more to applying the teaching of Scripture than quarrying short sections for uplifting thoughts. Graeme Goldsworthy comments, 'Evangelicals ... have traditionally propagated the idea of the short devotional reading from which a "blessing from the Lord" must be wrested. Failure to gain this undefined blessing is usually seen to be a function of the state of the reader than that of the nature of the text itself. This mentality is almost paralysed by such phenomena as the genealogies of the Bible.'[20]

Not only does this view fail to appreciate the diverse forms of biblical literature, it also fails to understand the variety of responses we can make to a passage. The application is not always simple, direct or immediate; but it can always be personal. For every part of the Bible deals with the purposes of God in history, and our personal history is bound up with this. As we saw earlier, our personal redemption is set in the wider context of God's kingdom and rule over all the world. With that view of the Christian life we can find the key to relating to and deriving benefit from all portions of Scripture. We simply wish to demonstrate here that the different kinds of literature in the Bible will have a different purpose and effect in building up our relationship to God.

Levels of investigation

Bible study involves a dialogue with the text, and this means that asking questions is integral to our approach to the Bible. Depending on the kinds of questions we ask, a study may be either 'academic' or 'devotional'. Perhaps this is the main difference between study in class and in our private devotions. The level of investigation is different. It is not that one is more intellectually rigorous or demanding than the other, but that we are seeking to discover different things from the Bible in each setting. Both should interact, informing and enriching each other, for both have the same ultimate purpose of enabling us to understand the message of the Bible for us today. The various forms of biblical criticism and historical study may seem far removed from personal application, but they are simply the earlier stages of our encounter with the Bible, the first part of our effort to receive it fully into our lives. Rene Padilla stresses that the two cannot be separated: 'The understanding and appropriation of the biblical message are two aspects of an indivisible whole – the comprehension of the Word of God.'[21]

Another way of seeing these different levels of enquiry is to consider the two contexts of any passage – the original and the contemporary. In class we are mainly dealing with the original context of both writer and hearers; we ask the question 'What did it mean then?' In our personal study we are more concerned with the present application: we ask the question 'What does it mean for me/us today?' We must be concerned about both contexts if we are to get the real message. The main point of tension and, perhaps, the reason why many divorce critical and devotional reading, is that critical study often seems to undermine the assumptions of devotional reading, namely the authority and clarity of the Bible. There is no simple solution here. We discuss the interaction of our critical and devotional study later in this essay. The point remains that there are different levels of investigation that are all part of our efforts to live by the Word of God.

Areas of application

Not only is the message of the Bible many-sided, but so is our existence also, and we can distinguish different dimensions to our life and our relationship with God that affect our Bible study.

Dimensions of life. Most of us are not sufficiently aware that we are persons-in-community, not just distinct individuals. Consequently our application of Scripture is too narrow. It can be even worse when the Christian life itself is seen as 'isolated soul-salvation'.[22] We have seen that salvation is bigger than that. Life also is bigger than the individual's concerns. We are part of a network of relationships that extends to the whole human community. We must apply God's Word to all these dimensions of our life: in family, in society, in church, in the nation. Then there are the many facets of society's life: the law, the state, politics, economics, the environment, conflicting ideologies. In other words, we are called upon to try to develop a Christian outlook on life, to build a Christian world-view as best we can. This requires much study and reflection; it is an ongoing endeavour, but it is no less devotional for that. It is the outworking of the simple belief that Jesus Christ is Lord. Through this we seek to acknowledge Christ's Lordship over all of life and glorify and serve him in it. Paul even speaks of it as spiritual warfare; he struggles to 'take captive every thought to make it obedient to Christ' (2 Cor. 10:3–5). Is our concept of devotion to Christ too narrow? This effort requires an in-depth grasp of the biblical message, comparing it with other views. It requires much thought and prayer. Yet it is very clearly both devotional and academic.

Dimensions of our relationship to God. Like our human friendships, our relationship to God develops over time. That development and change is both short-term and long-term. Our experience is both of a daily walk with God with all its ups and downs, and a life-long growth in our knowledge of him. We will call these the 'micro-level' and 'macro-level' of change.

Consider first how it works in a human friendship. Love grows imperceptibly through the sharing of countless experiences, thoughts and feelings. Most of the time the relationship is not analysed but lived and enjoyed. Occasionally, however, we have to reflect on the relationship: to make plans, solve a dispute, face a major crisis. Such change-points lead to a deeper understanding of the relationship and how it works; the new insights change things in the long-term. Love is deepened.

It may be less romantic for a couple to discuss financial matters than to have dinner by candlelight, but love needs both. We experience God in the same way.

The purpose of our daily devotions is to effect change at the 'micro-level', refreshing our spirit, rekindling our love, keeping our hearts and minds in tune with God, enjoying his presence. Change at the 'macro-level' is the accumulated effect of daily walking with

God, but it is more than that. It comes from seeking a deeper understanding of the dynamics of spiritual life, applying the Word to all areas, strengthening the foundations of faith.

Again it must be said that these two levels are not clear-cut in experience, but it is a way of seeing how we grow as Christians and how academic study of the Bible contributes to spiritual growth as much as does devotional reading. Another way of seeing the relationship is this: issues we only touch on in devotional reading we may cover systematically in academic study. The process of gaining an overall, coherent grasp of Christian doctrine and life represents 'macro-level' growth, but it also feeds into our daily communion with God. It makes us wiser and more secure Christians, enriching our worship and prayer. Areas of application then affect the character and emphasis of a study.

To summarize, then. All our Bible study proceeds upon the same principles of interpretation and contributes to the same ultimate purpose of knowing God. All study is both academic and devotional, but the emphasis may fall upon one or other depending upon the immediate intended effects. These are determined by the various factors noted above.

There is, however, one other factor which outweighs all others in determining whether or not our study will be pleasing to God and beneficial to us. That is a hunger for God himself. It is the pure in heart who shall see God, the hungry who shall be filled (Matt. 5:6–8). A burning desire to honour God and glorify him in all we do will transform all our study. The words of J. I. Packer express this eager longing to feed upon God's Word:

> Let us then take our Bibles afresh and resolve by God's grace henceforth to make full use of them. Let us read them with reverence and humility, seeking the illumination of the Holy Spirit. Let us meditate on them till our sight is clear and our souls are fed. Let us live in obedience to God's will as we find it revealed to us in Scripture: and the Bible will prove itself both a lamp to our feet and a light upon our path. May it please the divine author of Holy Scripture to give to us and to all his people that for

which the Litany asks: 'increase of grace, to hear meekly (his) Word, and to receive it with pure affection, and to bring forth the fruits of the Spirit'. For that will be life indeed.[23]

So it will, but we must ask God to give us this life and this longing, otherwise all our study will just accumulate knowledge that will stagnate and lead to pride and deadness of soul.

This thought leads us into our next main consideration: how theological students can maintain passion and vitality in their spiritual life.

Maintaining the spiritual life

The most important devotional exercise for every Christian, including students of theology, is daily time spent alone with God in meditation on Scripture and in prayer. No matter how prayerfully you approach your studies, they will not remove the need for time alone with God. Just because you are occupied in a sense with the things of God every day does not mean you have ceased to be Christian: you must make spiritual progress by way of the same spiritual disciplines as all other Christians. Indeed it is all the more vital for students of theology to seek God himself, for it so easy for them to grow weary of spiritual matters. Familiarity breeds contempt.

The need and the desire to withdraw into quietness before God are beautifully expressed in a prayer of Thomas à Kempis in his famous devotional work, *The Imitation of Christ*: 'O God the Truth, unite me with yourself in everlasting love. I often grow tired of reading and hearing so much – in you lies all I really wish or desire. Let all teachers fall silent, let every creature hold its peace before you. Speak to me yourself, and speak alone.'[24] Such a period of communion with the Lord we usually call 'the quiet time'.

The 'quiet time' is not taught in the Bible; it is a tradition. However, it is a well-tried and tested tradition that has the support not only of Christian experience but also of certain biblical principles and examples. Daniel prayed daily (Dan. 6:10). Paul surely did when we consider his references to his 'constant' prayer for people (Rom. 1:9–10; 1 Thess: 1:3; 2 Thess. 1:11; 2 Tim 1:3). Most important of all, Jesus himself, though he lived in constant, unbroken, intimate fellowship with his Father, felt the need to withdraw to solitude for seasons of prayer (Luke 5:16). Moreover, his teaching in Matthew 6:6 assumes that his disciples will do the same. Who among us then is beyond the need for such times of prayer?

Secondly, there is a principle of spiritual life which suggests we need to pray daily. It is that 'By the consecration of one special part, it becomes possible to consecrate the whole.'[25] Why does God want us to keep the Sabbath holy? Why does he want a tithe of our income? It is so that we will make every day holy and be proper stewards of all we possess. In the same way, if we set aside a short time each day specially for God, we will be able to reclaim the whole day for him. When we consciously focus on him, lift up our hearts to him, open our lives to his Spirit, we go into the rest of the day with a sense of his presence and in his strength. Definite times of prayer are not the alternative to 'praying without ceasing'; they are the necessary means to that end. It is giving God the firstfruits of our time.

Thirdly, no relationship develops without planned meetings and activities. Keeping a daily appointment with God is the way of safeguarding our fellowship with him; it shows he is the most important person in our lives. This is not a legalistic bondage, but a voluntary discipline. The alternative is to be in bondage to our moods and physical condition. The inevitable result is neglect through busyness, tiredness, laziness or just 'not feeling like it'.

This is not, of course, saying there is no place for spontaneity in our devotional practices. However, it is a mistake to think that prayer is at its most sincere when it is accompanied by intense emotion. The quality of our prayer, like everything else we do, is measured not by our feelings but by our faith. George MacDonald has this to say: 'That man is perfect in faith who can come to God in the utter dearth of his feelings and desires, without a glow or an aspiration, with the weight of low thoughts, failures, neglects and wandering forgetfulness, and say to him, "Thou art my refuge".'[26] It will generally be our delight to meet with God in prayer, but even at those times when it is not, it still remains our duty: we 'should always pray and not give up' (Luke 18:1).

The purpose of the 'quiet time' is communion with the Lord, conscious fellowship in worship, thanksgiving, confession, consecration and meditation. We seek the grace of Christ, enjoy the love of God and share the fellowship of the Holy Spirit. This is the reality of the Christian life. It is more than a system; it is a personal knowledge of God, a relationship in which we dwell in God and he in us. We are drawn into the very life of the Trinity (John 14:23; 17:20–23; Eph. 2:18). God initiated this union and he will sustain it, but we must seek his face. 'This background abiding relationship must be kept fresh and personal by a definite time of directness and openness with God.'[27]

In this time with God a reading of Scripture is basic. It is God as he speaks through his Word who draws us to himself. The Holy Spirit engenders real worship 'in spirit and in truth' by illuminating the great truths of the gospel. Knowledge about God is turned into knowledge of God when we 'turn each truth that we learn about God into matter for meditation before God, leading to prayer and praise to God'.[28]

There are five things the student of theology needs to remember in this matter of devotional Bible reading.

First, *to pray for a spirit of expectancy.* Our attitude should be that of the psalmist, who prayed, 'Open my eyes that I may see wonderful things in your law' (Ps. 119:18). It is a sad fact that the academic study of the Bible can often deaden its spiritual effect. Through handling the Scriptures constantly our response to them becomes jaded. The technical analysis, the academic atmosphere, the daily routine combine to weary our minds, dull our sensitivities and lessen our appetite for God's Word. The great truths do not thrill us. We need to ask God earnestly that his Spirit will make the Scriptures live to us, that we will hear the voice of God as we read in spite of all our weakness. Let us remember that God is not limited by our frailty and failure. It is his opportunity. A sense of helplessness is our greatest asset in prayer. We know Jesus knocks at the door of our hearts seeking fellowship. We need only to open the door and let him in and he will manifest his love to us. The answer to dryness is to pray, 'O Lord, send thou my roots rain.'[29]

Secondly, *the same principles of interpretation apply at all times.*

The meaning of the text does not change outside the classroom. Devotional reading is not an excuse for reading into the Bible whatever we like. We must still take care to be subject to the true meaning of the text.

Thirdly, *read large portions of the Bible*. Often in class passages dry up because we get bogged down in the details of textual criticism. Vitality can be restored if we read steadily through longer sections and find ourselves gripped again by the grand sweep of the history and message of redemption. Reading steadily through whole books reinforces our sense of the unity of the biblical message; it keeps the great fundamental truths in our mind and that helps to put other matters in perspective. Resolving the many textual difficulties somehow seems less urgent when we are feeling the thrust of the central themes of the gospel. It would be a good discipline perhaps to aim to read the Bible through once each year of your time at college.

Fourthly, *read passages you are not studying in class*. This is not to duck awkward questions. It just seems sensible that if you are dealing with a book for weeks in class it is going to be harder to come to it with enthusiasm in private. Variety here can be the spice of your spiritual life. If you find a passage is going dry, don't be afraid to just leave it for a while and come back weeks later. Relax! Scripture, as someone has said, is not like a lemon which we must squeeze till we get something out. It is like a fountain from which, in God's goodness, come springs of living water.

Fifthly, *learn the practice of meditation*. The godly man in Psalm 1 is like a tree planted by streams of water, which yields its fruit in season, and whose leaf does not wither because 'his delight is in the law of the LORD, and on his law he meditates day and night'. The secret of meditation is in taking time to let Scripture have its full effect. In our studies we can perhaps assimilate all the material mentally but we cannot digest it spiritually. It chokes us. The rush of life and the rush of our studies makes meditation all the more important. I make no pretence to being an authority on meditation, so must quote at length from the masters.

B. B. Warfield was a theologian of the late nineteenth and early twentieth centuries. In an address given to theological students in 1903 at Princeton he speaks about meditation, first quoting from

C. H. Spurgeon and then adding his own thoughts.

> Mr Spurgeon expounds ... the same lesson: Our
> bodies are not supported merely by taking food into
> the mouth, but the process which really supplies the
> muscles and the nerve and the sinew and the bone is
> the process of digestion. It is by digestion that the
> outer food becomes assimilated with the inner life.
> Our souls are not nourished by merely listening
> awhile to this, and then to that, and then to the other
> part of divine truth. Hearing, reading, marking and
> learning all require inwardly digesting to complete
> their usefulness, and the inward digesting of the truth
> lies for the most part in meditating upon it. Why is it
> that some Christians, although they hear many
> sermons, make but slow advances in the divine life?
> Because ... they do not thoughtfully meditate on
> God's Word ... From such folly O Lord deliver us, O
> Lord and be this our resolve this day, 'I will mediate
> on thy precepts'. [Warfield continues] Meditation is
> an exercise which stands somewhere between thought
> and prayer. It must not be confounded with mere
> reasoning; it is reasoning transfigured by devout feel-
> ing; and it proceeds by broodingly dissolving rather
> than by logically analysing the thought. But it must
> be guarded from degenerating into mere daydream-
> ing on sacred themes; and it will be wise in order to
> secure ourselves from this fault to meditate chiefly
> with the Bible in our hands and always on its truths.
> As meditation, then, on the one side takes hold upon
> prayer, so, on the other, it shades off into devotional
> Bible reading, the highest exercise of which, indeed,
> it is. Life close to God's Word is life close to God.[30]

Meditation may be a lost art today or something we feel is
beyond us, but in every spiritual exercise we are beginners. If we
have the resolve and are prepared to take the time which is needed,
we can learn to meditate.

Handling critical Questions

It is time now to answer this question: From the standpoint of our devotional life, how do we respond to critical theories which challenge our view of Scripture? The basic reply is that it is not dishonest to disregard critical questions in the 'quiet time' provided you are not disregarding them in the classroom. If we are able to defend an evangelical view of Scripture in our studies, then we can continue to assume it in our religious life.

What we cannot assume, however, is that we have formed a proper and perfect understanding of the infallibility of Scripture. Throughout our college years and beyond we are modifying our views; it is relevant here to try to understand the dynamics of this process. We come to college with certain assumptions about the Bible: that it is infallible, utterly true and reliable in all its teaching. We begin a course of study in which evidence emerges which appears to contradict and refute this view. We must face up to the problems, but we do not need immediately to suspend our original belief simply because we do not have an instant solution. We are not the first and will not be the last to find ourselves in this position. *There is no need to panic.*

What happens is that a slow and long-term process of reflection begins in which we test our assumptions in the light of new evidence and new ideas of all kinds.[31] We begin to refine and modify our views to find a position in which our assumptions and the evidence best fit together. There is room for manoeuvre, place for an ongoing dialogue as we try to move towards a more complete and accurate doctrine of Scripture.

This room for manoeuvre exists because 'the doctrine of inspiration does not prescribe the nature of the reliability which belongs to the inspired documents'.[32] 'In other words, the principle that "Scripture should always be interpreted on the basis that it is infallible and inerrant" still leaves open the question of the kind of infallibility and inerrancy to be ascribed to the Bible, and this can be determined only by an examination of what actually happens in the Bible'.[33] We seek, then, to integrate the Bible's teaching about its own nature with the actual phenomena of the text itself; there is a constant interaction between the two. Each is refined in the light of the other.[34]

The process is unending and we never clear up all the problems. Some we may have to 'shelve' for a later time; it is a practical impossibility to try to face fully every question as it comes. There are far too many. On some matters we will change our minds; we may find that certain of our preconceived ideas about the Bible were inaccurate and not included within a full recognition of Scripture as the Word of God. In the end we must remember we are finite creatures who will never know all the answers and must learn to live with some uncertainties. I. H. Marshall comments on this: 'To tread the path between the Scylla of suspending judgement on critical issues and the Charybdis of qualifying one's doctrine of the entire trustworthiness of Scripture is not easy. There is no simple formula which will enable us to solve all our difficulties. Faith is never free from risk or from the duties of self-examination and self-correction.'[35]

So hard questions must be respected but not allowed to make us unduly anxious. Face them as your thinking matures and your reading and discussion clarifies the basic issues. Get help in doing so, and be willing to alter your previous ideas. The ideal is an open mind, not an empty mind.[36] Again we stress that you do not need to abandon a belief as soon as you realize there are problems associated with it. There are problems with the belief that God is love in relation to the amount of suffering in the world. This is a major question, yet for other reasons, namely the cross of Christ, we maintain our belief.

Or take the doctrine of the Incarnation. Here is the central mystery which we cannot explain; but equally, because of the evidence of Jesus' life, death and resurrection, we cannot explain it away either. Uncertain ties or mysteries have to be set alongside the solid foundations on which evangelical doctrine rests. These foundations are not just intellectual. Experience can confirm them. Our experience of the power of the Scriptures is a relevant factor in what we believe about them. We said earlier that we have to take into account 'what actually happens in the Bible' when we are forming our ideas. This includes the power of the Scriptures to change us and bring us the salvation it proclaims. We can make trial of the Word to see if it is able to fulfil its own claims. Jesus said that the Sadducees were in error because they knew neither the Scriptures not the power of God (Mark 12:24). Apprehending the truth is not just an intellectual matter. Paul tells Timothy, 'continue in what you have learned and have become convinced of' (2 Tim. 3:14–17), and gives as the reasons the moral character of those who taught Timothy and also the effects of this teaching in Timothy's own life.

Let us be quite clear what we are doing here. This is not the very error we rejected under the response of segregation. There the notion was that experience stood on its own: it was self-justifying. That was shown to be false. What we are saying here is that our beliefs and our experience must be consistent, and that experience is a factor which can confirm or weaken our beliefs. To use again the example of the resurrection, if it could be shown conclusively that Jesus did not rise from the dead, then we could not claim to know him as a risen, living Saviour. But if in supporting our conviction that Jesus did rise, we are able to point to the experience of his power and presence in our lives, then our experience confirms and adds weight to our claim. Experience does not stand on its own, but it does have a vital supporting role. It is not, then, illegitimate to bring into consideration the effect of Scripture upon you, including the effects of your devotional reading and meditation.[37]

This is perhaps the place to say a little about doubt. Doubt is a painful experience; and the initial impact of religious studies can lead us to doubt many things – our beliefs, ourselves, our God. Doubts will cloud our enjoyment of God's presence, but they do not mean he is not with us, for in the end it is not our hold upon God that counts but his hold upon us. He will not let us be tested beyond what we are able to bear (1 Cor. 10:13). He loves us, knowing all our sins and failures. At no point will our behaviour disillusion our Father and forfeit his love; he knows the secrets of our hearts. In the midst of storms we need to remember that Christ will not let us be overwhelmed. If the disciples in the boat on Galilee had thought of that they would not have been overcome by fear.

A minister preaching on this incident once said: 'That boat

could have sunk, but if it had, it would have come up again with him in it. If he goes down with you, you are bound to come up again, however long it takes, because he cannot sink, and he won't allow you to sink: he will come up and so will you.' This is the foundation which cannot be shaken. Dietrich Bonhoeffer in his doubt did not lose sight of this great fact. Here is part of one of his poems:

> Who am I? This or the other?
> Am I one person today and tomorrow another?
>   Am I both at once? A hypocrite before others,
> And before myself a contemptibly woebegone weakling?...
>
> Who am I? They mock me, these lonely questions of mine.
>   Whoever I am, Thou knowest, O God, I am Thine![38]

Respond to doubt in this way and it will become the stepping-stone to stronger faith.

One final way in which academic study can affect our private study is in a loss of confidence in the clarity of the Bible. If we approach this rightly we can achieve a balance of confidence and caution. Critical study will make us aware that there are many more possible interpretations of some passages than we had thought previously. It will show that some of our interpretations were wrong. This is all a bit disturbing perhaps, but is this not why we come to the Bible? To be taught, rebuked and corrected? After all it is the Bible we believe to be infallible, not our interpretation of it. Our very conviction about the infallibility of Scripture should make us all the more careful and willing to work hard to interpret it correctly.[39]

We need to read it with great humility and honesty, to accept the valid insights and benefits of historical study. Search for light and truth with absolute integrity, begin willing to subject yourself to it wholly in mind and life. Jesus is the Truth and if we continue to be taught of him we shall be free indeed. But be assured: academic study will change the way you interpret the Bible. It will make you more rigorous and more cautious about how much you can draw with certainty from a passage. But if it enables you to interpret Scripture more accurately, rejoice!

The other side to this matter is a word of reassurance. God does not disappoint the humble believer who comes to hear his voice. The good Shepherd still leads his flock to green pastures (John 10:1–10). The Spirit of truth still teaches (John 16:13). The Father has not ceased to give bread to his children when they request it (Matt. 7:9–11). The supreme requirements for being taught of God are that we be humble, teachable, obedient, dependent on the enlightenment of the Spirit. These are spiritual conditions required of every Christian and student of the Bible. J. I. Packer writes:

> The first part of this task [interpretation] may call for a good deal of technical learning, but this does not mean that exegesis is work for scholars only: the decisive part of the task is the second part, for which the first is, at most, only ground-clearing, and in this the professional scholar does not stand on any higher footing than any diligent student of the test in any language. The supreme requirement for under-standing a biblical book ... is sympathy with its subject matter, and a mind and heart that can spontaneously enter into the author's outlook. But the capacity to put oneself in the shoes of Isaiah, or Paul or John and see with his eyes and feel with his heart is the gift, not of academic training, but of the Holy Ghost through the new birth.[40]

Take heart from this: God will teach us and reveal precious things to us if we earnestly seek his truth.

Beyond your studies

So far, in speaking of maintaining the spiritual life we have focused on the matters of devotional Bible reading and intellectual integrity. Now we turn to the common but serious problem of intellectualism.

The nature of their studies can lead theological students into an exclusive concern with the doctrines of Christianity to the neglect of God himself. Paul tells us that 'knowledge puffs up' (1 Cor. 8:1). We can be intoxicated or thrown off balance by the excitement of new discovery. We are not usually conscious of what is happening, but slowly we begin to drift towards spiritual dryness and apathy. Our hearts grow cold. Our desire for God, for prayer, ebbs away. We have become a victim of the lust of the mind, idolizing knowledge for its own sake. The mind is fixed in a habit of handling divine truth in a detached fashion. Our faith has become cold and cerebral; we have lost our spiritual glow. Some in this condition may realize what has happened and feel powerless and depressed. Others who are not alert to what has happened may become proud. Worst of all, we may end up treating God as if he were just an object of study.

We never overcome this problem once and for all, but there are seven definite steps we can take to avoid the danger and maintain a healthy spiritual life.

Turn your insights into prayer

Draw your studies into your private devotions. Let your new knowledge become the springboard for worship. As was said at the very outset, theology should end in doxology, and 'deep theology is the best fuel for devotion'. This happens through prayer alone. 'The practice of prayer is both the safeguard against spiritual decline and the means of drawing benefit from what has been studied.'[41] In this way your studies will lead you into the presence of God. There you will be kept humble and your love for God will be rekindled.

Pray regularly with your fellow-students

This includes not just joining in official college devotions (if there are such), but also informal gatherings when mutual problems and joys can be shared in an atmosphere of dependence on God and support for each other. Here is where the older students can be like Barnabas, 'son of encouragement'. Barnabas was a man of generous spirit. He accepted Paul when others suspected him; he recognized the grace of God at work among the Gentiles of Antioch; he was prepared to give Mark, the failure, a second chance. This is the kind of attitude which can help another struggling in spiritual darkness.[42] Love 'always protects, always trusts, always hopes, always perseveres' (1 Cor. 13:8).

Prayer and fellowship will not just bring encouragement, however. They can also warm up cold hearts. Stephen Winward writes,

> Corporate prayer also quickens and kindles the spirit of the individual as he shares in the common life and action. The experience of Martin Luther is typical. 'At home, in my own house, there is no warmth or vigour in me, but in the church when the multitude is gathered together, a fire is kindled in my heart and it breaks its way through' … This does not mean that the devotion of an individual languishes because it is private. It may grow cold because it is not also corporate.[43]

So 'let us not give up meeting together' (Heb. 10:25).

Be a faithful member of a local church

This should be done, of course, simply because it is the normal Christian life for a member of the body of Christ. But for the student who has moved from home there may be a temptation to drift from commitment to a local church. Do not let it happen. Not only does a church take you out of the intense atmosphere of theological college and help you to 'keep your feet on the ground', it is the place where you receive ministry. You are still a Christian who needs to be part of a worshipping congregation, to receive the ministry of Word and Sacrament. To cut ourselves off from the appointed ordinances of church life is disobedient and foolish. Better to be like the first believers who 'devoted themselves to the apostles' teaching and to the fellowship, to the breaking of bread and to prayer (Acts 2:42).

Get a regular pastoral check-up

It is the normal pattern of the Christian life to be under the pastoral care of leaders in the church. Whether or not you choose to go to your own pastor, or some wise and trusted Christian friend, find someone to whom you can go on a regular basis to discuss the state of your spiritual life. Prevention is better than cure, and they may be able to see ahead when you cannot. They may be able to discern causes of spiritual decline or give encouragement as they see signs of growth. The ideal person will have studied theology and have a sympathetic understanding of your experiences; but if they are a mature Christian whom you can trust, a 'Barnabas', that is enough.

Be involved in active Christian service

The threat of intellectualism looms when knowledge starts to become an end in itself. If we are serving God it will remind us that theology is at the service of mission.[44] The gospel is to be proclaimed, not just understood; and proclaimed in a way which all can understand. Serving God often is a spur to keep us dependent on God because we know someone else is depending on our ministry to them. Mission, or any kind of service, helps us further to keep our theology in perspective and relevant to the needs of others.

Read devotional literature

Read literature that will lift your soul as well as stimulate your mind. This includes not just writings on the spiritual life, but the biographies of great men and women of God, our rich heritage of hymns, written prayers, Christian poetry and the Creeds. Of the Creeds Warfield says,

> I esteem [them] the very highest of all for spiritual impression. He who wishes to grow strong in his religious life, let him I say, next to the Bible, feed himself on the great creeds of the church. There is a

force of religious inspiration in them you will seek in vain elsewhere.[45]

Then speaking of written prayers, Stephen Winward writes:

> [They] are also of great value in times of special difficulty, spiritual dryness, bodily weakness or illness, weariness or distress. We can rely on the help of others when the creative effort of making our own prayers is well nigh impossible. Their function at other times is like that of the self-starter in a car, which is no longer used when the engine has started up. A written prayer can quicken the spirit of devotion and prepare the way for extempore prayer.[46]

Devotional literature is a treasure which cannot fail to build us up in our faith.

Learn to relax

Most students do not need to be told to do this! It is simply to remind us that our physical condition affects our inner life. Without proper rest and exercise we will find that 'much study is a weariness of the flesh'. Christian students will take theological study very seriously, but it can get out of proportion. The advice here is to know yourself – your temperament, your strengths and weaknesses. Aim to have balance in your life. Physical and emotional health will contribute to intellectual and spiritual strength.[47]

Devotion makes us better theologians

We have just considered how we can safeguard our spiritual vitality during our period of study. It is therefore appropriate now to make the point that strong devotion will make us better theologians, for obedience is the path to deeper understanding. It is 'the opener of the eyes'.[48] The things of God cannot be appreciated and understood fully from a detached standpoint, but only as they are lived and experienced. Pascal said that 'human things must be known to be loved: divine things must be loved to be known'. It is a biblical principle that as we respond to the light we have, more light is given. Faith turns what are otherwise mere concepts in a system into realities in our hearts. A. W. Tozer writes:

> At what point then does a theological fact become for the one who holds it a life-giving truth? At the point where obedience begins. Theological facts are like the altar of Elijah on Mt Carmel before the fire came: correct, properly laid out, but altogether cold. When the heart makes the ultimate surrender, the fire falls and true facts are transmuted into spiritual truth that transforms, enlightens and sanctifies. The church or the individual that is Bible-taught without being Spirit-taught has simply failed to see the truth lies deeper than the theological statement of it. We only possess what we experience.[49]

Faith does not make us better scholars: we will not pass our exams on it; but it gives us the experimental knowledge of God which is eternal life. We do not wish in any way to denigrate scholarship or learning, but in the light of our eternal destiny in Christ it counts for nothing if we have not also godliness. We thank God for the mighty mind of the apostle Paul; yet Paul says if he could 'fathom all mysteries and all knowledge' but does not have love, he is nothing (1 Cor. 13:2). He looks at his past with all his knowledge of the Jewish law and tradition and says, 'I consider everything a loss compared to the surpassing greatness of knowing Christ Jesus my Lord' (Phil. 3:8). One of the greatest theologians and thinkers in history was Thomas Aquinas. It is a true story about him that towards the end of his life he had a great experience of God and afterwards refused to write any more, even though his great work, the *Summa Theologica*, was unfinished. He said, 'I can do no more: such things have been revealed to me that all I have written seems as straw, and I now await the end of my life.'[50] Here is the perspective to view from. Let us have learning, but let us have the experience of God too.

Martin Luther stated emphatically the need for the Spirit's ministry and for genuine experience if we would have full understanding:

> No-one can understand God or his Word who has not received such understanding directly from the Holy Spirit. But no-one can receive it from the Holy Spirit without experiencing, proving and feeling it. In such experiences the Holy Spirit instructs us as in his own school, outside of which naught is learned save empty words and idle fables ... *Sola experientia fecit theologum* (only experience makes a theologian). Experience is necessary for the understanding of the Word. It is not merely to be repeated and known, but also to be lived and felt.[51]

This strong statement is in a sense a summary of all that we have said about 'the way of integration'.

Pursuing the way of integration

We have explained and argued for an integrated approach to theological studies, a marriage of academic and devotional life. In addition we can consider three incentives for pursuing this path.

First, it is the way of *discipleship*. There is a cost to following Jesus, and if he calls us to study then that cost will include the expenditure of time and mental effort. This means supremely that we will try to think what Christ thought. Is that not involved in 'following him'? Jesus not only thought in a consistent way, he honoured God in all his thoughts. There is enough evidence even in the story of his visit to the temple at the age of twelve that Jesus spent much time in thought. Then he lived out what he knew to be true. This is our calling – to live as Christ lived, to think as Christ thought.

Secondly, it is the way of *witness*. Jesus never said the same thing to any two people we see him meeting in the gospels. He dealt with each differently. He had a genuine conversation with them, asking and answering questions. This is how we must witness too, not only in our encounters with people but with views different to our own. Can we afford to ignore serious questions put to us about our beliefs? Can we disregard alternative interpretations of the gospel which appear to us as 'another gospel'? Can we be content with a personal, cosy faith but fail to enter the battle for people's minds? By no means! Let us instead answer the objections to our faith; let us be ready 'to give an answer to everyone who asks you to give the reason for the hope that you have' (1 Pet. 3:15).

Thirdly, it is the way of *humility*. Evangelical Christians are bound by their own view of Scripture to approach it with humility. We who profess to wish to live under the authority of the Scriptures must be self-critical, examining our own traditions and interpretations. There is always more light to break forth from God's Word. Students who come to their studies with a completely closed mind, whatever the reason, will learn nothing, and are wide open to the charge that they think they have nothing to learn. The way of integration can be rejected only by those who think they have reached perfect understanding.

Opportunity and privilege

Up to this point our discussion, while we hope it has been positive, has been problem-orientated. We have sought to resolve some of the difficulties which Christian students encounter as they study academic theology. In this final section, however, we would like to see the study of theology as a great privilege and opportunity. Our studies can be offered to God for his glory and in service to his church. There are three main lessons which need to be learned.

We must do our work as unto the Lord

It has been said that 'the true end of the devotional life is the devoted life'.[52] Our work when done as unto the Lord becomes worship, an offering pleasing in his sight. This is true of course for all Christians. We are to glorify God in all we do. It has to do not with the substance of our work but the attitude we bear towards it. It is a matter of the right intention, the right spirit.

Christian students can adopt unbiblical views of study.[53] They may see their work as secondary to more 'spiritual' pursuits. They may see academic excellence as only for eccentrics, or think that if they make sacrifices for God by serving him instead of studying, he will help them pass their exams. The biblical command in Colossians 3:23 is, however, 'Whatever you do, work at it with all your heart, as working for the Lord, not for men.' God is not saying we must all be brilliant scholars, or calling us all to be 'bookworms', but he is saying we are accountable to him for how we work. One day the quality of our work will be assessed not by the academic standards of our lecturers, but by the expectations of our Heavenly Father (Eph. 6:7–8; 2 Cor. 5:10). There is nothing Christian about shoddy work, laziness, neglect or superficiality. We need what John White calls a 'godly conscientiousness'.[54]

We could do no better than to pray at the beginning of each day,

> May the words of my mouth
> and the meditation of my heart
> be pleasing in your sight
> O Lord, my Rock and my Redeemer.
>
> (Ps. 19:14)

This attitude is not only pleasing to God, it is foundational to God's work in our lives of building Christian character. 'You cannot build up a religious life except you begin by performing faithfully your simple daily duties', wrote Warfield. He goes on to say that theological students in particular should make their studies 'religious exercises'. 'Put your heart into your studies: do not merely occupy your mind with them, but put your heart into them. They bring you daily and hourly into the very presence of God: his ways, his dealings with men, the infinite majesty of his being form their very subject matter. Put off the shoes from your feet in his holy presence.'[55] Even if you feel it is not your faculty he is talking about, you can take his point!

We must pray about our studies

Earlier we noted the benefit of using what we learn as subjects for prayer and meditation. However, we should also bathe the whole of our academic life in prayer. Bring to God your successes and failures, doubts and delights, your essays and exams, your lecturers and fellow-students. Scan the entire sphere of your studies with the radar of prayer. Earnestly ask the Lord to lead and guide you, to make your studies a blessing, to teach you how to honour him in them. Seek to meet God in every facet of your experience as a student of theology by consciously giving them to him. This is his will for you and he will answer. Bring your studies into the presence of God and you will bring the presence of God into your studies.

We must look on our study as an opportunity to develop our gifts in Christ's service

People study theology for different reasons. Not all who read this will be training for the ordained ministry of their church. But if you are a member of the body of Christ then you have a ministry; and if you have the brains to get to an institute of third-level education, then you have a gift of mind which you must seek to develop for the service and upbuilding of the church. There is a work for God which is as uniquely ours as our own personality and our relationship with him. The good Shepherd calls his own sheep by name. His relationship with each one is unique; and the lessons he wants to teach us are uniquely related to the work he wants to do in us and through us. This truth about the uniqueness of the revelation made to each one of us is beautifully stated by George Macdonald:

> There is a chamber also (O God, humble and accept my speech) – a chamber in God himself, into which none can enter but the one, the individual, the peculiar man – out of which chamber that man has to bring revelation and strength for his brethren. This is that for which he was made – to reveal the secret things of the Father.[56]

This is not to take ourselves too seriously; it is to take God's call and service seriously. Do we not wish to be our best for him? To realize our full potential for him? Paul urged Timothy, 'Do your best to present yourself to God as one approved, a workman who does not need to be ashamed and who correctly handles the word of truth' (2 Tim. 2:15). It does not matter if we think that much, even most of our course is irrelevant to the work of ministry, it is still our responsibility to heed these words and make the most of our time at college. Perhaps we fail to appreciate the privilege, and hence the worth and potential, of a period of study such as we are given. But we have only to look at church history to see how crucial a role has been played by those who gave themselves to a serious study of the faith. Look at the confusion of modern life, the complexity of the issues facing Christians, the counterfeit religions on offer, the consensus of unbelief. We will need a secure grasp of the Christian message if we are to proclaim and defend it with conviction and effect in such a situation. Our studies give us the chance to develop this deeper understanding. 'Only a theology which goes deep and grapples with the profundity of the divine revelation to men can ultimately satisfy the longings of men's souls and provide the basis for an effective ministry of the Word. To be content with a superficial theology which has never stretched our God-given mental powers is to commit the sin of insult to God.'[57]

Only earnest study, then, will do justice to the greatness of God's Word and the demands of ministry. John Stott stresses this too: 'The higher our view of the Bible, the more painstaking and conscientious our study of it should be. If this book is indeed the Word of God, then away with slovenly, slipshod exegesis! We have to make time to penetrate the text until it yields up its treasures. Only when we ourselves have absorbed its message, can we confidently share it with others.'[58]

The long reflection, the struggle, turmoil, doubts, fears, delights and discoveries of study are all part of our personal preparation for service to God's people in an unbelieving world. Here is the final argument for, the ultimate purpose of forming an integrated approach to our studies; theology in the service of mission, theology that will not just bring us to know God but which we will proclaim so that others might know him too, that the church of Christ might be built up, the kingdom advanced. What a high calling! To be ambassadors of the gospel of Jesus Christ the Lord, to be given a part in declaring his glory and grace to the nations.

We began with a question: What has been the effect upon your spiritual life of studying theology? A vision of the devotional life of a theological student has been set out to help you answer that question. In it there lies a call – a call to know God and to fit ourselves for his service.

> The challenge to all of us who study theology is not to remain unchanged in our studies (though to remain faithful) but to sift the good and the bad and to work on the academic and spiritual sides of things. 'Quality theological education means that both the integrity of the academic classroom and the involvement of the personal dimension are needed to make us the men and women of Christ, who are capable persons, intellectually and spiritually, to lead and serve in and for the body of Christ.'[59]

May this be our vision and may God give us grace to fulfil it for the sake of his name and his church.

This edition © David Cupples, 2001

Notes

[1] Quoted in J. I. Packer, *Knowing God* (Hodder and Stoughton, 1975), pp. 13–14.
[2] See K. Howkins, *The Challenge of Religious Studies* (Tyndale Press, 1972) pp. 14–16.
[3] Os Guinness, *Doubt* (Lion, 1983), pp. 84–85.
[4] I. H. Marshall, *Biblical Inspiration* (Hodder & Stoughton, 1982), pp. 66, 71.
[5] F. Schaeffer, *The New Super-Spirituality* (Hodder & Stoughton, 1973), p. 26. The whole booklet is devoted to the subject of experience-orientated Christianity.
[6] For a lucid and succinct treatment of the place of the mind in the Christian life, see John Stott, *Your Mind Matters* (IVP, 1972).

[7] Books dealing with this subject are: James Sire, *The Universe Next Door* (IVP, 1977); Arthur Holmes, *All Truth is God's Truth* (IVP, 1979) and *Contours of a World View* (Eerdmans, 1983).

[8] For an explanation of the development of dualism, both Christian and secular, see F. Schaeffer, *The God Who is There* (Hodder & Stoughton, 1970) and in particular *Escape from Reason* (IVP, 1968).

[9] Quoted in H. R. Macintosh, *The Christian Apprehension of God* (SCM, 1934), p. 63.

[10] I. H. Marshall, *I Believe in the Historical Jesus* (Hodder, 1977), pp. 101–106.

[11] For a view of Christian life in the perspective of God's kingdom see R. Lovelace, *Renewal as a Way of Life* (Paternoster, 1985), ch. 2, and Tom Sine, *The Mustard Seed Conspiracy* (MARC Europe, 1985).

[12] F. Schaeffer, *A Christian Manifesto* (Pickering & Inglis, 1982), p. 19.

[13] Editorial, *Themelios*, Autumn 1975.

[14] C. Sugden, *Radical Discipleship* (Marshalls, 1981), p. 140.

[15] This statement is not my own, but I cannot trace its source.

[16] R. T. France, *The Living God* (IVP, 1970), pp. 48–49.

[17] An article on the clarity of Scripture is Sinclair Ferguson's 'The Book for all the People', *Christian Graduate*, June 1982.

[18] This theme is dealt with by F. Entwistle in the Editorial of *TSF Terminal Letter*, Autumn 1960.

[19] For this distinction see Dr C. Rene Padilla, 'The Interpreted Word: Reflections on Contextual Hermeneutics', *Themelios*, September 1981. This brilliant piece is a must for all theological students.

[20] G. Goldsworthy, *Gospel and Kingdom: A Christian Interpretation of the Old Testament* (Paternoster, 1981), p. 112. See also pp. 30–31 for a description of the variety of literature in the Old Testament.

[21] Padilla, 'The Interpreted Word', p. 21.

[22] This phrase is used by Dr Hans Burki in a paper delivered to an IFES gathering, entitled 'Jesus: the Word of God Incarnate'.

[23] J. I. Packer, *Under God's Word* (Lakeland, 1980), p. 104.

[24] Bk. 1, ch. 3, 'On Being Taught by the Truth'.

[25] S. Winward, *Teach Yourself to Pray* (Hodder & Stoughton, 1965),

p. 22. This whole book is of great practical value and good sense in regard to the whole private devotional life.

[26] *George Macdonald: An Anthology* (Fount, 1983), edited by C. S. Lewis, p. 1.

[27] Graham Claydon, *Time with God* (IVP, 1979), p. 27.

[28] Packer, *Knowing God*, p. 20.

[29] A prayer of the poet Gerard Manley Hopkins, quoted in the preface to a booklet by W. Trobisch, *Spiritual Dryness* (IVP, 1974).

[30] There are two articles by B. B. Warfield on the devotional life of students of theology which, although old, have much of value in them: 'The Religious Life of Theological Students', *B. B. Warfield: Selected Shorter Writings* (Phillipsburg, 1970), vol. 1, pp. 411–425, and 'Spiritual Culture in the Theological Seminary', *B. B. Warfield: Selected Shorter Writings* (Phillipsburg, 1973), vol. 2, pp. 468–496. This quotation is from vol. 2, pp. 484–485.

[31] The relationship between presuppositions and evidence is dealt with in Marshall, *I Believe in the Historical Jesus*, pp. 97–101.

[32] Ibid., p. 19.

[33] Marshall, *Biblical Inspiration*, p. 61. For an example of an attempt to formulate a doctrine of Scripture, taking into account 'what actually happens in the Bible', see 'The Chicago Statement on Biblical Inerrancy', *Themelios*, April 1979.

[34] This process is explained in an article by J. I. Packer, 'Hermeneutics and Biblical Authority', *Themelios*, Autumn 1975, pp. 7–9.

[35] Marshall, *Biblical Inspiration*, p. 91.

[36] See Howkins, *The Challenge of Religious Studies*, pp. 5–6 and David Field, 'Approaching theological study' in this volume, pp. 13–37.

[37] Cf. Marshall, *I Believe in the Historical Jesus*, pp. 94–101.

[38] Quoted in L. Newbigin, *Honest Religion for Secular Man* (SCM, 1966), p. 99.

[39] A. Stibbs, *Understanding God's Word* (IVP, 1976), pp. 9–11.

[40] J. I. Packer, *God has Spoken* (Hodder & Stoughton, 1979), pp. 73–74.

[41] Howkins, *The Challenge of Religious Studies*, p. 137.

[42] See R. T. France, 'Barnabas – Son of Encouragement', *Themelios*, September 1978.

[43] Winward, *Teach Yourself to Pray*, p. 86.

[44] See: Clark Pinnock, 'Building the bridge from theology to mission', *Themelios*, April 1984.

[45] Warfield, vol. 2, p. 492. Lists of devotional works can be found in R. Foster, *Celebration of Discipline* (Hodder & Stoughton, 1981), p. 62, and Warfield, vol. 2, pp. 488–493.

[46] Winward, *Teach Yourself to Pray*, p. 96.

[47] On this and other topics related to 'spiritual depression' you could do no better than read *Spiritual Depression: its Causes and Cure* (STL, 1983), by Dr Martyn Lloyd-Jones.

[48] *George MacDonald: An Anthology*, p. 28.

[49] Quoted in *Gems from Tozer* (STL, 1978), p. 7. Tozer is always very devotional in tone.

[50] Story told in D. M. Lloyd-Jones, *Joy Unspeakable* (Kingsway, 1984), pp. 112–113.

[51] Quoted in Dr Hans Burki, *Essentials* (IFES, 1975). This booklet is an introduction to the doctrinal basis of IFES.

[52] Winward, *Teach Yourself to Pray*, p. 122.

[53] See D. Hempton, 'Improving by Degrees', *Cubit*, Spring 1981.

[54] This phrase is from *The Fight* (IVP, 1977), p. 205.

[55] Warfield, vol. 1, pp. 415–416.

[56] *George MacDonald: An Anthology*, p. 9.

[57] I. H. Marshall, Editorial, *TSF Terminal Letter*, Autumn 1957.

[58] J. Stott, *I Believe in Preaching* (Hodder & Stoughton, 1982), p. 182.

[59] Editorial, 'The Relevance of Theological Education', *Themelios* January 1983. This article is well worth reading.

6. Perspectives on preaching
Martin Downes

Martin Downes graduated in Religious Studies and English from the University of Wales. He was a staffworker for the RTSF and is now UCCF Team Leader in Wales.

God and preaching

'What is the chief end of preaching? I like to think it is this. It is to give men and women a sense of God and His presence.'[1] So wrote Dr Martyn Lloyd-Jones, one of the most eminent preachers of the twentieth century. Of course, his words were not intended to convey all that is included in the art and science of preaching, but as an expression of its goal and aim they would be hard to improve on. A little closer to our day, John Piper has expressed the essence of the preacher's message and mandate:

> God himself is the necessary subject matter of our preaching, in his majesty and truth and holiness and righteousness and wisdom and faithfulness and sovereignty and grace. I don't mean that we shouldn't preach about nitty-gritty things like parenthood and divorce and Aids and gluttony and television and sex. What I mean is that every one of those things should be swept up into the holy presence of God and laid bare to the roots of its Godwardness or godlessness.[2]

God is the necessary subject matter of preaching because Christianity is God-centred and not man-centred. Furthermore because God has spoken and made himself known, preaching is the authoritative declaration of God and his ways and not the speculations of men and women about themselves and their world. 'For from him and through him and to him, are all things' (Rom. 11:36). The one true God who is Father, Son and Holy Spirit made all things, by his will and power all things were made and 'have their being' (Rev. 4:11). It is because God is the holy, infinite–personal Creator, who thereby possesses ownership rights over men and women made in his image, that sin is primarily an offence against him rather than against humanity. We are so attuned to the appalling inhumanity which is woven into the very fabric of history, and which continues unabated into the third millennium, that preaching which does not address these issues appears removed, remote, indifferent and irrelevant. Yet the truth remains that the social, economic and environmental effects of sin are but symptoms and side-effects of something that is much deeper and far worse. It is that we *do not know God*; that we are hostile in our minds towards him, that we are alienated from his life, and that we neither thank nor glorify him as God (Col. 1:21; Eph. 4:17–19; Gal. 4:8; Rom. 1:21–23, 28). Ultimately, all men and women, by virtue of their rebellion against a holy God, have provoked his anger, have incurred his wrath, and stand under his judgment both now and for ever (Rom. 2:1–9).

Preaching then must be God-centred precisely because it is estrangement from God that lies at the heart of the problem, and the gospel alone is God's gracious declaration of how sinners may know him and be accepted by him. In the gospel those who were without God in the world are brought near by the blood of Christ; those who did not know him have now come to know him and are known by him (Eph. 2:12–13; Gal. 4:8–9). Eternal life is nothing short of knowing God and his Son Jesus Christ (John 17:3). Of course, to say that the chief need of human beings is to 'know God' goes beyond the mere possession of true information about him. It is that, but it is much more than that. By his sin-bearing, substitutionary death, Jesus Christ the Father's Son received in himself the punishment that sinners deserved, he took all the consequences of sin upon himself and satisfied the righteous demands of a holy God. The result of his death was to justify those who trust in him alone, forgiving their sins, averting God's wrath, accounting them as righteous in God's sight by imputing Christ's righteousness to them, establishing peace with God, and granting access to God's presence. All this is made a reality on a personal level by the working of the Holy Spirit as he enables sinful men and women to understand these things and receive them by faith, and as he implants a new principle of life and a desire to know God and be like him. The Christian life, therefore, is one of knowing God, and knowing him better and better, both in this life and in eternity. The death of Christ rescues from this present evil age, which is destined for destruction, and makes believers citizens of a kingdom that will be consummated when Christ the King returns and ushers in an everlasting reign of righteousness.

What then is the chief end of preaching? It is, and must be, to bring men and women to a right knowledge of God, as the gospel of Jesus Christ is unfolded to them. Therefore, as the Bible is correctly taught, in relation to its central message – the gospel of God (Rom. 1:1–4) – God speaks and deals with human beings. The acceptance of the message brings eternal life; the rejection of it leaves individual men and women in a state of condemnation. Little wonder then that the Puritan Richard Baxter determined to preach 'as never sure to preach again, and as a dying man to dying men'. In an interview for *Christianity Today*, published in 1980, Carl Henry asked Martyn Lloyd-Jones why he seldom used humour in the pulpit. The veteran Welsh preacher answered in a way that is entirely in tune with the words of Richard Baxter: 'I find it very difficult to be humorous in the pulpit. I always feel in the pulpit that I am in the terrible position of standing between God and souls that may go to hell. That position is too appalling for humour.'[3]

True preaching inevitably, then, makes us aware of God's existence and character, of the divine origin and authority of the Bible, and brings a consciousness that God is dealing with us and addressing us. Whenever the Bible is expounded truly, because of the inescapable relations of its constituent parts, what is at stake is eternal life or eternal condemnation. And this is both in the direct sense that the gospel addresses our ultimate destination, and in the indirect sense that one is either persevering in the life of holiness, or playing with the knowledge of God.

The doctrine of God and preaching

Preaching is made or marred by the view of God that sustains it. If we imagine God to be other than he is, then we will speak of him in ways that correspond with our underlying theological assumptions. It is this that draws out from J. I. Packer an unfavourable assessment of contemporary evangelical life in comparison to former generations:

> Whereas to the Puritans communion with God was a *great* thing, to evangelicals today it is a comparatively *small* thing. The Puritans were concerned about communion with God in a way that we are not ... we do not spend much time, alone or together, in dwelling on the wonder of the fact that God and sinners have communion at all; no, we just take it for granted, and give our minds to other matters. Thus we make it plain that communion with God is a small thing to us ... it does not startle us that the holy Creator should receive sinners into his company; rather, we take it for granted![4]

If, as I have been arguing, preaching is to give us a sense of God and his presence, then the meaning of this must be filled out by Scripture and not by contemporary ideas and agendas, nor by taking God's attributes out of their scriptural harmony. Models for understanding God and his relation to the world and sinners must be taken from Scripture and not from the perceived needs and ideas of society. For example, God's immanence must never minimize his transcendence, or his love obscure his holiness. God can never be reduced to manageable proportions, he can never be related to on easy terms. True faith will always lead to the fear of a gracious God, for God is never less than holy. Therefore, where there is no awe, reverence, fear and repentance, there is no true knowledge of God. For it is these things that render God's love so amazing and his grace and mercy so astounding. Calvin's observations on the encounters with God recorded in Scripture are worth pondering:

Hence the dread and wonder with which the Scripture commonly represents the saints as stricken and overcome whenever they felt the presence of God. Thus it comes about that we see men who in his absence normally remained firm and constant, but who, when he manifests his glory, are so shaken and struck dumb as to be laid low by the dread of death – are in fact overwhelmed by it and almost annihilated. As a consequence, we must infer that man is never sufficiently touched and affected by the awareness of his lowly state until he has compared himself with God's majesty.[5]

Again this seems strangely out of place in contemporary worship and preaching, as Piper notes:

Most people today have so little experience of deep, earnest, reverent, powerful encounters with God in preaching that the only associations that come to mind when the notion is mentioned are that the preacher is morose or boring or dismal or sullen or gloomy or surly or unfriendly ... the result is a preaching atmosphere and a preaching style plagued by triviality, levity, carelessness, flippancy, and a general spirit that nothing of eternal and infinite proportions is being done or said on Sunday morning.[6]

The factor that accounts for the seriousness that ought to be found in the preacher, and the seriousness to be found in the hearers, is the nature of the Word of God and of the God who has spoken. The impression given by those whose task it is to preach the Word, and by those who listen and take part in corporate worship, speaks volumes about the kind of God we imagine God to be. Tony Sargent, in his survey of the preaching of Martyn Lloyd-Jones, comments that 'the doctrine you believe will shape the prayers that you offer'.[7] To this we might add all the other elements of public worship, including preaching. Great preachers and great preaching can be produced only where there is a vision of a great and holy God.

The message and the method must correlate

Preaching rests, therefore, on two theological foundations; first, God and his essential nature and, secondly, God's knowability through revelation. Both of these realities may be submerged by practices and methods that are not governed by the message itself and its theological bearings. Preaching ought never to be done in a cold detached manner as if the preacher stood in no emotional relation to the text. This is the antithesis of the way theological study is pursued in the academy, where 'objective scholarship' is a virtue. But it is impossible to approach the text of Scripture in a value-neutral way and therefore to handle it with analytical detachment.

Again, to imply that we may sit in judgment over the teaching of Scripture, or preach in such a way that is designed to explain away the text and emasculate it, merely indicates that we are operating from a different theological base than that of the self-revealing holy God of Scripture. Preaching that is infected by a theology that is not subservient to inscripturated revelation is calculated only to parade its learning or piety, and impoverish the spiritual lives of those upon whom it is inflicted. Even an orthodox view of Scripture and its teaching that leads to dullness and indifference in delivery is inadequate and unacceptable. Such preaching shows signs of being unconvinced that the Bible really is the Word of God or that the dire predicament of humanity in sin is really that bad, or the solution offered so great.

Jonathan Edwards has been described as a preacher who continually stood in awe at the weight of the truth he was charged to proclaim.[8] It is all the more remarkable when we consider Edwards' daily commitment to study and preparation, his immense learning and intellectual endeavours, which all but dwarf contemporary models but which did not produce a method of preaching that lacked conviction and intensity.[9] For Edwards it was an impossibility that a preacher could believe in heaven, and particularly in hell, and yet preach in a way that implied indifference to these truths. To do so betrays a contradiction, for the manner of the preaching is then clearly at odds with the subject.[10] Rather, the words of J. C. Ryle, one time Bishop of Liverpool, used to describe the great evangelists of the eighteenth century (themselves contemporaries of Edwards), must be true of all preachers:

> They preached *fervently* and *directly* ... they spoke with fiery zeal, like men who were thoroughly persuaded that what they said was true, and that it was of the utmost importance to your eternal interest to hear it. They spoke like men who had got a message from God to you, and must deliver it ...[11]

It is not that pulpit fire-works are evidence of true fervour or spirituality; exuberant delivery may be no more than the amplification of natural personality. Ryle's words strike at the fundamental convictions about God and the truth of the gospel that produces deadly earnestness in preaching. If these are some of the dangers that may work their way into the pulpit from the academy, there are other errors that may intrude from popular sources. If our temptation is not to appear scholarly, it may well be to appear affable, humorous and entertaining. This is not to say that humour has no place in preaching, but that it is ever subservient and secondary to the preacher's first task. Humour and illustrations are only in place to draw appropriate attention to the actual teaching of Scripture. If they fail in this task then they simply draw attention away from God and his Word. Moreover, as Martyn Lloyd-Jones explained (see p. 182) there are subjects that are too solemn for jocularity. Unless humour and illustrations are checked by the message, they are liable to cheapen and lighten subjects that are weighty, serious and precious.

Again we return to controlling principles. The apostle Paul's charge to Timothy was to 'preach the Word'; an imperative issued against the backdrop of the return of Christ, the judge of 'the living and the dead' (2 Tim. 4:1–2). This is harder to do in an age where entertainment reigns and consumerism is the order of the day. It is far easier to pander to the demands of the moment. After all, we are seeking to communicate to people in the twenty-first century, and how can we do so if we do not adopt the methods and techniques of our society? Yet to adopt this course of action uncritically would be to forget that God has condemned this world and its passing fads and fashions. It is not antiquated modes of communication that hold the church back, but a lack of preachers who know God. Os Guinness has stated it well:

> ... transcendence is the source of all true proclamation. What did Jeremiah say of the false prophets? 'Which of them has stood in the presence of the Lord?' The Word is transcendent and those who bear the message of the Word must come from there. When I was a boy being brought up in evangelicalism, you could see from the very demeanour of the preacher coming into the pulpit where he had come from. I don't often see that now amongst modern evangelical preachers, the sense of awe at having received a message from the King of kings and which is about to be delivered to the people.[12]

True knowledge

Thus far we have concentrated on the message and the effect it has on how preaching ought to be done in a general way. As important as it is to note the several steps and stages, and all the other constituent elements that make up preaching, our focus has been on the end result of preaching and its relationship to God. Without this, preaching is of no value. Techniques and aides may prove useful in preparation and delivery, but the big picture is the knowledge of who God is and how we relate to him.

This brings us to an absolute prerequisite in the life of the preacher (which is also applicable to anyone who shares the gospel, or who gives a talk to a group of any age, or who is studying the Bible with a friend). Quite simply, *you must be born again* (John 3:3). If there is an absence of a work of grace in your life, if you have not repented of your sins and are not trusting in the death of

God's Son for your acceptance with God, then your speaking is worthless.

Without doubt the greatest blight that the church has faced is Christian leaders who do not believe the gospel or have not experienced its power in their lives. How can men and women see their sins as infinitely offensive in the sight of a holy God if the preacher regards sins as the vestigial remains of an outdated morality, or of a God who is so loving that he can smile on wrong-doing with benign indifference? How can people know true conviction and repentance, or seek holiness of life, if God is presented as happy to accept any lifestyle provided it is tolerant of others? Why should anyone trust in Jesus Christ and him crucified, when God is said to welcome those of all religions or none? Who need fear hell and judgment when all will go to heaven and punishment is deemed incompatible with love? Why read the Bible when all it contains are human insights and best guesses at what some people imagined God to be like, but which we may take or leave as we see fit?

Again it is not only overt liberal diversions from the truth of Scripture that may ruin the spiritual welfare of the preacher, but also a dead, or merely cerebral, orthodoxy. It is possible to outline what faith in Christ is, and yet the description of it will do us no good if we know nothing of actually trusting in Christ to save us. Likewise, to wax eloquent about walking with God is of no use if there is no reality of it lived out day by day. What advantage is there in declaring God's holiness if we know nothing of the fear of the Lord and think little of offending him?

It is possible, therefore, to live on preaching and doctrinal correctness and not to live on Christ; to condemn sin with the lips but to cherish and tolerate it in one's life. This is a snare and temptation for all true Christians, but it is not impossible that there may be great learning, even evangelical orthodoxy, but no personal acquaintance with God. The way to begin the Christian life is also the way to maintain it, and the absence of applied truth is nothing short of spiritual disaster. Few have seen and stated this as clearly as John Owen:

When the heart is cast into the mould of the doctrine

that the mind embraceth ... when not the sense of the words only is in our heads, but the sense of the things abides in our hearts; when we have communion with God in the doctrine that we contend for, then shall we be garrisoned, by the grace of God, against all the assaults of men. And without this all our contending is, as to ourselves, of no value. What am I the better if I can dispute that Christ is God, but have no sense of sweetness in my heart from hence that he is God in covenant with my soul? What will it avail me to evince, by testimonies and arguments, that he hath made satisfaction for sin, if, through my unbelief, the wrath of God abideth on me, and I have no experience of my own being made the righteousness of God in him? ... Will it be any advantage to me, in the issue, to profess and dispute that God worketh the conversion of a sinner by the irresistible grace of his Spirit, if I was never acquainted experimentally with the deadness and utter impotency to good, that opposition to the law of God, which is in my own soul by nature, [and] with the efficacy of the exceeding greatness of the power of God in quickening, enlightening, and bringing forth the fruits of obedience in me? ... Let us, then, not think that we are any thing the better for our conviction of the truths of the great doctrines of the Gospel ... unless we find the power of the truths abiding in our own hearts and have a continual experience of their necessity and excellency in our standing before God and our communion with him.[13]

Owen is contending for the reality of gospel truth as it displays itself in the experience and personal lives of theological students and all involved in Christian ministry. One of the many dangers that face evangelicals in the Western world is the assumption that intellectual affirmations of the gospel are a sufficient indication of spiritual life. The gospel, then, may be assumed to be, but may not actually be, the central reality of Christian belief and experience, with what it means to 'encounter God' being filtered through other, experiential, criteria. Similarly, creedal affirmation may be taken as a substitute for a genuine work of conversion.

Richard Baxter, a contemporary of Owen, set out the tragedy of those who are ordained but ultimately worship an unknown God, preach an unknown Christ, pray through an unknown Spirit, and thus recommend a state of holiness and communion with God and a glory and happiness that is unknown to them.[14] Baxter's words, as with Paul's in 2 Corinthians 13:5–6, are not a description of imaginary people. It is therefore wrong to assume that all professions of faith and Christian life are genuine. The tragedy of this is magnified in those who teach and have pastoral responsibility for others.

Knowing God

The preparation needed for a sermon can be plotted in two ways. Along one axis is the specific time needed for exegesis, interpretation, structure and application of a particular text for a one-off message or a series of sermons. Along another axis is the necessary preparation of the spiritual life of the preacher. This task is continual and far more difficult to manage. It is also the backdrop to the specific task of preparing a particular message. We can sum it up in one important word: godliness. Furthermore it can be subdivided into the private or secret life of communion with God, and the outward observable life of holiness. Jonathan Edwards prized the importance of secret fellowship with God:

> Some are greatly affected when in company but have nothing that bears any manner of proportion to it in secret, in close meditation, secret prayer, and conversing with God, when alone and separated from all the world. A true Christian doubtless delights in religious fellowship and Christian conversation, and finds much to affect his heart in it, but he also delights at times to retire from all mankind to converse with God ... True religion disposes persons to be much alone in solitary places for holy

> meditation and prayer. So it wrought in Isaac, Gen.
> 24.63. And which is much more, so it wrought in
> Jesus Christ ... The most eminent divine favours that
> the saints obtained that we read of in Scripture, were
> in their retirement ... True grace delights in secret
> converse with God.[15]

It would be easy to mark this off as the source of true power in preaching, as if the cultivation of the inner life was the magic wand that produced great preachers and will do so again. What is at stake is the distinction that needs to be made between technique and substance. When addressing a group of ministers, Martyn Lloyd-Jones was closer to the mark when he said that failure to spend time in prayer was due to an insufficient desire for God, and that we do not desire him because we do not know him.[16] Once more it is not techniques that are needed but a recognition that to know God and be known by him is the only thing that matters both now and for eternity. It is a measure of our spiritual well-being both how we think about God and how that knowledge shapes the people we are, the people that we want to become, and the way we order our lives in the meantime.

The traditional evangelical 'quiet time', the daily setting apart of Bible reading, prayer and reflection, has fallen somewhat on hard times as it has had to compete with the demands of the modern world on our lives. Yet although some circumstances in life squeeze out time for personal devotion, which ought not to drive anyone into a state of guilt, there is a question of spiritual appetite that needs addressing. If meeting with God in secret is not a priority, that in itself may be an indication that we simply do not know God as we ought to. In a sermon entitled 'The Most High a Prayer-Hearing God' Jonathan Edwards remarked:

> We may learn how highly we are privileged, in that
> we have the Most High revealed to us, who is a God
> that heareth prayer ... we have the true God made
> known to us; a God of infinite grace and mercy; a
> God full of compassion to the miserable, who is ready
> to pity us under all our troubles and sorrows, to hear

our cries, and to give us all the relief which we need
… How highly privileged are we, in that we have the
holy word of this same God, to direct us how to seek
for mercy! … If we enjoy so great a privilege as to
have the prayer-hearing God revealed to us, how great
will be our folly and inexcusableness, if we neglect the
privilege, or make no use of it, and deprive ourselves
of the advantage by not seeking this God in prayer.[17]

There is no substitute for private prayer and meditation on
Scripture in order for us to be better acquainted with God. This is
the staple diet of the spiritual life for all Christians, and so where
it is neglected in preachers and teachers, it must have an ill effect
on their listeners. John Owen once remarked that if the Word does
not dwell with power in us then it would not pass with power from
us.[18] Neglect of the inner life is the cause of much of the weakness
we experience in preaching.

At this point the resources and help that can be gleaned from the
biographies of preachers used of God in the past are invaluable.
Robert Murray McCheyne, the nineteenth-century Scot, recorded
this as his goal for 'Reformation in Secret Prayer':

I ought to spend the best hours of the day in
communion with God. It is my noblest and most
fruitful employment, and is not to be thrust into any
corner. The morning hours, from six to eight, are the
most uninterrupted, and should be thus employed, if
I can prevent drowsiness.[19]

Andrew Bonar, his friend and fellow minister, noted
McCheyne's reflections on the ministry of preaching 'Jesus to
dying men' in a letter to a colleague in Scotland: 'speak for eternity.
Above all things cultivate your own spirit. A word spoken by you
when your conscience is clear, and your heart full of God's Spirit,
is worth ten thousand words spoken in unbelief and sin'.[20] This he
sought to do by 'giving the eye the habit of looking upward all the
day, and drawing down gleams from the reconciled countenance'
and by the daily enlargement of his heart in fellowship with God.[21]

The value of building a secret history with God and its effects on ministering to others draws the following comment from Bonar concerning McCheyne's preaching:

> From the first he fed others by what he himself was feeding upon. His preaching was in a manner the development of his soul's experience. It was a giving out of the inward life. He loved to come up from the pastures wherein the Chief Shepherd had met him – to lead the flock entrusted to his care to the spots where he had found nourishment.[22]

While it is possible, regrettably, to live a surrogate Christian life from the experiences of others, both past and present, nevertheless there is great help to be gained from knowing church history better and learning from Christians who have already walked on the way that leads to life. There are no short cuts in the Christian life, and no final conflict between a life of disciplined living and grace. If we can say that 'to know him properly is a life full of peace',[23] and we can state our aim as gaining Christ and being found in him (Phil. 2:8–9) and know the reality of those words, then the priorities of our lives will be ordered by the great and glorious God who is Father, Son and Holy Spirit.

Holiness and the preacher

Having considered something of fellowship and communion with God, we now turn to the necessity of holiness of life for the preacher. It is not too much to say that personal holiness is indispensable for Christian service. Positively this will mean dedication to God and the bending of all our faculties and powers for his service. Negatively it involves 'mortification', to use the old word, or the 'putting to death of sin' (Rom. 8:12–13; Col. 3:5–8). For the Christian this is carried out in the context of union with Christ in his death and resurrection, so that by the Spirit this union is brought to bear on sin and its dethroned mastery (Rom. 6:1–14; Col. 3:1–4). It also includes the reality of indwelling sin, this side of the resurrection of the body, and the subsequent frustrations and struggles that constitute the normal Christian life (Rom. 8:9–13, 22–23; Gal. 5:16–18).

With piercing clarity Robert Murray McCheyne set the requirements for fruitful preaching ministry in the context of holiness: 'In great measure, according to the purity and perfections of the instrument, will be the success. It is not great talents God blesses so much as great likeness to Jesus. A holy minister is an awful weapon in the hand of God.'[24]

In the final analysis we can all admire and aspire to the gifts and abilities of others, but unless they play a secondary role to the pursuit of holiness, our priorities are frankly askew. Paul lays out for Timothy the pattern of his ministry as it will be seen by his personal example. The things Paul lists – speech, life, love, faith and purity (1 Tim. 4:12) – are not only to be present for others to see but cover the private life of the preacher also. The battle for godly character is won or lost in the way that we go about the small things in daily life. It is not big sins, as we perceive them, that constitute the greatest threat, but the daily acts of disobedience and neglect that pave the way for greater falls. Thus Paul's exhortation to 'watch your life and doctrine closely' (1 Tim. 4:16) needs to be worked out obediently all day, every day, in a humble and contrite walk with God.

Richard Baxter warned ministers of the dangers of unsaying with their lives what they say with their tongues, and of living in the sins that they preach against in others.[25] The neglect of holiness saps preaching of its life:

> This is the way to make men think that the Word of God is but an idle tale, and to make preaching seem no better than prating. He that means as he speaks, will surely do as he speaks ... We must study as hard how to live well, as how to preach well. We must think again, how to compose our lives, as may most tend to men's salvation, as well as our sermons.[26]

The qualifications for overseers in the pastoral epistles, in addition to doctrinal purity and teaching ability, place holiness and consistency of life high on the agenda for Christian service (1 Tim.

3:1–13; Titus 1:6–14). It is not that Paul is recommending these things for *effective* service to be achieved; rather they are the basic prerequisites of any, and all, Christian work. To lower these standards is to tarnish and undermine the purpose of the ministry of the gospel that is 'the knowledge of the truth that leads to godliness' (Titus 1:1b).

Much more can and ought to be said on the nature of sin and sins, of the necessity of high standards, and the maintaining of a close walk with God, and this must be the dominant thought in the life and preparation of preachers. Who is fit then to preach the Word? Is there anyone whose conscience is clear, who feels no regret over past sins or condemnation for their present behaviour? It is an axiom of the Christian life that the longer it goes on the better acquainted with indwelling sin you become. John Newton once wrote to advise a friend on this subject:

> Every sin, in its own nature, has a tendency towards a final apostasy; but there is a provision in the covenant of grace, and the Lord, in His own time, returns to convince, humble, pardon, comfort and renew the soul … we begin at length to learn that we are nothing, have nothing, can do nothing, but sin. And thus we are gradually prepared to live more out of ourselves, and to derive all our sufficiency of every kind from Jesus, the fountain of grace. We learn to tread more warily, to trust less to our own strength, to have lower thoughts of ourselves, and higher thoughts of *Him*.[27]

J. I. Packer summarized the stated aims of Charles Simeon's sermons as 'to humble the sinner, to exalt the Saviour, and to promote holiness; and it was the second aim that gave point to the first and meaning to the third'.[28] What Simeon intended to produce in his hearers is the very thing that must first be worked out in the life of the preacher. God's holiness would overwhelm us entirely if it were not for the blood of Christ. And it is to Christ's blood that the apostle John directs us if we are to walk in the light and go on being cleansed from our sins (1 John 1:5 – 2:2). One who deeply understood the nature of his own heart and the unqualified demands of holiness put it like this:

> I am persuaded that I shall obtain the highest amount of present happiness, I shall do most for God's glory and the good of man, and I shall have the fullest reward in eternity, by maintaining a conscience always washed in Christ's blood, by being filled with the Holy Spirit at all times, and by attaining the most entire likeness to Christ in mind, will, and heart, that is possible for a redeemed sinner to attain to in this world.[29]

We would do well to ponder these words and be persuaded of them for ourselves.

Why preaching matters

The students who entered Westminster Theological Seminary, Philadelphia, in the summer of 1944, did so whilst many of their peers were fighting and laying down their lives in Europe and the Pacific. They were addressed by Professor John Murray who presented the seriousness of the choice they had made, and the vocation they would take up:

> You are preparing yourselves in pursuance of a divine call for the ministry of the Word without which the whole world perishes in sin, in misery and death. You are training for the most militant service in that kingdom that is an everlasting kingdom and in that dominion which shall not be destroyed. Militant service, indeed, for we wrestle not against flesh and blood, but against principalities, against powers, against the rulers of this darkness, against the spiritual hosts of wickedness in high places. All of this lays upon you an exacting obligation.[30]

With the brevity of life a daily reality in the far off summer of

1944, the choice of training for the ministry ahead of military service, and hence studies over hardship, may well have appeared close to cowardice. Certainly the distinguished English preacher John Stott knew acute family pain as he chose ordination over military service in the early 1940s.[31] Yet it is because eternal issues are at stake, issues that eclipse the struggles and suffering of this world, that preaching is not an occupation designed to provide an escape from the hardships of life or an alternative to other careers. John Piper has unfavourably contrasted Jonathan Edwards' grasp of eternal realities to present standards:

> Compelling preaching gives the impression that something very great is at stake. With Edwards' view of the reality of heaven and hell and the necessity of persevering in a life of holy affections and godliness, eternity was at stake every Sunday. This sets him apart from the average preacher today. Our emotional rejection of hell, and our facile view of conversion and the abundant false security we purvey have created an atmosphere in which the great biblical intensity of preaching is almost impossible.[32]

Without the knowledge of God as the holy Creator and Judge of all, and of human beings as rebellious sinners who are held accountable for their actions and who are thereby under God's just condemnation, the urgency of being right with God solely through Christ's death is dissipated and undermined. Without this true knowledge of God, preaching is reduced to a tiresome monologue or second-class entertainment. Great preaching is utterly dependable on the vision of God that sustains it, and it requires men and women of God to produce it.

B. B. Warfield saw no disparity between the office of the theologian and that of the preacher, for it is the knowledge of God that produces both: the knowledge of a holy God, personally grasped and daily lived out in his presence, among his people and before a watching world.[33] Is this vision too much to ask? Is it too high an ideal for the evangelical church in the twenty-first century? In the words of the apostle Paul, '... who is equal to such a task?'

His own answer drives us back to the One who makes and sends out preachers, 'in Christ we speak before God with sincerity, like men sent from God' (2 Cor. 2:16–17).

Theology and preaching

> Though he was a scientific theologian who intended, God helping him, to establish solid doctrinal foundations in the Reformed Churches; and though he was also a lecturer to the students who met in the College at Geneva ... nevertheless it was not to these activities so much as to the pulpit itself that the major part of his time was given. His primary obligation was not to fellow scholars, nor even to his students, but to the ordinary people ... who crowded St. Peter's day by day to listen to his sermons.[34]

So reads the introduction to a modern reprint of John Calvin's sermons on Ephesians. It is historically indisputable that Calvin was pre-eminently *the* theologian of the Protestant Reformation in Europe, whose thought has shaped theology in the church and the academy for over four centuries. And yet, for Calvin theology was to be preached, and preaching was none other than the exposition of the Word of God.

In the previous section we noted that the aim of preaching is to bring men and women to a right knowledge of God, as the gospel about God's Son is unfolded. Preaching ought to be shaped by the knowledge of the holiness and majesty of God, and both public worship and the private life of the preacher must be moulded by the same truths. In this section we will consider something of the relationship between theology and preaching, particularly systematic theology. In an age where biblical illiteracy is rampant, and privatized beliefs are the norm, it is essential that the whole revealed will of God is known both in the church and in the world.

Our aim therefore is fairly modest. Preaching ought to be expository, explaining what the Bible says and what it means, and doctrinal, articulating the truths that the Bible teaches and how they relate to each other. To engage in theology is to begin to answer questions such as 'Who is Jesus Christ?', 'What is salvation?', 'How can someone be saved?', 'What happens to people when they die?', 'How can God be sovereign and human beings be accountable for their actions?' and so on. The answers to those questions will be culled from the total knowledge someone possesses of God, the sum of individual parts of the Bible rightly or wrongly understood, as well as thoughts derived from outside of the Bible. Forming appropriate answers to these questions is the task of systematic theology. The challenge to anyone who preaches is whether they are explaining the Bible correctly, and whether they are enabling their listeners to form a right understanding of the whole of Christian truth.

What is theology?

Put succinctly, theology is the knowledge of God.[35] Christian theology is drawn from the data of revelation. This comprises general revelation in creation, providence and in human beings made in God's image; and special revelation in God's redemptive acts, in Scripture and in the incarnation of the second person in the Godhead. David F. Wells has argued that theology should mean the same thing whatever the setting (the lecture room, church service, hall group, Bible study or Sunday-school class). Furthermore theology is made up of three constituent elements that have become fragmented in the modern world and have undermined the subject:

1. A confessional element.
2. Reflection on this confession.
3. The cultivation of a set of virtues that are grounded on the first two elements.[36]

The meaning of these elements for evangelical theology, with its roots in the Protestant Reformation, is clear. Confession is what the church believes and is derived from and dependent on the Word of God. Even where there is disagreement on the precise details of what the Bible teaches, nevertheless, it is the sole and final authority in all things. Confession, says Wells, 'must be at the center of every theology that wants to be seen as *theologia*, the knowledge of God'.[37] Reflection is the attempt to understand confession in the present by ranging over the whole of God's disclosure in Scripture, humbly recognizing and receiving the labours and insights of the church throughout history, and finally untangling what is confessed from the prevailing trends of the day that intrude upon the life and thought of the church.[38] The cultivation of virtues is the logical outworking of wisdom for life 'built on the pillars of confession and surrounded by the scaffolding of reflection', viewing God as holy, spirituality as centrally moral, and Christian life as the practice of truth not a matter of technique.[39] It is the estimation of David Wells that evangelicals are substituting the confessional centre with a new set of principles and are drifting away from the point where they can meaningfully be called historic Protestants, not so much by denying what is central, but by orchestrating evangelical practice in such a way that doctrine does not define how things are done. Technique replaces truth and theology disappears, or rather a different kind of theology replaces it.

Borrowing Wells' three-part framework we may note the various sub-disciplines that are to inform reflection and feed the cultivation of virtues.[40] There are at least ten, and it would be hard to improve on J. I. Packer's summary:

> The first is *exegesis*, for which the question always is: what was this or that biblical text written to convey to its readers? The second is *biblical theology*, for which the question is: what is the total message of the canonical books on this or that subject? The third is *historical theology*, the bonding glue of church history, exploring how Christians in the past viewed specific biblical truths. The fourth is *systematic theology*, which rethinks biblical theology with the help of historical theology in order to restate the faith, topic by topic and as a whole, in relation to current interests, assumptions, questions, hopes, fears and uncertainties in today's church and world. The fifth is *apologetics*, which seeks to commend and defend the faith as rational and true in face of current unbelief, misbelief and puzzlement. The sixth is *ethics*, which

systematizes the standards of Christian life and conduct and applies them to particular cases. The seventh is *spiritual theology* ... which studies how to maintain sanctifying communion with God. The eighth is *missiology*, which aims to see how God's people should view and tackle their gospel-spreading, church-planting and welfare-bringing tasks across cultural barriers worldwide. The ninth is *liturgy*, which asks how God is best and most truly worshipped, and how true worship may be achieved in existing churches. The tenth is *practical theology*, embracing pastoral theology, family theology and political theology as it explores how to further God's work and glory in home, church and society.[41]

Systematic theology, although it appears fourth in the list, forms the apex and fulcrum for the other nine disciplines. It is the sum of the material of the first three and the source of material for the remaining six. Whether theology is ever taught and consistently practised in this manner is another question. Evangelical theology and scholarship must be committed to pursuing all ten disciplines, and that in a unified and coherent way. And it is not too much to say that the preacher, as with all believers, must be a theologian.

The primacy of systematic theology

Systematic theology is easy to malign and misunderstand. It does not imply that any other theological disciplines are less than logical or that they are haphazard in their arrangements. Neither is it dependent on proof-texting in order to produce its results. Nor does it treat texts as a-temporal and a-historical, thereby ignoring historical and cultural settings and literary context. To be sure it may be guilty of both these errors, but not as a matter of course. Rather, systematic theology seeks to answer the following question in the following way:

> 'What does the whole Bible teach us about a given topic?' Stated more technically, systematic theology is

> that methodological study of the Bible that views the
> Holy Scriptures as a *completed* revelation, in
> distinction from the disciplines of Old Testament
> theology, New Testament theology, and biblical
> theology, which approach the Scriptures as an
> *unfolding* revelation. Accordingly, the systematic
> theologian, viewing the Scriptures as a completed
> revelation, seeks to understand holistically the plan,
> purpose, and didactic intention of the divine mind
> revealed in Holy Scripture, and to arrange that plan,
> purpose and didactic intention in orderly and
> coherent fashion as articles of the Christian faith.[42]

This quotation from the Presbyterian theologian Robert Reymond
helpfully illuminates why systematic theology is primary, and
what undergirds it. Systematic theology is only as good as the
biblical theology that it has attempted to collate, which in itself is
made up of the exegesis of various parts of Scripture from the
stages of redemptive history. Evangelicals hold to fundamental
convictions about the authority of the Bible, its nature as a
completed revelation and its sufficiency for faith and life. It is
God's final Word that reliably teaches salvation through faith in
Jesus Christ. The end task, then, of all departments of theology is
to contribute to the total understanding of God's self-revelation in
Scripture.

Systematic theology is not revelation; it merely deals with the
subject matter of revelation and arranges it logically and
coherently for the benefit of the church. The value of a systematic
theology is determined by its presuppositions regarding the
sources of revelation and their authority. It is the consolidated
reflection on the confession of the Christian church, to borrow
Wells' categories. Furthermore, the task of systematic theology is
never complete. The Christian life is not just about the
transformation of character but also the renewing of the mind.
There is to be progression in knowledge as bad theology is excised
and truth built into the framework of our total understanding of
God and his ways. In short the Christian must be committed to
loving God with his or her mind and does so as the Bible shapes

his or her total understanding of Christian truth.

No church or Christian can ignore the task of systematic theology because it is simply unavoidable. Any, and all reflection on God, drawn from whatever source, and leading to whatever results, is a form of systematic theology. What is needed for Christians who are seeking to grow in their individual and corporate relationship with God is thoughtful reflection on this process and the willingness to do it as best they can. One thing that is definite is that this cannot be avoided, because, as Gerald Bray has said:

> The message of the Bible is a message of spiritual truth addressed to the human mind. Dogmatic definitions of its content are not an aberration, but the logical outcome of the process of revelation itself. Salvation for the whole man cannot bypass the mind, but must use it for the powerful weapon which it is.[43]

How theology can mar preaching

There are two ways that theology can mar preaching.

First, it is clear from the New Testament that preaching, which is after all the communication of theological truth, can be ruined if the theology that feeds it is wrong. Throughout the history of the church, largely until the Enlightenment's erosion of orthodoxy, Christians have operated with the categories of truth and error and therefore have understood there to be such a thing as false teaching and heresy. False teaching is the perversion of Christian truth that stems from rival sources of authority to Scripture, wrong exegesis, the isolation of particular truths (and therefore the misshaping of a particular truth), and/or the addition and subtraction of truths. Given that for the past two centuries theology in the academy and in seminaries has been shaped by Enlightenment ideas about reason and revelation (and now by late- or post-modernity, the stepchild of the Enlightenment project), the waters of Christian orthodoxy have been muddied and poisoned. So much so that to hold on to categories of orthodoxy and heresy has become the only heresy that remains.

The effect of this, as it has trickled down from the university to the pulpit to the pew, has been to empty churches and lives. In this sense theology has had a catastrophic effect on preaching because its controlling principles, in the Word of God correctly handled, have been eroded and replaced by reason and experience. It is little wonder then that the dangers still facing believing students in university theology departments remain those of bowing to the god of scholarship, crafted by the results of 'higher' learning and the whims of what the scholarly guild will allow. It is understandable to feel intimidated by tutors with several degrees, years of teaching their discipline and general life experience. Nevertheless, and with all due respect, theology has not always been taught in this way, nobody is free from bias (particularly the intellectual effects of sin) or thinks in a value-neutral way, and there are inevitable consequences in life from the view of God that is being offered. The results of liberalism have been disastrous for the church and particularly for preaching.[44] It is remarkable that a senior church figure has said that 'liberalism is a creative and constructive element for exploring theology today'.[45] One finds it hard to imagine the apostle Paul speaking so warmly about error given his words in Acts 20:28–31 (assuming of course that the Paul of Luke–Acts is not a figure constructed by the author, who pays a passing resemblance to the author of some of the New Testament epistles that bear his name).

The second way that theology can mar preaching may take a number of forms. The pulpit, or platform, can be the place where someone parades his or her learning and voluminous reading, implying that only those who are aware of the latest research, or who can cite what the most notable authorities have said on this or that verse, are qualified to handle texts. This is not intended to disparage learning. It is very easy, however, to keep the Scriptures and their meaning in the hands of a new breed of priests. Again it would be wrong to suggest that parts of Scripture are not very difficult to understand, and that the church does not owe a great debt to those who have dedicated their lives to theological research.

What needs reflecting on is the capacity for the preacher, or theology student, to be puffed up with intellectual pride like a swollen toad. Martyn Lloyd-Jones summed up this attitude well:

> 'A little learning is a dangerous thing.' That does not
> mean, of course, that there is no danger in much
> knowledge. There is. But I am not sure that in this
> respect there is not a greater danger in a little, because
> it always means that the element of the tyro or novice
> who imagines that his little knowledge is all
> knowledge comes in ... That in turn expresses itself
> in the use of slogans, clichés, tabloid expressions and
> phrases which always characterizes this condition ...
> That is unfailingly indicative of a little knowledge, a
> lack of true knowledge, and above all of this lack of
> balance of knowledge.[46]

At least one temptation that arises from this is to turn the pulpit into a lecture theatre, a platform to impart to a congregation all the complex issues that they have never thought about but that you think they simply must consider. Once more the subtle threat is to display learning rather than to teach and edify.

The test of true preaching, including that which is trying to stimulate better theological understanding, is whether it is *motivated by love*. To leave people impressed with your knowledge, dazzled by your intellect and frustrated by their supposed ignorance, is to fail as a Christian preacher. Anyone can repeat theological terminology, but it requires skill and craft to take complex subjects and to explain them at a level that is accessible, whilst being motivated by a desire to see people grow and mature in Christ.

As the tyranny of learning can be inflicted on congregations, so can the fog of ignorance. If a preacher fills out the meaning of a passage not by explaining what is there (exegesis) but by importing ideas from elsewhere then the capacity to skew right understanding is a real threat. Preachers and teachers are responsible for the spiritual welfare of their listeners, even if they are visiting speakers, and must let the weight of this impress itself on how they prepare and what they deliver. Each sermon has the capacity to advance or retard a congregations' understanding of God and his ways and will contribute to or hinder each individual's capacity to think authentically about God, Christ, sin, salvation, the world and themselves.

Earlier we stated the truism that everyone has a theology because any thoughts or discussion about God means that we are theologizing. What is needed is a good theology rather than a bad one. Good theology is formed as we submit our thoughts to the authority and teaching of the Bible so that our thinking is not coloured by a few verses here and there but by the whole counsel of God. Part of the process of possessing a renewed mind is the ongoing experience of grasping the meaning of individual parts of Scripture. This is in fact what Christians do if they are asked why they believe certain things (for example, 'How is someone right with God?' or 'How can one God be three persons?'). The answers to these questions rely on previous understanding of particular parts of Scripture. Therefore while there may be nothing pernicious or deliberately misleading in announcing a text and then giving a talk that fails to derive its structure and content from that text, its long-term effects weaken the ability of listeners to construct a right understanding of God.

Where a talk has explicit truth content, the material is patently biblical, but fails to explain the passage it is meant to be based on, the immediate effects may be very beneficial but not necessarily so helpful if this occurs week in week out. The reasons why this occurs are varied and may not be universally or acutely present. At one level it may merely demonstrate insufficient training or inappropriate models of ministry. For churches that do not have full-time ministers, or speakers who also have other occupations, there is the difficulty of insufficient time for preparation and personal study. Whatever the setbacks involved, churches that seek to uphold the authority of Scripture and preach the gospel need to aim for excellence in teaching the Bible.

On the other hand, it is possible that a failure to structure sermons around a section of Scripture may indicate an element of unbelief about the importance and sufficiency of Scripture. Either as a preacher or as a member of a church, it is worth reflecting on how the Bible is being taught and what criteria are being used to teach it. Are hard passages being avoided or explained away? If the preaching is topical or subject-based rather than sequential and expository (verse by verse, chapter by chapter, book after book) who decides on the subjects, and why? Are important truths being neglected and ignored? Do certain subjects dominate? Why are many books of the Bible unfamiliar and unexplored? The Bible is open to massive abuse in the hands of church leaders and preachers; not only can they misinterpret it but they may also preside over which parts are taught and which parts are passed over. In the end such malpractice deforms our vision of God for we are encouraged to think of him as other than he is.

Lurking behind this failure is a faulty theology, for if what 'Scripture says, God says',[48] then teaching the whole Bible must be the priority of every church. Anything less than this betrays a different manifesto for the role of the Bible in the church than the one laid down by the apostle Paul (2 Tim. 3:16).

How theology helps preaching

If theology that mars preaching ultimately stems from a failure to teach the Bible, then the starting point for faithful preaching must stem from a right view of the authority and life-giving nature of holy Scripture. After all, God's words are not idle but are our very life (Deut. 32:46–47). Indeed the perennial question that must be faced by all theologies is that of ultimate authority. Classical liberalism subverted the authority of 'Scripture alone' and supplanted it with reason and experience. Both of these replacement authorities continue to clamour for the high ground by relativizing Scripture's demands on belief and behaviour by appealing to the cultural context of language, symbolic non-literal history, and by the kind of deft exegetical ingenuity that can make Scripture say whatever you want it to say.[48] Thus the authority of Scripture is upheld but is hollowed out by what it is made to say.

How then do theology and preaching relate? In the main, preaching must be the exposition of the Word of God, explaining and unfolding what the text says, what it means, and how it applies. Because exposition is not the same as giving a running commentary on a passage, preachers may begin with contemporary assumptions and attitudes about God from both within and without the church and show how the text addresses these and corrects them. The goal is to expound and apply what the text says and to do that effectively the preacher may anticipate the conclusions that the audience already hold on the subject in hand, as well as the conclusions that he wishes to steer them towards. Whenever a passage of Scripture is read or expounded there is a framework present in how we move from text to application, and therefore how we articulate what God is saying to the contemporary Christian, the church and the world.

We may identify a minimum of four steps or stages:

1. What does the text say?
2. What does the text mean?
3. Where does the text fit in the unfolding revelation in Scripture and how does it fit into the total system of Christian truth?
4. How does the text apply today?

Preachers must do the hard work of exegeting a passage. This necessitates working from a good translation and carefully reading the passage, noting its literary type, structure, language patterns and so on. Closely related is the task of establishing what the text meant to the original readers. This will be dependent on what the text says and will provide the basis for the meaning for today. Unless the meaning of a text is established from what the text says, the constant danger is that its meaning will be filled out by the reader or preacher's own understanding. The third step is crucial in aiding correct interpretation. Whenever we read or expound a text we do so from a particular context (a chapter or book), from a distinct genre or corpus (wisdom literature, gospels, Pauline epistles, and so on.) and from a certain stage in redemptive history (Old and New Testament, pre- and post-resurrection). In this way we must recognize where the text fits, and how it contributes to, the unfolding purposes of God from Genesis to Revelation. Moreover, we are then able to see how the text fits into the total system of Christian truth and how that system contributes to our grasp of that particular text.[49]

The process of correctly applying a text can now be approached, safeguarded by the interplay between exegesis, hermeneutics and biblical and systematic theology.

Biblical and systematic theology

The twentieth century witnessed the rise of a biblical theology movement and a renaissance, in its last quarter, of the writing of systematic theologies. The emergence of the latter is striking given the academic antipathy in biblical studies towards any form of unity between Old and New Testament theology and even between individual authors. The Bible should not be viewed as a unity but as a collection of overlapping and, at many points, conflicting theologies. To even suggest, as we have been doing, that there is agreement in concept, a unity of theology amidst diversity of style, between Moses, Isaiah, John, Paul and the writer to the Hebrews, is to swim against the tide of much scholarship. To outline a defence of the possibility of biblical and systematic theology is beyond the scope of this essay and would ultimately include an articulation of the very foundations of evangelical theology.[50] Both biblical and systematic theology are possible because of the nature of God and his ability to reveal himself through personal and verbal revelation to fallen men and women in space and time. It is the unity provided by the one divine author who stands behind, initiates and superintends the work of the human authors that makes systematic theology possible, and by implication also makes the task of biblical theology a viable reality. Both branches of theology must be pursued by the preacher as he seeks to understand the progressive unfolding of revelation in each stage in redemptive history and the logical relations of each part of the completed revelation.

John Murray helpfully explains the interconnection of the two disciplines:

> Systematic theology deals with special revelation as a finished product incorporated for us in Holy Scripture. But special revelation in its totality is never conceived of apart from the history by which it became a finished product. As we think of, study, appreciate, appropriate, and apply the revelation put into our possession by inscripturation, we do not properly engage in any of these exercises except as the

panorama of God's movements in history comes within our vision or at least forms the background of our thought. In other words, redemptive and revelatory history conditions our thought at every point or stage in our study of Scripture revelation. Therefore, what is the special interest of Biblical theology is never divorced from our thought when we study any part of Scripture and seek to bring its treasures of truth to bear upon the synthesis which systematic theology aims to accomplish. Furthermore, the tendency to abstraction which ever lurks for systematic theology is hereby counteracted. The various data are interpreted not only in their scriptural context but also in their historical context ... Texts will not thus be forced to bear a meaning they do not possess nor forced into a service they cannot perform. But in the locus to which they belong and by the import they do possess they will contribute to the sum-total of revelatory evidence by which biblical doctrine is established.[51]

Biblical theology acts as a corrective against reading texts in isolation, as if they are hermetically sealed off from the storyline of redemptive history. Positively it enables the preacher to stimulate good habits of Bible reading in the church and to enrich the understanding of Christians as they see the plan of redemption foretold, patterned, promised and fulfilled in the incarnation, death and victorious resurrection of Jesus Christ.

Why preaching must draw on systematic theology

The effect of culture upon the church is similar to a moth being drawn to a light bulb. The power of attraction continues whilst the health of the fluttering insect is being impaired. In the previous section on 'God and preaching' we argued that the worth and value of preaching is determined by the theology that sustains it, and therefore where the doctrine of God falls short of his greatness and majesty, the pulpit is inevitably moulded into the shape of the idol it serves. One of the most beneficial remedies for the evangelical church in the twenty-first century is the rich history of theology and preaching from former generations. It is only presumption of the worst kind that imagines that the present is the benchmark for true spirituality. In spite of the educational advances of the last two hundred years and the availability of Bibles in contemporary language, the standards of biblical literacy and articulate theological definition are far from acceptable. In large measure the fault is attributable to the lack of theological preaching in the churches. That is not to say that it is entirely absent at present, and it must be borne in mind that truth is not necessarily popular or sought after (2 Tim. 4:3–5). Nevertheless, it is the task of preachers to teach the Word of God. Positively, this involves enabling believers to know what they believe, and why they believe it, so that they will speak the truth in love and be built up in Christ; negatively, the warning about false teachers and every wind of teaching that leaves believers 'tossed back and forth by the waves' is no idle threat (Eph. 4:14–16).

Systematic theology aids the preacher's task and forms an integral part of the goal of preaching for the following reasons. We naturally think in terms of subjects that can be stated as questions. In fact, this is the way non-Christians most often enquire about what Christians believe and why. An example would be 'What happens to people when they die?' The way in which we answer this question involves at the very least eschatology (the last things, heaven and hell and so on), our doctrine of what a human being is (are we more than biological entities? do we have immortal souls?), and the doctrine of sin. The form of our answer will be both propositional and a summary of biblical teaching. We may state it in the following way, 'The Bible says that death is the punishment for sin. Death isn't natural because we were made to know God and relate to him. When people die the Bible says that they will be judged...' and so on. This answer is made up of our reading of the Bible and other Christian books, the results of reflection and discussion, personal views and what we have been taught at home and church.

If our questioner were to probe a little further, then all the component parts of our answer will need to be substantiated from the book that we regard as our ultimate authority. How many verses would we turn to? Have we understood these verses in context and their implications for other parts of our answer? Assuming that we have listened well, a significant resource in forming our answer will have been the teaching we have received in church; or, for the preacher, one hopes that the people who listen week by week have been equipped to give a satisfying answer.

It is in part because we think in terms of subjects that are logically related to other subjects that preaching must aim toward establishing a good understanding of the system of Christian truth. Another example would be how a series of expository sermons deals with doctrines as and when they arise in the text. John, in the prologue to his Gospel, tells us that the Word was with God, the Word was God, and that the Word became flesh. Assuming that the amount of text to be covered and the amount of time in which to expound it are not disproportionate, some thought ought to be given to how John 1:1–18 contributes to the understanding of what Scripture teaches about the person of Christ and the doctrine of God. The likely answer, 'Who is Jesus?' will be based on the doctrinal understanding of who Jesus is (eternal God, who became incarnate, and so was fully God and fully man; or more simply the Son of God, equal with the Father). to the question Therefore, it is necessary to show that John affirms the full deity of Christ as do the other New Testament writers.

The doctrine of the person of Christ runs throughout the New Testament not only in the passages that explicitly call him God (theos), but also in those that attribute to Jesus the titles and names of God and the prerogatives of deity. In this way the audience are given a fuller picture of what Scripture teaches and why this truth is so important. Conversely, it also gives an opportunity to look at verses that allegedly deny Christ's deity (and why opponents put weight on them) and what the implications would be if one part of Scripture contradicted another.

Granted that systematic theology is an ongoing process, it would not be out of place to consider how Christians in the past have faced these issues (there is an obvious connection with the Arian controversy and the debate that ensued about the identity of Jesus).

Clearly John's prologue should not become the platform for a series of lectures on Christology but, nevertheless, John introduces us to the One who was a baby lying in a manger and yet at the same time was God over all, blessed for ever. Thus in teaching the text there is also the possibility of equipping the congregation to think rightly about Jesus Christ as they range over the teaching of the New Testament.

The deity of Christ is a major doctrine that all Christians need to understand as best they can, but what of God's sovereignty? Justification by faith alone? Penal substitution? Regeneration? Sanctification? Sin? Exposition and systematic theology feed each other. As we understand individual texts, we inform our understanding of doctrines and how doctrines interrelate; the better informed our framework of truth is, the better able we are to interpret individual texts. It is the responsibility of the pulpit to teach people how to think theologically. It is not enough just to teach the passage in hand. There must be a serious attempt made to teach people biblical doctrine.

Unless there is a recovery of doctrinal preaching, not only will the gains of the past be buried under the semblance of Christian truth that is served up today, but also the church will become a shadow of what it is intended to be. D. A. Carson's words are incisive:

> Above all the problem lies in the pulpit. Too few preachers have so married content and passion that they have taught their people to think biblically and love and honour God passionately. The books on many church bookstalls are a disgrace-thousands of pages of sentimental twaddle laced with the occasional biblical gem. There is very little effort to build up a biblical mind in our churches ...[52]

Remarkably the same point was made by Martyn Lloyd-Jones at the close of the 1940s. His biographer records an incident that illustrates this:

He was also persuaded that too often Christians had

no grasp of truth as *a system* because of the type of preaching to which they had been chiefly accustomed. 'The great trouble of our time is the lack of theological preaching,' he told students at Spurgeon's College when he spoke there in January 1948 ... Before concluding that address he anticipated the question likely to be put to him, 'Will people listen to this kind of preaching?' To which he replied 'they have more or less given up listening to the other kind! The low level of the life of the church today is due to the lack of doctrinal preaching. This is a question never to be asked: we have a commission to preach; a commission to God; not the call to satisfy the popular palate. Preach the Word. Our one concern should be to preach the truth.[53]

The passing of time has not diminished the need for this kind of preaching that builds the church, confronts error and calls the world to listen to the voice of God.

God and preaching revisited

The plea for a more doctrinal form of preaching is not an attempt to champion one form of preaching over another. Neither can it be accomplished by the mere recitation of truths logically arranged and cogently presented. Systematic theology finds its *raison d'etre* in its panoramic vision of the greatness of God and his ways. What C. H. Spurgeon once called the loftiest piece of writing in the human tongue, the epistle of Paul to the Romans, at the climax of eleven chapters of rich theology breaks out into adoring praise at the mystery of God and his judgments (Rom. 11:33–36). It is the absence of awe and reverence at the greatness of God's being that marks the deepest poverty of preaching that does not put God and his glory as its central focus. A. W. Tozer lamented this state of affairs:

The Church has surrendered her once lofty concept of God and has substituted for it one so low, so ignoble, as to be utterly unworthy of thinking, worshipping men ... The decline of the knowledge of the holy has brought on our troubles. A rediscovery of the majesty of God will go a long way toward curing them. It is impossible to keep our moral practices sound and our inward attitudes right while our idea of God is erroneous or inadequate. If we would bring back spiritual power to our lives, we must begin to think of God more nearly as he is.[54]

The theology student, church member, Christian Union leader, fledgling preacher, all alike must make the knowledge of God their starting point for study, worship and life. The greatest threat to this knowledge is not necessarily the theology of the lecture theatre but the life of the church. David F. Wells has the final word:

Unless the evangelical Church can recover the knowledge of what it means to live before a holy God, unless in its worship it can relearn humility, wonder, love and praise, unless it can find again a moral purpose in the world that resonates with the holiness of God and that is accordingly deep and unyielding, unless the evangelical Church can do all these things, theology will have no place in its life. But the reverse is also true. If the Church can begin to find a place for theology by refocusing itself on the centrality of God, if it can rest upon his sufficiency, if it can recover its moral fiber, then it will have something to say to a world now drowning in modernity.[55]

© Martin Downes, 2001

Notes

[1] D. Martyn Lloyd-Jones, *Preaching and Preachers* (Hodder and Stoughton, 1985), p. 97.
[2] John Piper, The Supremacy of God in Preaching, (Kingsway, 1998), 12.

[3] Quoted in Christopher Catherwood (ed.), *Martyn Lloyd-Jones: Chosen by God* (Highland Books, 1986), p. 104.

[4] J. I. Packer, *Among God's Giants: the Puritan Vision of the Christian Life* (Kingsway, 1997), pp. 282–283.

[5] John Calvin, *Calvin: Institutes of the Christian Religion*, Vol. 1, edited by John T. McNeill (Westminster Press, 1960), 1.1.3.

[6] Piper, *The Supremacy of God*, pp. 51–52.

[7] Tony Sargent, *The Sacred Anointing: The Preaching of Dr Martyn Lloyd-Jones* (Hodder and Stoughton, 1994), p. 133.

[8] Piper, *The Supremacy of God*, p. 103.

[9] See the comments in I. H. Murray, *Jonathan Edwards: A New Biography* (Banner of Truth, 1996), pp. 137–151.

[10] See the comments on this in 'The Distinguishing Marks of a Work of the Spirit of God' in *The Works of Jonathan Edwards*, vol. 2 (1834; Banner of Truth, 1996), pp. 265–266.

[11] J. C. Ryle, *The Christian Leaders of the Last Century* (T. Nelson and Sons, 1891), p. 25.

[12] Os Guinness, 'The Word in the Age of the Image', in Melvin Tinker (ed.), *The Anglican Evangelical Crisis: A radical agenda for a Bible-based church* (Christian Focus Publications, 1995), p. 170.

[13] Cited in Packer, *Among God's Giants*, p. 285.

[14] Richard Baxter, *The Reformed Pastor* (1656; Banner of Truth, 1997), p. 56.

[15] Cited in I. H. Murray, *Jonathan Edwards*, p. 136.

[16] I. H. Murray, *D. Martyn Lloyd-Jones: The Fight of Faith, 1939–1981* (Banner of Truth, 1990), p. 372.

[17] 'The Most High a Prayer-Hearing God' in *The Works of Jonathan Edwards*, vol. 2, pp. 116–117.

[18] Quoted in Packer, *Among God's Giants*, p. 377.

[19] A. A. Bonar, *Memoir and Remains of Robert Murray McCheyne* (Oliphant, Anderson and Ferrier, 1892), p. 158.

[20] Bonar, *Memoir and Remains*, p. 93.

[21] Ibid., p. 55.

[22] Ibid., p. 36.

[23] Murray, *Martyn Lloyd-Jones*, p. 220.

[24] Bonar, *Memoir and Remains*, p. 282.

[25] Baxter, *The Reformed Pastor*, pp. 63, 67–68.

[26] Ibid., pp. 63–64.

[27] John Newton, *The Utterance of the Heart* (1780; Baker Book House, 1979), pp. 13–14.

[28] Packer, *Among God's Giants*, p. 376.

[29] Bonar, *Memoir and Remains*, p. 150.

[30] John Murray, *Collected Writings*, vol. 1 (Banner of Truth, 1989), pp. 105–106.

[31] T. Dudley-Smith, *John Stott: The Making of a Leader* (Inter-Varsity Press, 1999), pp. 157–178.

[32]. Piper, *The Supremacy of God*, p. 103.

[33] B. B. Warfield, *Studies in Theology: The Works of B. B. Warfield*, vol. 9 (1932; Baker, 1991), pp. 86–87, quoted on pp. 236–237 of this volume.

[34] *John Calvin's Sermons on Ephesians*, trans. Arthur Golding (Banner of Truth, 1987), p. vii.

[35] For the purposes of this essay we will not address the fact that any religion that has a place for a god or goddess (or gods and goddesses) is strictly speaking engaging in theology.

[36] D. F. Wells, *No Place for Truth: Or Whatever Happened to Evangelical Theology?* (Eerdmans, 1993), p. 98.

[37] Ibid., p. 99.

[38] Ibid., p. 100.

[39] Ibid.

[40] Carl Trueman comments: 'it is rather misleading to speak of theology or divinity as a university discipline. More often than not, it is a disparate collection of various subjects, methodologies, and philosophies that just happen to be in the same department for reasons which have more to do with institutional history and administration than any inner-coherence or mutual relationship'. See his essay 'The importance of being earnest: approaching theological study', in this volume, p. 219.

[41] J. I. Packer, 'The Preacher as Theologian', in C. Green and D. Jackman (eds.), *When God's Voice is Heard: Essays on preaching presented to Dick Lucas* (Inter-Varsity Press, 1995), p. 80.

[42] R. L. Reymond, *A New Systematic Theology of the Christian Faith* (Thomas Nelson, 1998), pp. xxv–xxvi.

[43] G. Bray, *Creeds, Councils and Christ: Did the early Christians misrepresent Jesus?* (Mentor, rep. 1997), p. 37.

[44] See the incisive statistics and comments in M. J. Erickson, *The*

Evangelical Left: Encountering Post conservative Evangelical Theology (Paternoster, 1998), pp. 1–6.

[45] The words of Dr George Carey, Archbishop of Canterbury, quoted in I. H. Murray, *Evangelicalism Divided: A record of the crucial change in the years 1950–2000* (Banner of Truth, 2000), pp. 142–143.

[46] D. M. Lloyd-Jones, *The Puritans: Their Origins and Successors* (Banner of Truth, 1987), pp. 28, 32–33.

[47] B. B. Warfield, *Revelation and Inspiration* (Baker, 1991), pp. 283–332.

[48] See the excellent articles by M. Tinker, 'Currents of change: trends in Anglican Evangelical theology today' and G. Bray, 'Whatever happened to the authority of Scripture?', in M. Tinker (ed.), *The Anglican Evangelical Crisis*, pp. 42–71.

[49] See, for example, G. Goldsworthy, *Preaching the whole Bible as Christian Scripture* (Inter-Varsity Press, 2000).

[50] An excellent starting point is the essay by D. A. Carson, 'Unity in Diversity in the New Testament: the possibility of systematic theology', in D. A. Carson and J. D. Woodbridge (eds.), *Scripture and Truth* (Inter-Varsity Press, 1983).

[51] J. Murray, *Collected Writings of John Murray 4: Studies in Theology*, (Banner of Truth, 1982), pp. 20–21.

[52] D. A. Carson, *The Gagging of God: Christianity Confronts Pluralism* (Apollos, 1996), p. 484.

[53] Murray, *Martyn Lloyd-Jones*, p. 166.

[54] A. W. Tozer, *The Knowledge of the Holy* (O. M. Publishing, 1994), pp. 7–8.

[55] Wells, *No Place for Truth*, p. 301.

7. The importance of being earnest: Approaching theological study[1]
Carl Trueman

Carl Trueman was Senior Lecturer in Church History at the University of Aberdeen, and is now Associate Professor of Church History and Historical Theology at Westminster Theological Seminary, Philadelphia, USA. He is editor of Themelios.

Introduction

There can be no more pressing question to be addressed by the theological student than that of how academic theological study proper is to be related to his or her everyday life as a Christian believer. Now, this is a vast subject, and scarcely one that can be covered adequately in one essay. It is, after all, an issue with which some of the church's greatest minds have wrestled for a lifetime and yet never come up with a fully satisfactory answer. It is important at the start, therefore, that I clarify precisely what specific issues I intend to address here, in order, as the advertisers would say, to prevent disappointment later on. My aims will be modest. I shall not deal with specifics, merely with the general framework within which your studies should be approached.

I should make it clear from the start that although I recognize the head–heart dilemma as one that is peculiarly relevant to those engaged in full-time theological study, it is something that affects all thoughtful Christians everywhere. It is, of course, a cliché that all Christians are theologians – but it is none the less true. Anyone who reflects on God or thinks about who God is and what he has done; anyone who has ever been puzzled or challenged by an apparent problem in the biblical text, or confused by the church's teaching; that person has been confronted with an issue of theological importance, has entered the world of theology proper

219

and has faced, perhaps unconsciously, the perennial head–heart dilemma. It is thus not something peculiar to university bedsit discussions late at night; it is the inevitable result of the fact that the Christian faith, while challenging human beings as human beings, yet has an intellectual content that needs to be faced up to in some form and at some level by all Christian believers.

Having said all that, the head–heart dilemma is peculiarly relevant to full-time theologians because the issue lies so close to their existence on a relentless daily basis, and because it confronts them left, right and centre. Challenges to their view of Scripture, God, Christ and salvation occur daily, requiring much hard-headed intellectual effort in response. This embattled environment then creates an overwhelming temptation to abstract doctrine from the practical context of life and to make it an end in itself. Thus, the Bible becomes a book we argue over, not something we build our lives upon; the Trinity becomes an exercise in logic and metaphysics, not the cornerstone of creation and salvation, and so on. Belief and practice, doctrine and life, are thus rent asunder and the Christian faith is, to put it bluntly, emasculated.

Now, many questions crowd into our minds when we approach the subject of how to relate theological studies to our everyday lives. A lot of these, however, deal with specifics: how does text criticism fit in with my evangelicalism? What is the relevance of hermeneutics to my daily Bible reading? What can history tell me about church-life today? These are important questions, but they represent specific manifestations of a deeper problem: for theologians, the issue is ultimately one of how to integrate the task of treating the Bible both as an object of analysis in their studies and as the source of devotion in their Christian life. Problems raised by text criticism, systematic theology, philosophy of religion, church history, and so on, all ultimately resolve themselves into variations on this one basic theme. What is needed, therefore, is a model of the Christian life which provides a framework that allows for the integration of analysis and devotion.

A framework for integration

To construct such a model, we need first of all to define what theology would be in an ideal world (and I stress that we are talking 'ideal world' here. I will come to the real world in a while). At this point, I confess my debt to John Calvin who, at the start of his *Institutes*, while not using the word 'theology', highlighted the fact that knowledge of God and knowledge of ourselves are intimately linked to the extent that it is not easy to see which precedes the other. Calvin's definition is useful here because it highlights the fact that theology has two poles that stand in relation to each other: on one side, there is God who reveals himself; on the other side there are human beings who receive that revelation. As Calvin will go on to say, that revelation of God is accommodated to human capacity – not that it is an imperfect, misleading and inadequate synthesis of the human and the divine, but that it is divine truth expressed in a manner which human beings can grasp. In short, the nature of theology is determined both by the God upon whom it depends and upon the humanity that receives it. This means that whatever model we develop to understand how theological study and Christian devotion are to be integrated must proceed on the basis of who we understand God to be, who we understand ourselves to be, and therefore the relationship that exists between the two.

The fundamentals of this relationship from an evangelical perspective can be sketched briefly as follows: the triune God created the world with humanity as the crown of creation; humanity fell into sin, which darkened the whole of its existence, including those areas traditionally referred to as intellect, will and emotions; through the incarnation of the second person of the Trinity, God redeemed a people for himself; that people now enjoy fellowship with God the Father through Christ the Son via the personal ministry of the Holy Spirit; while Christians have a foretaste of their eschatological perfection in this life, however, they remain as those who look forward to the full consummation of their salvation at the end time, not those who enjoy it here and now other than by way of anticipation.

Given the reality of this basic framework for understanding our existence, it becomes obvious that the conditions for a healthy life as a theological student are, as one would expect, determined to a large extent by the conditions for a healthy spiritual life in general.

What are these conditions? Well, to use a phrase beloved of the Puritans, these conditions consist primarily in careful and faithful attendance to the means of grace. That is where healthy spiritual life begins, and that is something which must take priority if we are ever to achieve a proper integration of our working lives with our broader Christian existence. We must all look to these bread-and-butter issues first before turning our minds to the more refined details.

What are these means of grace? Very simply, they are, on a corporate level, involvement in the worshipping life of the church, with its preaching of the Word and its celebration of the Lord's Supper, and, on an individual level, prayer and Bible reading. Get these right, and you are well on the way to putting into place a life policy that will help you resolve difficulties you may have with relating your Christian life to your studies.

Of course, at this point some may be tempted to sneer. You wanted a university academic to tell you some clever and brilliant ways of tying together the different parts of your life; you don't want to be told to go to church, to pray and to read your Bible. Like Naaman wanting to be cured of his leprosy, you want something sophisticated and elaborate that will solve the problem. Well, if that is how you react to my argument so far, I would like to make a number of observations:

In my experience as a university academic, I have known a number of evangelical students come unstuck during their studies. They have found the critical assaults on the Bible, or the radical attacks from philosophy and theology, or the relativizing effects of historical and phenomenological studies, to be too much to bear and have ultimately found it easier to abandon their evangelicalism than to stand against the deluge of alternative arguments being hurled at them from all sides. This is without doubt a tragedy and has, on more than one occasion, called me to question my own position as a member of departments where such things take place. And yet, in every single case of which I have personal experience, the problem has never been purely, or even primarily, an intellectual one. In conversations with such students, the problem has always started in another sphere: church attendance has slipped; Bible reading has slipped; the life of principled obedience has slipped. And it is this practical decline in daily Christian walk that has provided the framework for the impending intellectual crisis. Indeed, on one or two occasions, it would appear that the intellectual crisis was itself primarily the result of the individual concerned trying to justify to him or herself a course of moral or practical action that he or she had adopted already. Of course, I would hesitate to generalize, but the pattern is at least suggestive; and when we take seriously our existence as whole, spiritual, sinful beings, with all of the irrationality that inevitably entails, we must be wary of overestimating the amount of intellectual honesty and integrity that really motivates our intellectual convictions.

We must always remember that human beings are not simply intellectual automata. Our beliefs are not simply the result of value-neutral logical processes working from self-evident truths. This is something that the collapse of Enlightenment rationalism in the wake of postmodern critiques has made very clear indeed; and yet this is something that Luther and Calvin could have told us five hundred years ago, that Paul had spotted way back in the first century, and that the serpent so brilliantly exploits in Genesis 3. Christian belief is therefore a moral as well as an intellectual stance. The reason that individuals do not believe in Christ is because they are in a state of moral and intellectual rebellion against God. This is not to say that non-Christians are as bad as they could be; but it is to point to the fact that objections to Christian belief all contain a fundamental moral element which refuses God's claims. After all, Christ points us to our sinfulness, our moral turpitude; he stands in judgment on our self-righteousness; he calls us to repent, die to self and live for him, though every instinct in our minds and bodies militates against this; and, surprise, surprise, we do not like this at all. Furthermore, while we remain on this mortal plain, we will continue to struggle against our basic human desire to be free of God. Loss of faith, like lack of faith, is thus never simply a problem of epistemology; it is also a problem of morality. In the same way, the failure to integrate any particular aspect of our lives into the larger reality of our union with Christ, from our studies in the university library to our behaviour within the marriage bond, is not simply a problem of technique but also a problem of morality.

My first basic point, then, is this: don't imagine that you can integrate your theological studies with your daily Christian walk successfully, unless you have first established the latter on a sound footing. Are you praying daily for spiritual help, not just for your work, but for your life in general? Are you reading God's Word every day not simply to pass your examinations but to familiarize yourself with salvation history and with God's revelation of himself, so that you can understand more fully the God who has redeemed you and your own identity as one of the redeemed? Are you attending a local church regularly (and I must stress at this point that the Christian Union is no substitute for church) where the word is preached faithfully and the Lord's Supper is duly administered? If not, then you might as well stop now, for I have nothing more of use to say to you here; if you have not laid such basic foundations for integrating your studies with your faith, then you are simply not ready to address the more specific issues that academic theology raises for the Christian.

If, however, you are one who attends carefully to those things that are the basic staple of the Christian life, both at an individual and corporate level, then we can move on to the next level of getting the integration right. If my first point refers to your general life as a Christian, then my second point refers specifically to how you should understand your studies to function. What is the model you should use when attempting to set your studies in the context of your Christian life as a whole? Here, I would like to make two points and, again, neither of them is unique to the calling of the theological student. The first (in order of priority) is that theological study, like everything else we do in this life, is something to be done first and foremost to the glory of God; and that is to inform and shape the attitude with which it is pursued. Such a point is, I hope, self-evident. Second, theological studies are to be seen as an opportunity for, and an avenue of, service to the church in general.

It is worth taking this latter point to heart: the fundamental model of all Christian activity is that of servanthood. Christians are not those who live for self, who strive to gain personal glory, but those who give of themselves to others. 'From each according to his abilities, to each according to his needs' – a slogan of Marxist origin, I know, but not a bad watchword for the Christian in general and the theological student in particular. The Christian is, by definition, someone to whom great privileges have been given; and with great privileges come great responsibilities for serving others. And the theological student, by dint of what he or she studies, is somebody with particularly marvellous privileges and thus especially daunting responsibilities.

How does this play out in practice? Well, first, we must rid ourselves of any notion that we are, so to speak, God's gift to the Christian church. We may know more theology than the person sitting next to us on the pew at a Sunday morning service; we may well be able to beat them hands down in a debate concerning some theological point in the context of a church meeting or even an informal discussion over coffee; but that does not mean we are in any sense a more effective, God-glorifying Christian than they are. If Christianity involves the intimate union of belief and practice, of knowledge of God which finds its being through piety, as Calvin would say, that is, the godliness of the true Christian, then technical mastery of the niceties of scholarship in no way counts by itself as genuine Christianity. As a result, mere technical accomplishment does not qualify you to take a leadership role within your local congregation, or provide an occasion for you to lord it over others. Many of us are quite capable of reading and mastering the ins and outs of a car-maintenance manual; but I would hesitate to recommend myself as capable of changing the brake blocks on my own car, let alone that of someone else. Thus, knowing what prayer means is not the same as knowing what it means to pray; knowing what the Chalcedonian definition *says*, for example, is not the same thing as knowing the Chalcedonian definition's *personal significance*.

Luther captured this truth nicely when he distinguished between his own theology and that of his opponents by contrasting the existential impact and personal demands of Christian doctrine as he understood it with the position of others. His enemies, he said, knew that Christ had died and been raised from the dead; but he knew that Christ had died and been raised from the dead *for him*. The difference is between a scholar reading a note from the library archives that says the cavalry are on their way to save the beleaguered troops, and actually being one of the beleaguered troops who receives the note.

All this is to leap ahead of ourselves, but it does underline the fact that knowledge of an abstract, impersonal kind should never be mistaken for that personal, doctrinal knowledge which lies at the heart of the Christian life, faith and church. The simple point, therefore is: when you leave the lecture theatre and walk through the door of the church, remember first, who you are – a sinner saved by the grace of God in Jesus Christ, nothing more, nothing less. Second, remember that while you may have gifts, great gifts, to offer the church, that is for the church to recognize and for you to offer in all humility. Your attitude should be that of the servant who sees his or her skills as an opportunity for the more effective serving of others, rather than a basis for exalting yourself above the level of those who have not had the privilege of a theological education.

As a result, the next step towards getting theological study right, after the foundation of personal and corporate worship, is involvement as a servant at whatever level in the day-to-day running of the church, whether as a Sunday school teacher, a youth club leader, or a church cleaner. Even Christ stooped to wash feet – and we should be prepared to make ourselves no less humble.

This, of course, is no less than is demanded of every believer: all should work hard within the local church as a natural part of their Christian existence. What I am arguing all along is that true integration of faith and learning is possible only within a balanced and healthy Christian life in general, and this aspect of practical church service, in whatever form, is simply another part of this. Nevertheless, there are many tangible benefits that can accrue to the theologian in particular from certain kinds of service, in addition to the general spiritual benefits of a life of principled obedience.

Sunday school, for example, is one excellent means of developing a truly theological (as opposed to merely academic or scholarly) mindset. Here the theologian is faced with a class of youngsters who are probably not yet old enough to be either indifferent or hostile, or some lethal combination of the two; and yet they are also theologically unlearned. Children may have the basic Bible stories, they may even have a certain amount of theology proper; but the twin challenges of explaining difficult concepts to them in ways that they can understand, and of making these concepts relevant to how they live their lives and think each day is a profound challenge of which the average ivory-tower theologian has but the vaguest notion. This is where the rubber hits the road; this is where you get your hands dirty; this is where the real challenge of the relevance of theology to real life as lived by real people begins to be felt.

Theology as a university discipline

This, in a roundabout way, now brings us at last to the issue of academic theology. As I wrote at the beginning, I am neither qualified nor keen to address the specific questions you may have about biblical criticism, religious philosophy and so on, that you may feel impede the integration of your faith and your studies. I do, however, wish to highlight one problem at the very core of academic theology that, I am sure, provides much of the context for the problem of relating faith and studies with which some readers struggle. This is the issue of theology as a university discipline. I need to be careful that I am clear about what I mean here, and thus it is necessary to give a little historical background.

Anyone who has any knowledge of theology as it was pursued in the patristic era, as it developed in the Middle Ages, or as it was elaborated by the Reformers and the Puritans in the sixteenth and seventeenth centuries, will know that it was a practical discipline, intimately connected with the life of the church precisely because it arose out of the life of the church. It was integral to the church's life and testimony, and thus intensely practical. Not that it was reducible to mere praxis or reflection upon religious experience and never engaged in any deep analysis of doctrine – such is self-evidently not the case. But it was generally pursued as part and parcel of making sense of the church's confession in worship that Jesus is Lord. Debates about the Trinity, about the person of Christ and about grace all arose within the life of the church as the church itself faced up to various internal and external challenges to its position and sought to clarify its testimony in the world. I am of course aware that this is something of a simplification; after all, any attempt to reduce 1,800 years of theological reflection to a single cause or theme is bound to involve a considerable amount of generalization. Nevertheless, in the precritical world there was a unity of purpose involved in the theological enterprise provided by its practitioners (people involved in the day-to-day life of the church), its target audience (those who made up the church), its foundation (the personal revelation of the personal God), and its overall context (the worship of the church). Precritical theology was thus doxological, terminating in the praise and glorification of God by the men and women who made up the worshipping congregations. This is an element that has been lost, particularly in the sphere of university theology courses.

The reasons for the loss are manifold. The privatization of religion that the Enlightenment witnessed served to push existential questions concerning the personal nature of religious truth to the background. In addition, central aspects of Christianity's historic testimony, notably the whole idea of Scripture, of special revelation, and of reconciliation as embodied in the great creeds and confessions of the church, became something of an embarrassment, given the epistemological and ethical assumptions of the time. Theology had long been described using the language of science, but Enlightenment notions of what was and was not scientific meant that if theology was to retain scientific status within the university, it would have to undergo a fundamental divorce from its roots in the life and worship of the community of faith.

In addition – and here I guess I tread a more controversial path – the very existence and pursuit of theology within universities was not, I would argue, either helpful or appropriate. While many had Christian origins, the university at the Enlightenment became, and remains, a secular phenomenon, where the structures of what does and does not count as knowledge were set (and continue to be set) by the philosophies of Enlightenment Europe (postmodernism being, in my view, fundamentally continuous with modernity in highly significant ways). The founding of the University of Berlin, along with the debates about whether theology had any role to play, and if so, what kind, are a microcosm of what was happening all over Europe.

The outcome of the enlightening of the universities was devastating for theology precisely because the Enlightenment demanded that theology give an account of itself not in terms of itself, its own inner dynamics and ultimate purposes, but in terms of the universal criteria that had been established for judging what was and was not plausible within the university framework. Basic to this, of course, was the loss of the idea that the Bible was a supernaturally inspired book and that God was in Christ reconciling the world to himself. As Stephen Williams has argued persuasively in his book *Revelation and Reconciliation*,[1] the former offended Enlightenment epistemology, the latter outraged Enlightenment morality. At the time, this was not considered to be too serious to the Christian faith: the self-confidence of the Enlightened Christians, bolstered by the fact that Christianity was, after all, utterly dominant in the cultural realm, led them to continue to believe that Christianity was self-evidently superior to other religions and belief-systems, even without a supernatural Bible and saviour understood in terms of Chalcedon.

That the theological toothpaste was well and truly out of the tube at this point became evident only later. Nobody at the time ever thought that Christianity would have to justify its special place in life and thought, so obviously superior did it seem to all the other alternatives. Indeed, the fact that the Bible was not inspired in the traditional sense of the word, and that Christ was not saviour in the traditional sense of the word, did not mean that both were not still that much better than the rest. Nevertheless, in conceding these two points, Enlightenment theologians conceded the two points which actually supported the pursuit of theology as one discipline possessing its own integrity. Now, without any epistemological or soteriological centre to hold it together, the stage was set for the discipline to fragment hopelessly, not just as a result of the external pressures created by the rising tide of information and of sub-disciplinary specialization in academic culture in general, but also by its own lack of any internal basis for providing coherence and unity. The result is that today it is rather misleading to speak of theology or divinity as a university discipline. More often than not, it is a disparate collection of various subjects, methodologies and philosophies that just happen to be in the same department for reasons that have more to do with institutional history and administration than any inner-coherence or mutual relationship.

Some lessons

There are a number of lessons to be drawn from this brief historical observation. First, be aware that the discipline or disciplines you study today did not drop straight out of the sky. They possess no ideal existence. Their form and content, the questions asked and the answers given, are not immune from the more general flow of history. Rather, they are profoundly shaped in form, purpose and content by the world from which they have emerged. One factor is, therefore, Enlightenment presuppositions as to what constitutes valid method, what is plausible, and what is unacceptable as an academic argument. For you, in the twenty-first century, more significant factors are, I suspect, how the managerial culture that so dominates universities, combined with the crude vocationalism with which teaching philosophy and political policy is so riddled, is changing not just the way you are taught, but the whole way in which education is understood within the context of the wider society. For all the talk of the impact of postmodern epistemologies on education, my own belief as one working within the system is that the epistemological discussions within the academy are a side-show to the main event, a case of academics fiddling while Rome burns. State-funded university theology's main problem at the moment is not actually one of justifying itself on espistemological grounds but of justifying itself on commercial and economic grounds. The great danger to thoughtfulness, intelligent debate and real learning comes from the fundamentalist mullahs of management control and consumerism who, not content with having reduced society at large to worshipping the false gods of modern materialism, wish to do the same with higher learning. When the purpose of education becomes merely serving the commercial market-place, Arts subjects in general are placed in grave peril, and theology in particular looks decidedly unstable.

But I digress. The real lesson here, then, is *learn the history of your chosen discipline.* Why do New Testament scholars think the way they do when they reject the virgin birth? Is it to do with the historical evidence? Is it to do with an epistemology that rules out *a priori* the possibility of this having happened? Is it to do with the tradition of theology to which they belong that simply discounts the need for the virgin birth? All are legitimate questions to ask. This, of course, is a simple but important point. Obviously, the evangelicals who specialize in these different fields are the ones who are competent to guide you in these matters; but in general do not be fooled by outward displays of scholarly objectivity – find out what the agenda is, and how it is shaping the way your lecturers think and teach.

The second point is of somewhat more importance: be aware, as you seek to integrate your faith and your studies, that the very context of your studies, the very university tradition within which you stand, is profoundly opposed to precisely the integration you seek. The world of university theology is an unnatural one. It is one where a subject that developed specifically within the context of faith as a means of nurturing the people of God has been taken out of its context and stripped of its most important presuppositions. This is where I think most danger lies, and indeed, it is what concerns me most about the evangelical obsession with academic success. Theology is not just a question of content, it is also a question of context; and if we simply replace liberalism with evangelicalism with regard to content whilst remaining happy with the overall context, we will have failed.

A medical analogy

Let me elaborate this as follows using a silly, but I hope pointed, analogy. Let's imagine that at some point in the future it is decided that the discipline of medicine needs to be reformed. This is done first of all by denying that certain medicines had curative properties that others lacked. Initially, it is assumed that, while antibiotics are obviously superior to baking soda in curing infections, the difference in curative power is one of degree, not kind; but gradually, over time, all compounds come to be regarded as having equal power to cure. In addition to this first claim regarding curative powers, the reformers also deny that there are any diseases out there that need to be cured. Again, it is initially assumed that the very ill person is actually not very ill but simply in possession of less health than others; gradually, however, the logic of the position works itself out and it becomes an act of cultural imperialism to claim that any one person is more or less ill than any other. Indeed, such a claim will certainly lose you your job within the medical faculty. The results, of course, are predictable – the discipline of medicine, whose very purpose was reflection upon and the curing of human diseases, fragments because there is nothing to keep it together, no central concern or conviction which can provide a positive base for disciplinary integrity. In addition, the hospitals run by the students of these great men of medicine gradually empty as their patients are either killed off by the treatments offered, and other people simply go elsewhere for treatment, knowing instinctively that what is on offer is not adequate for their needs.

Then, along come a group of students who, for whatever reason, gradually become disillusioned with what they are being taught. For some, it does not match up to their own experience; for others it is singularly useless when they themselves are ill; for yet others it is because they have been reading some other books on medicine that, while not featuring on any reading list they have been given, seem to make a good deal of sense. Over time, they formalize themselves into a Pharmaceutical and Medical Students Fellowship, where they meet once a week to discuss medical questions and to attack the received academic orthodoxy. Indeed, once a year they even arrange a conference where the speakers are a bunch of crazed fundamentalists who have somehow managed to get jobs on medical faculties despite being committed to the outlandish ideas that medicine is good for you, poison is bad, and people actually suffer from diseases (though, interestingly enough, many of these speakers hold faculty positions in the history of medicine, or the interpretation of medical texts, not in medicine proper).

There is a problem with this group, however. Yes, they are intellectually committed to the old reactionary notions of disease and cure; yes, they want to think through the medicinal issues for themselves; but, at the end of the day, all they do is talk. They consider their task done when they demonstrate to Professor Smith and Dr Jones that it is *plausible* even within the setting of the medical school to believe in disease and cure; and at base, all they really want is for Smith and Jones and their ilk to accept them and their viewpoint as having a legitimate place at the discussion table. They don't actually want to go out and apply what they have learned to themselves or to the sick lying in hospital; they are fearful even in their fellowship groups of ever using the old offensive terminology of illness, cure, poison and remedy; and they certainly don't want to imply that Smith and Jones don't make interesting and legitimate contributions to debate. Indeed they often laugh loudest when Smith cracks a joke about ignorant medical fundamentalists of the past such as Louis Pasteur and Alexander Fleming. These students just want to be known as clever men of medicine who, despite their intellectual commitment to curing people, are nevertheless on the whole perfectly decent and user-friendly and not going to rock the boat by actually trying to cure people. They have rejected the shibboleths of contemporary medical theory, but they have done so within the same context and culture as their opponents: not that of curing people, but that of juggling with clever and interesting ideas.

You get the point? Of course, the analogy is not perfect and medical science will never, we hope, go down such an absurd path. Yet the modern university's approach to theology would appear as absurd to a medieval scholar as the above scenario would appear to a modern medic. The modern university has divorced theology from its proper place in the life of the church and has abandoned the traditional language of doxology, orthodoxy and heresy. You can set up all the RTSF meetings you like, but the problem is not just the liberal theology you learn at university but the whole university culture and ethos, of which you and I are a part. The university is ultimately not interested in those claims that make Christian theology so important: revelation, sin, Christ, redemption. For the university, at best, these are artefacts to be examined and discussed; at worst, they are irrelevant in an education which looks only to economic criteria as constituting real truth; they are certainly never to be applied. Yet these are things the very truth or falsehood of which demand not just an intellectual response with our minds but an existential response with the whole of our beings. We simply cannot talk about them in a disinterested way and remain true to their original import. It is not enough to reject the liberal theology of your lecturers; that is a task worth doing when done thoughtfully and in an informed manner, but it is not a task worth doing as an end in itself, nor is it the most difficult task you will face. Indeed, if that is all you as an evangelical theology student are interested in, you might as well not bother.

Far more subtle and far more serious than being damaged by the *content* of what you are taught is being damaged by the *context* of university discourse, with its tendency to neutralize all the imperatives of Christian theology. Now don't misinterpret me here – I am not saying that we should not be aware of and interact with the best contemporary scholarship, the most thoughtful liberal theology and the most sophisticated challenges to orthodoxy. My own historical heroes, Augustine, Aquinas, John Owen, Charles Hodge, B. B. Warfield and W. G. T. Shedd, to name but six, did all of these things. None of them felt the need to cut themselves off from the scholarly world, but they did not pursue orthodox theology for its own sake. They did so because they thought that such theology was faithful to the biblical text and was therefore of overwhelming importance both for themselves and for others. Don't be fooled by those evangelicals who today spend their time praising the insights of liberals and non-evangelicals while trashing or mocking our evangelical forefathers for their intellectual peccadilloes. Make no mistake, God will be the ultimate judge of this contemporary evangelical tendency to turn a blind eye to great blasphemies in liberal theologians who happen to say the odd useful or orthodox thing, while excoriating evangelicals of the past for their mistakes. Too many gnats are strained out, while too many huge elephants are being swallowed whole.

Our forefathers were not idiots, neither were they uncouth louts who responded with knee-jerk abuse and anger to any who disagreed with them, but neither were they prepared to play happy families with those whose theology was fundamentally opposed to the gospel. The issues at stake, issues, after all, of eternal consequence, were, are and always will be just too important to be reduced to intellectual parlour games or restricted by the protocols of academic diplomacy. Yes, interact with liberals in an informed and thoughtful manner – the church needs men and women for such a task; but please do not buy into the contemporary culture of evangelical academic protocol that leads only to a useless blurring of what is good with what is bad. Making unconditional peace with heresy should never be mistaken for a proper integration of faith and learning.

Conclusion

In a way this brings me back to the points with which I started. You want to integrate your faith with your studies? It simply cannot be done in the purely academic environment of the university because the modern university in its very essence is designed to reject the kind of integration for which you seek. It can be done only when theology is given its proper place within the church, within the worshipping community. And that is why it is not just a matter of principled Christian obedience that you are actively involved in a local church fellowship; it is also a matter of sanctified common sense if you wish to pursue your university studies with true Christian zeal.

Why is this? Because church is the place where you will be reminded again and again of what it really is that you are studying and how it affects you. You may debate sin in a theology class, but in a sermon you will be told something you will never hear in a university lecture theatre: that you are yourself a sinner, intimately involved in the very thing you talked about so abstractly at the seminar. You might talk about atonement with your supervisor, but only the preacher will tell you that Christ died for you. You might study eschatology for an essay assignment, but only in church will you take the Lord's Supper, remembering that you do this until he comes again in glory. In other words, you need not only to supplement the liberal stuff your lecturers teach you with sound, orthodox evangelical theology, you also need to place yourself in an environment where the indifference to and distance from real life that academic theological study engenders can be alleviated. And that place is church.

I hope this prospect excites you. When you hear on Sunday that you worship the God who rules over history, who is sovereign, who is powerful to save, and yet who stoops to take flesh himself, to care for the poor and the needy – does it not make your heart burn within you when you come to deal with issues of theology and biblical studies on a Monday morning? Of course, much of your studies will be tedious, frustrating, antithetical to the faith you hold dear; but the bottom line is, don't let it grind you down, and don't let the university set your theological life agenda as it sets your theological studies curriculum. Make sure that your head and heart are filled with enough good stuff to enable you to deal with dross as and when it comes your way. See your theological work as you should see all of your work: an act devoted to the glory of the God who bought you with his precious blood and will one day glorify you in heaven.

I close, therefore, with the words of one much better placed than I am to speak of the theological scholarship of his own day, liberal and conservative, Catholic and Protestant; one who was accomplished across a whole range of academic disciplines in a way that would now be impossible; a man honoured by one of the great universities of Europe for his contribution to theology; but also a man who knew the love of Christ in his own heart and who sought through his writings, scholarly and devotional, to shed that love abroad. I speak, of course, of the great Benjamin Breckinridge Warfield. Writing on 'The Idea of Systematic Theology', he wrote the following:

> The systematic theologian is pre-eminently a preacher of the gospel; and the end of his work is obviously not merely the logical arrangement of the truths which come under his hand, but the moving of men, through their power, to love God with all their heart and their neighbours as themselves; to choose their portion with the Saviour of their souls; to find and hold him precious; and to recognise and yield to the sweet influences of the Holy Spirit whom he has sent. With such truth as this he will not dare to deal

in a cold and merely scientific spirit, but will justly and necessarily permit its preciousness and its practical destination to determine the spirit in which he handles it, and to awaken the reverential love with which alone he should investigate its reciprocal relations. For this he needs to be suffused at all times with a sense of the unspeakable worth of the revelation which lies before him as the source of his material, and with the personal bearings of its separate truths on his own heart and life; he needs to have had and to be having a full, rich, and deep religious experience of the great doctrines with which he deals; he needs to be living close to his God, to be resting always on the bosom of his Redeemer, to be filled at all times with the manifest influences of the Holy Spirit. The student of systematic theology needs a very sensitive religious nature, a most thoroughly consecrated heart, and an outpouring of the Holy Ghost upon him, such as will fill him with that spiritual discernment, without which all native intellect is in vain. He needs to be not merely a student, not merely a thinker, not merely a systematizer, not merely a teacher – he needs to be like the beloved disciple himself in the highest, truest, and holiest sense, a divine.[2]

Such was Warfield's vision. Impossible, you say, impossible to achieve that level of integration between devotion and study. Well, yes, with us these things are impossible – but with God, all things are possible. Let us pray that the great God of grace might grant us some measure of that Christian experience in our studies and teaching which Warfield describes so eloquently!

This edition © Carl R. Trueman, 2001

Notes

[1] This essay first appeared in *Themelios*, 26 (1), 2000, pp. 34–47.

[2] Stephen Williams, *Revelation and Reconciliation* (CUP, 1996).
[3] B. B. Warfield, 'The Idea of Systematic Theology' in *Studies in Theology* (Banner of Truth, 1988), pp. 86–87.